Family Ambiguity and Domestic Violence in Asia

CONCEPT, LAW AND PROCESS

THE SUSSEX LIBRARY OF

Asian Studies

Series Editor: Dr Mina Roces, School of History, The University of New South Wales

The Sussex Library of Asian Studies publishes academic manuscripts in various disciplines (including interdisciplinary and transnational approaches) under the rubric of Asian Studies – focusing on Economics, Education, Religion, History, Politics, Gender, and comparative studies with the West and regional studies in Asia.

Published

The Politics of Dress in Asia and the Americas
Edited by Mina Roces and Louise Edwards, UNIVERSITY OF NEW SOUTH WALES, SYDNEY AND UNIVERSITY OF TECHNOLOGY, SYDNEY

Chinese Identity in Post-Suharto Indonesia: Culture, Media, Religion and Language
Chang-Yau Hoon, SINGAPORE UNIVERSITY

Han Shan, Chan Buddhism and Gary Snyder's Ecopoetic Way
Joan Qionglin Tan, HUNAN UNIVERSITY, CHINA AND UNIVERSITY OF WALES, LAMPETER

China's Rising Profile: The Great Power Tradition
Harsh V. Pant, KING'S COLLEGE LONDON

The Independence of East Timor: Multi-Dimensional Perspectives – Occupation, Resistance, and International Political Activism
Clinton Fernandes, UNIVERSITY OF NEW SOUTH WALES

Forthcoming

Pool of Life: The Autobiography of a Punjabi Agony Aunt
KAILASH PURI (CO-AUTHOR OF *THE MYTH OF UK INTEGRATION*) AND ELEANOR NESBITT (UNIVERSITY OF WARWICK)

Sports Media in China: Making Spectacle
Haiqing Yu
UNIVERSITY OF NEW SOUTH WALES

Family Ambiguity and Domestic Violence in Asia

CONCEPT, LAW AND PROCESS

Edited by

Maznah Mohamad and
Saskia E. Wieringa

SUSSEX
ACADEMIC
PRESS
Brighton • Chicago • Toronto

2 4 6 8 10 9 7 5 3 1

First published 2013, in Great Britain by
SUSSEX ACADEMIC PRESS
PO Box 139
Eastbourne BN24 9BP

and in the United States of America by
SUSSEX ACADEMIC PRESS
Independent Publishers Group
814 N. Franklin Street, Chicago, IL 60610

and in Canada by
SUSSEX ACADEMIC PRESS (CANADA)
8000 Bathurst Street, Unit 1, PO Box 30010, Vaughan, Ontario L4J 0C6

British Library Cataloguing in Publication Data

A CIP catalogue record for this book is available from the British Library.

Library of Congress Cataloging-in-Publication Data

Family ambiguity and domestic violence in Asia : concept, law and process / edited by Maznah Mohamad and Saskia E. Wieringa.
pages cm
Includes bibliographical references and index.
ISBN 978-1-84519-555-7 (alk. paper)
1. Family violence—Asia. 2. Family violence—Law and legislation—Asia. 3. Families—Asia. I. Maznah Mohamad, editor of compilation. II. Wieringa, Saskia, 1950– editor of compilation.
HV6626.23.A78F36 2013
362.82′92095—dc23

2012050211

MIX
Paper from responsible sources
FSC® C013056
FSC
www.fsc.org

Typeset & designed by Sussex Academic Press, Brighton & Eastbourne.
Printed by TJ International, Padstow, Cornwall.
This book is printed on acid-free paper.

Contents

Series Editor's Preface

The Sussex Library of Asian Studies Series publishes original scholarly work in various disciplines (including interdisciplinary and transnational approaches) under the rubric of Asian studies — particularly Economics, Education, Religion, History, Politics, Gender, Comparative Studies with the West, and Regional Studies in Asia. The Series is keen to publish in emerging topics that demand attention in the Asian context — from the politics of dress to the heteronormative in India and Indonesia for example. Seminal works and approaches will find a home here. The Series also welcomes single-country studies or anthologies that explore one important theme across a number of Asian contexts. We expect the Series to contribute to the scholarly debates on topical issues, highlighting the importance of the region.

Feminist scholars have previously tackled the issue of domestic violence in Asian societies. Maznah Mohamad and Saskia Wieringa's edited volume adds a new dimension to scholarly studies on the topic by focusing on the ambiguity of the family; in particular the "harmonious Asian families" that produce "gendered expectations of women's behavior". In this sense this seminal anthology shows how society's expectations of women's roles in maintaining the unity of the family prevent women from speaking out while legitimizing the violence perpetuated against them. Using case studies from several countries including Malaysia, Indonesia, India, Singapore and the Philippines, this book analyzes the ways in which the mythologized ideal heteronormative Asian family (and heteronormativity here is interpreted as violence), the process of passing anti-violence laws, and the challenge to implement them, has had a poignant impact on women victims. The novel perspective and conceptual approach of this multi-sited and interdisciplinary work makes it essential reading for women's studies scholars including those interested in law and how it interacts in practice in the Asian cultural and patriarchal context.

MINA ROCES
University of New South Wales, Australia

Acknowledgements

We document our appreciation to a number of institutions and people that made this volume possible. This book is the result of a workshop titled, "Domestic Violence in Asia: The Ambiguity of Family as Private–Public Domain", held in October 2010 in Singapore. The project was first conceived by the Kartini Asia Network for Women's and Gender Studies at its 2009 Bangkok meeting, whose members, among others, comprise the editors and Nursyahbani Katjasungkana, one of the contributors to this volume. The Kartini Network focuses on five interconnected themes — women's studies, fundamentalisms, sexuality, conflicts (including domestic violence) and livelihood. The workshop itself was sponsored by the Asia Research Institute (ARI) of the National University of Singapore and brought together 15 paper presenters to the Singapore meeting. We thank ARI for providing the initial impetus through the workshop for the eventual production of this volume. Our debt of appreciation is especially owed to Professor Lily Kong, then Director of ARI, and Professor Gavin Jones, Research Leader of the Changing Family in Asia Research Cluster of ARI, for without their support this project would not have culminated in this volume.

Other speakers at the workshop who contributed their ideas and expertise towards the final conceptualization and improvement of the volume, and for whom we are deeply thankful, include Kumaralingam Amirthalingam, Marianne Hester, Siti Hawa Ali, Santosh Jatrana, Rashidah Shuib, Umme Busra Fateha Sultana and Shofia Romas. The deliberations at the workshop were ably moderated by Teo You Yenn, Lai Ah Eng, Zhang Yanxia, Chee Heng Leng, Melanie Budianta, Noor Aisha Abdul Rahman, Gavin Jones and Melody Lu. For assistance at the publication stage, we thank Mina Roces, Series Editor of the Sussex Library of Asian Studies, Sussex Academic Press, for her encouragement and faith in this volume. Our language and copy editors, Veena N. and Raji Chacko, contributed greatly to the overall quality of the book. We, as editors, thank each other for the collegiality and friendship which made working on this volume such a rich experience. Needless to say we bear responsibility for all of the shortcomings of the book. Finally, this book is dedicated to all victims of domestic violence in the hope that some of its findings and recommendations will contribute towards the resolution of one of the most pervasive, everyday forms of violence in the world.

MAZNAH MOHAMAD (*Singapore*)
SASKIA E. WIERINGA (*Amsterdam*)

Family Ambiguity and Domestic Violence in Asia

Introduction
Why the Book?

MAZNAH MOHAMAD AND SASKIA E. WIERINGA

Although Violence Against Women (VAW) has received significant attention from scholars, social activists, policy makers and international agencies, the scourge of violence in homes is far from diminished. Therefore, we continue to scrutinize domestic violence (DV) as the most pervasive form of violence against women and keep it alive as a societal problem that needs to be understood, grasped, revisited and dealt with in its breadth and depth. Although a universal phenomenon, VAW is also context-specific. As domestic violence, per definition, takes place within a family setting, the specific forms of families and the ideologies surrounding the family greatly affect the specificities of domestic violence in particular contexts. Putting together this volume allows the question of family ambiguity to be explored. Comparative Asian experiences allow an examination of the effectiveness of family regulations and laws in diverse national, cultural and religious settings. The chapter on European policies adds depth to some of the most critical debates, particularly the one on "gender neutral wording", which is gaining prevalence in the Asian region as well. In deconstructing and critiquing the limitations of human rights discourse and gender determinism in resolving family conflicts, we also hope to inject new ways of understanding an ostensibly familiar problem.

Our Concerns

By addressing family ambiguity as a central issue of domestic violence, we investigate the gaps between concept, law and process. As has long been acknowledged, the family is no longer seen primarily as a site of production and reproduction but as a point of tension and conflicts, with violence among intimate partners being one of its manifestations. Veena Das calls the home a site of many "domesticities", not just a haven of peace and comfort but also a dominion of masculine power and coercion (2008: 292). The family is but one of many power systems that rely on force and violence to subjugate and control their members (Goode 1971). Another approach to this issue is the feminist perspective that centralizes patriarchy as a root cause of not just domestic violence but of oppression and inequality in society (Jaggar 1983). This is sometimes complemented and even contradicted by the behavioural approach, linking factors such as psychological deficiency to violent actions (Hamberger and Hastings 1988, Gottman et al. 1995, Fernández-Montalvo and Echeburúa 2008). Yet another is the family demographic approach that links wife-abuse to multiple variables, from poverty to educational status to access to financial credit (Awang and Hariharan 2011, Clark et al. 2008, Yount and Carrera 2006, Koenig et al. 2003, Bates et al. 2004). Eradicating domestic violence lies at the heart of the matter and that it has not yet occurred highlights the failures of state intervention in regulating behaviours and norms within intimate relationships. By tracing the root of the problem to the private–public debate over family, this collection of research articles aims to uncover some of the sources of the difficulties and paradoxes in understanding and stopping domestic violence as an all-encompassing problem, from its legal to its cultural dimension.

Chapters in this volume highlight all of the above and start from the conceptualization of the family as both a public as well as private domain. When the state intervenes in family matters (as in policies on reproductive health and employment), the family is treated as a public concern (Amirthalingam 2005: 706). However, the state takes a liberal stance of respecting individual human rights or even multicultural rights, when the sacredness of the family as a private domain is emphasized. There are also extremes in the extent of state intervention upon the family. States that enforce Syariah or Muslim laws do not even limit the extent of their intervention upon private, individual and family lives, but for the most part, reinforce masculine dominance. Other states are selective about when and how they intervene. A developmentalist state that projects long-term demographic goals in terms of marriage, reproduction and ageing trends will enact legislations and direct resources towards private behaviour and choices in its favour. If domestic violence is conceptualized as a private hurt that leads to public harm, the state criminalizes the offence, but when domestic violence is presented as rooted in gender inequality in need of more than just a legal solution, then the nature of state intervention may be more ambivalent. Three main focal points, namely, concept, law and process, explicate how some of these issues and arguments are being addressed in this volume.

Concept

Under the rubric of "concept", chapters that follow capture some of the more salient debates surrounding the issue of domestic violence. Some conceptual issues have still not been reconciled or continue to be disputed and thus, contribute towards how advocacy, law, policy and cultural norms are being shaped.

Culture as defence

One of the more prevalent justifications of violence in the home is that certain cultural and religious doctrines allow for its use, and that by using it, cultural and religious distinctiveness are safeguarded. Hence, domestic violence can be viewed as a culture in itself, explains Zarizana Abdul Aziz in her chapter. However, she cautions that culture merely represents a socio-political symbolic discourse that changes over time. By analyzing several international cases of domestic violence, Aziz examines how and why domestic violence continues to be erroneously placed within culture and why the intersecting issues of privacy, culture and honour have come in the way of granting justice to victims of domestic violence. The culture defence discourse and the right to family privacy act to seal the family as an isolated and autonomous unit. A human rights perspective is needed to re-situate the family within the justice system. State action and inaction sometimes work against this goal as they tolerate, if not encourage, domestic violence. In some landmark cases discussed in the chapter, the state was in the best position to eliminate domestic violence, but it did not. This chapter argues that instead of justifying domestic violence in the name of culture, culture should be enlisted to create a non-violent society.

Domestic violence: Neutral or gender-based?

Another conceptual paradigm that has muddied the debate is the question of whether domestic violence should be seen as a neutral wrong rather than one specific to a gender. In highlighting this debate, Renée Römkens discusses some major transformations that have taken place in Europe and the EU over the past four decades. The profound ambiguities that these debates reflect are relevant to the Asian context. They show how universal the idea of family and its link to the perceived dichotomy between private and public have become. Current developments in Europe reflect a paradox where conflicting paradigms co-exist. As our Asian case studies in this volume also illuminate, at one level there is successful mainstreaming of the domestic violence issue implying feminist collaboration with social welfare, health care or criminal justice systems. However, the latter are not necessarily in tune with the feminist position on domestic violence as a form of violent discrimination against women. In mainstream paradigm, violence and aggression are treated as human behaviours that affect men and women equally and are not gender-specific. However, Römkens argues that although men are victims too, women constitute the majority of the victims of domestic violence, especially of severe domestic violence.

Thus, she argues that men's victimization at the hands of their female partner is neither a public health nor a large scale safety concern, and therefore does not qualify as a State concern, nor as a form of discrimination, unlike — unfortunately — a substantive part of women's victimization at the hands of known men. Given all these, she fears that "Domestic violence is at risk to be neutralized and in a way privatized again". While the human rights approach has succeeded in having the state treat domestic violence as a crime, preventive and protective support measures are also essential. However, there is still scant recognition that violence is intrinsically related to gendered inequality between women and men, a conceptual flaw that would need to be addressed in both Europe and Asia.

Family as a state construction

The family as a social construction forms part of the problem of domestic violence. Just as state prerogatives have shifted, so has the image of the family. Amrita Nandy traces the trajectory of family regulation vis-à-vis domestic violence in India, where there have been major shifts in legislation and its discourse. Outlining the ancient Indian family's attempts at self-regulation to modern state-based regulation, Nandy's chapter makes note of different forces that have buttressed the notion of family privacy and sanctity all along. She argues that rights to conjugality have always superseded those of the individual.

In locating family as a state construction, Narayanan Ganapathy analyzes the tenor of state paternalism when the proposed Bill on Family Violence was rejected after 30 days of parliamentary debates in Singapore. The reason given was that it would be detrimental to the family. The bill was said to be at odds with the state's defined role for the family, seen as "the 'fundamental building block' out of which larger social structures can be stably constructed". Law as a tool to legislate protection for victims of violence was also interpreted to be Western since it is litigious and confrontative as opposed to a more Asian and less legalistic, more consensus-seeking way of preserving the family. Popular sentiment has it that criminalization is neither an appropriate nor an effective method to deal with wife abusers and that social service agencies are preferred over police intervention.

Provisions in the 1987 Philippine Constitution define Filipino sexuality and shape Filipinos' "consciousness of what is acceptable and unacceptable, what is normal, and what is deviant or perverse", Cheryll Alipio argues. Marriage, the family and the nation are interlinked. The Constitution "recognizes the Filipino family as the foundation of the nation" and, therefore, the state will actively promote its development.

Additionally, "The Family Code" of 1988 explicitly proclaims that parental authority over the person, property and children is given to the father/husband, whose decision shall be paramount over the mother/wife. Thus, the implication that the husband has absolute authority over his wife and children and the impossibility of divorce enhances the belief that the man can do no wrong. This partly explains why women are reluctant to report abuse and to leave violent relationships even if their lives are at risk. However, in uncovering strategies to obviate this, Alipio's study finds that by going abroad women use their bodies as their voice. This is seen as a silent but appropriate strategy to leave abusive relationships, especially given that divorce is illegal in Catholic Philippines.

Nursyahbani Katjasungkana similarly discusses the pervasiveness of violence against women that is reinforced by the state conception of family as a private matter and the notion that the harmonious family is the foundation of the nation. Male authority over the family and the women in it is further imposed as a religious norm. This prevailing culture of patriarchy is entrenched in the 1974 Marriage Law that affirms the unequal sexual division of labour within the household, stating that "a husband is the head of the family and a wife is a housewife" and that a husband is "obliged to protect his wife and provide her with everything needed for the livelihood of the household, according to his ability".

In Malaysia, there is no "family code" explicitly worded as in the Philippines and in Indonesia. Hence, the family debate is largely captured under the rubric of Islam as analysed in Maznah Mohamad's chapter. Due to the dominance of Islam in governance and the widening of Syariah law for Muslims, the Domestic Violence Bill was initially opposed because of the belief that the law (by encompassing Muslims and non-Muslims) would usurp the Syariah's jurisdiction over the Islamic family. Unlike the Philippines, India and Singapore, the notion of family protection and privacy was not the main narrative of that debate; instead, it was a power struggle between Islamists and feminists over legal jurisdictions. Interestingly, the objection around "marital rape" being defined as a form of domestic violence was only rejected by the Islamic faction. In Malaysia, it is as though Islam has become the de facto representative of all patriarchal forces and assumes its role as the main builder and gatekeeper of the essential "moral" family.

Heteronormativity as violence

Another crucial set of concepts explored in this volume is heteronormativity and passionate aesthetics and its link to violence in the family. Saskia Wieringa argues that in maintaining the internal cohesion of heteronormativity, violence is exerted in the physical and symbolic sense. Her research on widows, sex workers and prostitutes suggests that there is enormous violence involved in the perpetuation of the myth of heteronormativity as creating or preserving the harmonious Asian family.

Wieringa explains the meaning of aesthetics in situating violence within heteronormativity. It refers to a set of principles that underlie the making of morality. Heteronormativity as a system of values is subjective; at the same time, it is believed to have universal relevance. Any aesthetic distinction is based on subjective views, yet acquires a hegemonic power in a given context. Violence, as explored in Weiringa's chapter is intrinsic to passionate aesthetics that underlie heteronormativity. Even when psychic and sexual violence occurs, the ideal of the harmonious heterosexual family remains intact. Women internalize their shame and guilt rather than blame their perpetrators, thus attesting to the power of the symbolic violence of heteronormativity. Dejected women do not see each other as allies but as differently abject. Their point of reference remains the heterosexual patriarchal family, not "the commonality of their positions as falling outside of its boundaries". Widows and sex workers do not blame the heteronormative construct for their state of abjection, but rather their own individual misfortune. All of them internalized heteronormative society's repulsion of their own self and accepted the violence and violations inflicted upon them. The power of these aesthetics can be seen in how even women in non-heterosexual relations aspire to heteronormative values, while women who have experienced violence continue to love or live with their perpetrators.

Law

Besides "concept", this volume centres its analysis of domestic violence in Asia around the issue of "law". Almost all chapters touch on the role of law in bringing the issue of domestic violence into the public realm. Asia's first legislation on domestic violence was passed in Malaysia. The Malaysian Domestic Violence Act (DVA) was passed in Parliament in 1994 but was implemented only two years later. The two-year limbo was due to pressure from various quarters, significantly the Islamic faction that did not want Islamic family matters to be governed under what was perceived as a civil and, therefore, "secular" law. Mohamad's chapter argues that in Malaysia the state tried to be responsive to both feminists as well as the Islamic factions, resulting in a "diluted" law that made it difficult for domestic violence to be charged either as a criminal offence or a civil wrong. Although the Malaysian DVA exists as a law in itself, the criminalization of offenders must depend on the use of the Penal Code, making it no different from Singapore (which rejected the Family Violence Bill), where only Protection Orders are utilized under the DVA.

In Singapore, the first legislative change dealing with domestic violence came about in 1997 when the Amendments to the Women's Charter (Chapter 353) were made to provide protection for family members. A breach of the conditions of any of the Protection Orders was made a seizable (arrestable) offence. While the Amendments to the Women's Charter have been designed to eliminate the discretionary powers of police officers by directing them to arrest abusers whenever there is a violation of a Protection Order, the structural-legal premise upon which this legislation rests is still problematic. Most cases of domestic violence escape criminalization due to the absence of support structures for victims. The paternalistic and patriarchal state also impedes women's empowerment by prescribing the limits of police intervention in domestic violence. In a paternalistic discourse, protection takes precedence over empowerment or equal treatment.

In the Philippines, despite the enactment, in 2004, of Republic Act 9262 [The Anti-Violence Against Women and Their Children (VAWC) Act], violence remains pervasive throughout the country, where reported cases of rape and acts of lasciviousness are high. Alipio argues that the protection of women's rights does not end with the enactment of a law. It needs follow-through in implementation. Six years after the act was enacted, loopholes in the implementation remain. Lack of economic resources, inaccessibility to courts and other institutions, lack of awareness of rights, lack of knowledge of services available, and cultural and social reasons such as stigma and shame mean that most women do not go to the courts to seek protection from abuse.

Besides similar problems of implementation, Katjasungkana analyses several national laws that are in conflict with DVA stipulations. This constitutes one of the biggest structural barriers to the successful implementation of the DVA. The laws include the 1974 Marriage Law, the 1991 KHI and the Labour law. Another problem is Indonesia's system of Legal Pluralism, a legacy of Dutch colonialism. Additionally, there is the dichotomy between civil and criminal legal and court jurisdiction; domestic violence straddles both. Regional peculiarities such as the comprehensive implementation of Syariah in the Aceh province also contribute to the difficulty of enforcing laws based on the principle of gender rights as human rights.

Poor conviction rates in domestic violence cases and unwieldy court procedures have made legal remedies less useful for women. Hence, the passage of India's Protection of Women from Domestic Violence Act (PWDVA) did not radically transform the notion that family privacy was sacrosanct. Many surveys in India, as discussed in Nandy's chapter, confirm the popular perception that "domestic violence is a family affair". The privacy of family will continue to sustain gendered hierarchies that are often dependent on the deployment of male domination and violence. In such a situation, law "becomes a site of ambiguity instead of a force against these acts [acts it condones, controls and penalizes]".

In relation to culture, Nandy's chapter also describes how counselling rather than conviction and punishment of domestic violence offenders has emerged as the closest "private" solution to the issue, making the "heightened presence of law in family matters [. . .] a mere chink in the armour of the private family". Her point is that while law might be able to re-order the family, law itself can be restrained by culture.

Alipio's chapter attempts to arrive at a clearer cultural understanding of why women prefer to remain silent in cases of abuse. In the region where Alipio conducted her study, women have limited personal, community and state resources to aid them in their pursuit of justice. Hence, the silence of Filipinas may not be as detrimental as usually perceived, since women could be using "silence" as a strategy to free themselves from abuse. Many overseas Filipinas explain their decision to go abroad in terms of fate, which is construed as an act of faith, where one gambles on the chance of another future free from abuse. However, in migrating to escape abusive relationships, Filipina mothers also face guilt and criticism from others who control and normalize the regime of male domination. Thus, transnational migration is a contradictory process, where both freedoms and costs collude, as in gambling. Alipio's finding also show that it is the significant role played by NGOs, rather than law, that makes the difference. They provide crisis intervention and support services and prevent victims from resorting to religious and spiritual doctrines or migration for solutions.

As Mohamad's chapter shows, Malaysia's domestic violence law is a limited success story. The "compromise" law does not satisfy all parties nor does it fully criminalize the offence of domestic violence. The ambiguous status of the law, being both civil and criminal, has become an obstruction to the solution. Mohamad's study shows that gendered violence, even if defined within the ambit of the Malaysian Penal Code, will still not be sufficiently addressed by it, given the complex nature of "hurt" and "harm" inflicted by intimate partners on each other.

Römkens' chapter alerts us to current debates within the European Union (EU), where a substantive minority of EU member states are arguing to extend the scope of the international convention on domestic violence to include male victims. They perceive this as necessary to entrench the principle of gender neutrality of the law. Römkens points out that this ignores existing international legal standards contained in the Convention on the Elimination of Discrimination Against Women (CEDAW), which declares that violence against women is a form of gender-based discrimination and a human rights violation. In contrast, the European Court of Human Rights (ECHR) has asserted that domestic violence is indeed a form of discrimination and has ruled that it is the state's duty, under the due diligence principle, to take measures to provide protection and avoid risk for victims in potential danger of violence. Law is indeed empowering but it is also constraining. Römkens concludes with Foucault's observation that law, although unique in its powers, has long lost its "all-powerful disciplinary position".

Process

A third crucial layer, after "concept" and "law", is "process"— how actors and stakeholders participate in making domestic violence an agenda for national and global engagements and interventions.

In Mohamad's chapter, the Malaysian DVA is presented as one of the most outstanding examples of drafting a law from the basics, involving the participation of a spectrum of interest groups. The major players were women's civil society groups, political parties, government institutions, the police and the print media. Significantly, the VAW movement was also led by the middle-class, which depended significantly on newspapers (particularly the English language press) for its voice and legitimacy. The passage of Malaysia's DVA is discussed as a terrain upon which the narratives of human rights, autonomous subjects, emancipated women and multicultural citizenship are outlined, disputed, claimed and carved.

The campaign and social movement behind the establishment of the DVA in Indonesia is another significant social process, creating rights consciousness around gender-based violence. Katjasungkana documents how NGOs like LHB-APIK and Rifka Annisa collaborated with state agencies like the Gender Unit of the Ministry of Religious Affairs and the Indonesian National Commission on VAW to push for legislation on domestic violence. APIK, the lead organizer, uses the concept of the triangle of empowerment involving civil society, parliament and government. The women's movement, feminist politicians and feminist civil servants (femocrats) converged and proved to be powerful players in the eventual passage of the DVA. The drafting team consisted of Members of Parliament, the Parliamentary Forum on Population, established academics, law professors and members of APIK. The law was finally enacted on 14 September 2004, and became effective on 22 September 2004, during the term of President Megawati Soekarnoputri.

The above triangulation of civil society, politicians and bureaucrats finds similar resonance in the Malaysian domestic violence movement. The campaign for a DVA in Malaysia started as early as 1985 although the law was only passed in 1994 and enforced in 1996. Like in Indonesia, the drafting of the bill was an inclusive process that engaged many different representatives of civil society and government, including the religious bureaucracy.

Ganapathy's study reveals that police response to domestic violence is largely circumscribed by a state discourse that discourages its criminalization. The most readily available remedy is the Protection Order. However, Ganapathy argues that protection subjects women to further abuse, as it gives significant room to the state to be both "motivator and dispenser of that protection". The police are entrusted with setting the boundaries on what constitutes "deserving" or "undeserving" violence. The chapter details how the police are, in fact, drawn into a (social) process whenever they respond to women who report violence. They define which forms of abuse are to be criminalized and made arrestable and which are to be condoned or excused. Policing violence furtively then reproduces the general order of social divisions based not only on gender, but class and race in a stratified Singapore society.

In making sense of the process, Römkens observes, "violence against women has become the domain of many social and political actors aiming to regulate the field and in doing so, discipline citizens." She contends that the public–private dichotomy has been useful for many different political agendas, such as politicians and social scientists inscribing the nature of gender relations in the home, when it comes to domestic violence. With many different actors, including civil society, shaping how violence against women is eventually legislated, this is a challenge for feminist activists, scholars and women's NGOs to entrench their positions within current debate and policy. More than anything else, the domestic violence cause has shown that "crucial decision making processes in legislative domains", as noted by Römkens, are no longer under the authority of only the state or legislative bodies, but include the participation of many institutions and actors.

Conclusion

We have sketched the outline and main arguments of the chapters in this volume. By contextualizing the analysis of domestic violence within the notion of family ambiguity, many complex, if not incomprehensible aspects of the issue can be explored. At the policy level, it is hoped that these questions can throw new light on how the state should relate to the family as an "ambiguous" unit, often used to represent the unified state, yet in contrast to the state itself. By theorizing and presenting field evidence around the issue of "family ambiguity", this volume studies the various intervention measures upon the family, especially their positive and negative possibilities towards the resolution of domestic violence in society.

References

Amirthalingam, Kumaralingam (2005) "Women's Rights, International Norms, and Domestic Violence: Asian Perspectives", *Human Rights Quarterly*, Vol. 27(2) (May, 2005), pp. 683–708

Awang, Halimah and Hariharan, Sharon (2011) "Determinants of Domestic Violence: Evidence from Malaysia", *Journal of Family Violence*, Vol. 24 (6), pp. 459–464.

Bates, Lisa M., Sidney Ruth Schuler, Farzana Islam and Md. Khairul Islam (2004), "Socioeconomic Factors and Processes Associated with Domestic Violence in Rural Bangladesh", *International Family Planning Perspectives*, Vol. 30 (4), on Gender-Based Violence and Reproductive Health, pp. 190–199.

Clark, Cari Jo, Jay Silverman, Inaam A. Khalaf, Basem Abu Ra'ad, Zeinab Abu Al Sha'ar, Abdullah Abu Al Ata and Anwar Batieha (2008) "Intimate Partner Violence and Interference with Women's Efforts to Avoid Pregnancy in Jordan", *Studies in Family Planning*, Vol. 39(2), pp. 123–132

Das, Veena (2008) "Violence, Gender, and Subjectivity", *Annual Review of Anthropology*. Vol. 37, pp. 283–99

Fernández-Montalvo, J., Echeburúa, E. (2008) "Personality disorders and psychopathy in men convicted for severe intimate partner violence", *Psicothema*, 20 (2), pp. 193–198.

Goode, William J. (1971), "Fear and Violence in the Family", *Journal of Marriage and Family*, Vol. 33(4) Part 2, pp. 624–636.

Gottman, J.M., Jacobson, N.S., Rushe, R.H., Wu Shortt, J., Babcock, J., La Taillade, J.J., Waltz, J. (1995) "The relationship between heart rate reactivity, emotionally aggressive behavior, and general violence in batterers", *Journal of Family Psychology*, 9 (3), pp. 227–248.

Hamberger, L.K., Hastings, J. (1988) "Characteristics of male spouse abusers consistent with personality disorders", *Hospital and Community Psychiatry*, 39 (7), pp. 763–770.

Jaggar, Alison (1983) *Feminist Politics and Human Nature*. Sussex: Harvester Press.

Koenig, Michael A., Saifuddin Ahmed, Mian Bazle Hossain and A. B. M. Khorshed Alam Mozumder (2003) "Women's Status and Domestic Violence in Rural Bangladesh: Individual- and Community-Level Effects", *Demography*, Vol. 40(2), pp. 269–288

Yount, Kathryn M. and Carrera, Jennifer S. (2006) "Domestic Violence against Married Women in Cambodia", *Social Forces*, Vol. 85(1), pp. 355–387

CHAPTER

1

Domestic Violence

An Introduction to the Debates

Saskia E. Wieringa and Maznah Mohamad

Violence Against Women (VAW), including Domestic Violence (DV), its most prevalent form, is a human rights and a women's rights concern as well as a public health issue. DV is generally underreported, ongoing and pervasive, though both prevalence and forms may be context specific. In an unequal gender regime, where DV is both an effect of women's subordination and an instrument to maintain it, victims are often blamed or they blame themselves for the violence they experience. Such a situation has compelled officials of the United Nations (UN), including the office of the Secretary-General, to recognize domestic violence as "one of the most pervasive and pressing human rights concerns faced by the international community" (Meyersfeld 2010: vii). Reliable statistics being rare, a rough estimate has it that in 1999, one in three women at some stage in their lives experienced a form of VAW. This figure, by Heise and others (1994), has been widely quoted as a window to the gravity of the problem (see also Garcia-Moreno, Heise, Jansen, Ellsberg and Watts 2005). Apart from direct economic costs (loss of work time, costs for health services), the high human and emotional costs warrant urgent attention. Yet, at the national level, DV is still often seen as a private concern, not deserving of systematic state attention. Therefore, committed scholarship must persist in mapping the problem and analyzing issues of prevention, advocacy and resolution.

The discourse on VAW and DV in most countries is significantly initiated and shaped by the women's movement (see Htun and Weldon 2012 and chapters by Mohamad, Katjasungkana and Römkens in this volume). Since the 1970s, activists and researchers have underscored the serious consequences of this most prevalent form of violence that many women experience. Human rights institutes and public health officials have also taken up the issue and play an increasingly important role in both research and policy making. However, a great variation in levels of prevalence —

due to underreporting, differences in research methods, definitional concepts and sampling techniques — has made it difficult to establish actual prevalence rates of DV in any context. For instance, on the basis of an analysis of over 50 population-based surveys, Watts and Zimmerman report that between 10 and 50 percent of women who have ever had partners have experienced physical violence by an intimate partner at some point in their lives (2002: 1233). This wide variation indicates serious methodological discrepancies. Nevertheless, a comparative overview of figures indicating women's experience of domestic violence has demonstrated its widespread prevalence in both developed and developing societies (see Yount and Carrera 2006: 356).

In Asia, although relative numbers of those abused may vary from one regional or national context to the other, there is still a common thread — that women are the most vulnerable targets of violence within their own homes (see Koenig et al. 2004). Although there are numerous studies that have attempted to find the causal link between the preponderance of domestic violence and factors such as poverty, lack of female education, religious values or access to credit (see for example, Bates et al. 2004), none have conclusively established the root cause of the problem. Still, there is widespread agreement among researchers, activists and concerned policy makers that VAW is a social bane in need of analysis and solution and that the only sure protection for women against violence is the improvement of their social status (Jewkes 2002). Their status is related to patriarchal systems. A broad study of various forms of direct, indirect and structural forms of violence against women in Asia pointed to the prevalence of patriarchal notions of honour, shame and sexual purity linked to VAW (Manderson and Bennett 2003). Most recent research and policy making has concentrated on assessing the substantive harm and social costs that domestic violence has imposed upon society.

Discourses on DV

Domestic violence arose as a major issue in the wake of a so-called second wave of feminism. In the West, slogans coined by feminists, such as "the personal is political", stimulated women to speak out about their sufferings and shame and revealed the family to be an institution capable of covering up and justifying violence. Brownmiller's claim that rape is nothing more or less than a conscious process of intimidation by which all men keep all women in a state of fear (1975) highlighted the ubiquity of private and public VAW. In consciousness-raising groups, women discovered that the protective sanctuary of the home is also the most dangerous place for many women. The discovery that the perpetrators of sexual violence were not just unknown rapists but were more likely to be intimate partners came as a shock. From the mid-1970s, interpersonal violence could no longer be recognized as a private problem that was the misfortune of select women being battered by select dysfunctional men.

By politicizing DV, the women's movement succeeded in redefining the public–private divide, making it possible to conceptualize DV as a human rights issue related to bodily integrity and the right to autonomy. Resolution of such violence then is no longer a private affair, but a state concern, extending to international law. The right to be free from intimate harm has since become a "steady theme in international law" (Meyersfeld 2010: 316). However, intimate partner violence is still not incorporated systematically into mainstream international affairs and legislation. An issue of contention is the compatibility of human rights with group cultural rights, the touchstone of the latter being gender-based inequalities (and of homophobia), according to some of their proponents. However, the contention over this position only shows that cultural or religious norms can never be endorsed as an excuse for injury (see Aziz in this volume). In fact, the failure of some states to comply with anti -VAW laws can be seen as complicity, especially their acts of omission in not taking adequate steps to prevent the risk of violence among the vulnerable (Meyersfeld 2010: 206).

During the first few decades of the second wave of the women's movement in the West, VAW was seen as a single issue related to women's subordination. Its interconnections with other variables in women's lives, such as class, caste, sexual orientation, ethnicity and religion were often ignored. Crenshaw (1991) was among the first authors to point to the danger of white women essentializing the category of woman in the discourse on VAW, just as antiracist politics tended to essentialize racism as the problem of Black men. Since then, many authors (Collins 2000, Lockhart and Danis 2010, to name a few) have enriched our understanding of the complexities of identity politics. Single-issue solidarity politics gave way to strategically informed affinity politics (Wieringa 2009). The emphasis on intersectionality allows researchers and practitioners to understand the unique experiences of each victim of violence within a multi-layered context of individual and psychological traits intersecting with social, cultural, political and religious relations. In this way, both systemic oppression and marginalization, resulting from multiple, imbricating levels of subordination and the individual situation of the victims of gender-based violence can be understood. This avoids simplistic single-factor analyses and allows for an exploration of the various pathways to empowerment. Different levels of education and social and economic status, for instance, bring with them specific forms of social capital that survivors can draw upon. As Brah and Phoenix (2004) stress, the diverse identities of people cannot be separated into discrete and pure strands. One element (poverty or sexual orientation) is always inseparably interlocked with other elements that make up the complex, unique configurations of our subjectivities and identities.

In the global South, DV arose as an issue linked to various factors. In several countries, including Argentina, Brazil, Chile and Indonesia, attention was drawn to VAW in the context of struggles against military dictatorships. As women mobilized to fight state repression, they also decided it was time to end the violence they experienced in their homes. The end of apartheid in South Africa brought with it the political realization that violence within the home was as unacceptable as violence against citizens on the streets.

DV as human rights violation

Another impetus for global debates on VAW came from the UN Decade for Women (1986–1995) and the mobilization of women worldwide on the basis of human rights and development. Women's NGOs in the global South were originally set up to stimulate increased participation of women in development, but had already identified VAW in their early days as being a major impediment to women's progress (Yudelman 1987). Interestingly enough, at that time gender and development theorists, predominantly from the West, largely ignored such "personal" issues as DV and sexuality (Wieringa 1994).

Feminist global activists, however, argued for the recognition of VAW as a human rights issue. As Bunch passionately argued:

> Significant numbers of the world's population are routinely subject to torture, starvation, terrorism, humiliation, mutilation, and even murder simply because they are female. Crimes such as these against any group other than women would be recognized as a civil and political emergency as well as a gross violation of the victim's humanity. Yet, despite a clear record of deaths and demonstrable abuse, women's rights are not commonly classified as human rights. (1991: 3)

Or, as Ashworth had noted a few years earlier: "violence against the female sex, on a scale which far exceeds the list of Amnesty International victims, is tolerated publicly; indeed some acts of violation are not crimes in law, others are legitimized in custom or court and most are blamed on the victims themselves" (1986:8).

In 1979, the Convention on the Elimination of All Forms of Discrimination Against Women (CEDAW) was adopted by the UN General Assembly. Unfortunately, CEDAW has no specific clause on domestic violence although it addresses many issues of discrimination against women. The UN officially recognized VAW in 1992, when the CEDAW Committee recommended (Resolution 48-104) that periodic country reports should include information about the prevalence of VAW and the measures being taken to protect women.

Since it is a convention, CEDAW is similar to state law for the countries that have ratified it — to date, over 180. This is unlike documents with more far-reaching feminist language, such as the 1995 Beijing Platform for Action (reconfirmed in the Beijing +15 conference in 2010). Unfortunately both CEDAW and the Beijing PFA are among the many documents built on international consensus that governments can put aside once they have pocketed the international goodwill that comes from signing it. CEDAW has legal legitimacy although it has no formal means of enforcement.[1] It can only shame, not bully, countries into compliance. However, as Merry (2003) argues, it is instrumental in fostering a process of cultural change where women's human rights require legitimacy at the local level. It does so primarily through the periodic reports countries are required to submit. Civil society is actively involved in this review process by the presentation of "shadow reports" at CEDAW meetings, hence providing the "checks and balances" to government reports.

It was due to persistent feminist pressures that the Second World Conference on Human Rights in 1993 addressed VAW as a serious international concern. The United Nations High Commissioner for Human Rights defined VAW in 1993 as:

> any act of gender-based violence that results in or is likely to result in physical, sexual or psychological harm or suffering to women, including threats of such acts, coercion or arbitrary deprivation of liberty, whether occurring in public, or in private life, and including domestic violence, crimes committed in the name of honour, crimes committed in the name of passion, trafficking in women and girls, traditional practices harmful to women, including female genital mutilation, early and forced marriages, female infanticide, dowry-related violence and deaths, acid attacks and violence related to commercial sexual exploitation as well as economic exploitation. (quoted in Wies and Haldane 2011: 2)

The European Court of Human Rights followed suit as recently as 2009, while the European Council is only now working on a convention to address VAW as a form of gender discrimination. In Asia, the rise of international and regional networks of women's NGOs such as the International Women's Rights Action Watch of the Asia-Pacific (IWRAW-AP) and the Asia-Pacific Women in Law and Development (APWLD) have facilitated the exchange of information on VAW and strategies to combat it. Recently, ASEAN has begun paying more attention to VAW issues (UNIFEM 2009) and to human rights issues in general. However, there is great concern among feminists about the wording of the ASEAN Human Rights Declaration which was recently endorsed by leaders of the 10-member association in Cambodia in November 2012. Critics, consisting of some 50 civil society groups, including Human Rights Watch and Amnesty International pointed to clauses which could open up room for human rights violation in the name of national security, public order and public morality, among others (Kozlovski 2012). Before this the Women's Caucus of ASEAN had already circulated a petition to strike out the "public morality" clause from the Declaration. Members of the caucus feared that the introduction of "public morality" as a collective interest limits human rights and will eventually be used to deny women's human rights, especially sexual and reproductive health rights.[2]

Over the last decade, the Millennium Development Goals (MDGs) have also provided a major impetus for development issues. International and national actors have committed to reach a number of goals by 2015, including steps to diminish gender inequality. The MDGs stipulate that the UN and all its member states recognize that equal rights and opportunities for women and men are a prerequisite for human development. This entails that VAW must be addressed within the agendas for health, development, equality and human rights.

If VAW is seen as a human rights issue by the very nature of the human rights instruments that it is subjected to, it readily becomes a public issue. However, human rights concepts need to be translated into relevant policies and national laws for them to become effective. In this regard, the main human rights principles applicable in the context of VAW are freedom of expression, protection from violence and the guarantee of personal security.

Public health

Besides its human rights aspect, VAW is now widely recognized as having serious implications for the health of women and children. The 15-sites WHO study on women's health and domestic violence of 2005 charts the impact that VAW has on women's health.[3] The study points out that interpersonal violence (IPV) is an important cause of death among women (caused by both homicides and suicides) and contributes to high maternal mortality rates and an increased number of induced abortions. The study affirms that most of this violence remains hidden, as few women report it to the police and women tend not to seek health services. The physical and mental effects of VAW could be long lasting and are linked to emotional distress and suicide attempts (Garcia-Moreno et al. 2005). The study further found that there was a significant association between lifetime experiences of partner violence and self-reported poor health and specific health problems occurring in the previous four weeks, such as difficulty in walking and with daily activities, pain, memory loss, dizziness and vaginal discharge (Ellsberg et al. 2008). The researchers conclude that intimate partner violence is "associated with serious public health consequences that should be addressed in national and global health policies and programmes" (Ellsberg et al. 2008: 1165).

VAW is also a major mental health concern. The 2005 WHO multi-country research concludes that suicidal tendencies among women have a strong association with violence. The study recommends that violence be recognised as a major risk factor for women's ill-health and that mental health policy take this into account (Devries et al. 2011:85).

A national survey conducted in the US (1800 respondents) on VAW found that 60 percent of the respondents experienced at least one form of violence since age 18. Specific groups of women, such as biracial or multiracial women, native women, women receiving public assistance and lesbian and bisexual women, were at higher risk of experiencing violence in their lifetimes (Moracco et al. 2007). This study too points to the physical and mental health consequences of DV and the implications for the public health sector.

While crucial in controlling the incidence of DV, public health policies, such as those informed by the MDGs, can also be seen as a form of biopolitics in their focus on techniques, services and management of bodies. Together with the legal and policy apparatus, based on CEDAW and other international human rights instruments set in place in most countries, the anti-DV arrangements can be seen as a classic Foucauldian disciplinary system.[4] Nevertheless, this technology of power produces "modern" cultural meanings that question local religious and cultural traditions in which VAW might be condoned.

Anti-feminist backlash

Recently, a debate has surfaced on the perceived feminist bias of the domestic violence discourse. Advocates of the "family violence" concept argue that men fall victim to DV too. Proponents of this approach, which is gaining currency in policy and research circles, as Römkens demonstrates in this volume, use "gender neutral wording", wherein conflicts are seen as a normal part of family life. However, studies that document such violence fail to distinguish between aggressive and defensive acts and between the severity and frequency of various acts. While all forms of violence must be prosecuted, it has to be stressed that the majority of DV victims are women and that in general they are in a much more vulnerable position vis à vis the perpetrators and in courts that may reinforce stereotypes of the ideal "good woman" accepting her male partner's authority. Inevitably, in this "gender neutral" approach, sexual and economic VAW will be underestimated or overlooked.

The review of national surveys of intimate partner violence by Esquivel-Santoveña and Dixon (2012) is driven by a concern that the problem is usually framed as men's VAW, and that the level of men's victimization is underestimated. Excluding sexual, economic and psychological aggression, they maintain that the US Family Violence Surveys that report approximate symmetry between men and women are the most reliable instruments and that they should be applied more widely. In these surveys, partner violence is normalized as everyday family conflicts and only mild forms are identified as family violence. More extreme forms of violence are excluded from the survey, in addition to sexual forms of aggression, as the questionnaire was "already lengthy" (Esquivel-Santoveña and Dixon 2012:216). Presenting their work as based on "surveys of sound methodology" they advocate that "if the true nature of the problem is to be understood", future surveys on intimate partner violence must "adopt a gender inclusive approach and further methodology conducive of both sexes reporting their experiences" (2012: 217).

In this battle on methodology, it is, therefore, imperative to pay close attention to the definitions of VAW that are being used. VAW as defined by the UN High Commissioner in 1993, and quoted earlier in this chapter, is wide and has the advantage that it focuses on women and girls.

Other concepts used to understand VAW have different connotations. While the more neutral term "interpersonal violence" (IPV) applies to any violent act between individuals, irrespective of their relationship, the term "family violence" focuses on family members. In both cases, it is usually unclear that women and girls are the majority of the victims. The kind of violence deployed, whether aggressive or defensive, and the nature of the harm or pain inflicted is not mentioned. "Family violence" also leaves out such phenomena as stalking, eve teasing, rape, gender-based violence in the public sphere and harassment in the workplace. On the other hand, "gender-based violence" points specifically to acts of violence associated both with gender positionality and sexual orientation and includes violence against individuals identifying as Gay, Lesbian, Bisexual, Transsexual or Intersexual (GLBTI). In the case of GLBTI, perpetrators are not necessarily family members or intimate partners, although these forms of violence are included. It has to be noted that underreporting of intimate partner violence in gay and lesbian relationships is common.

The 2009 UNIFEM report on DV legislation in ASEAN countries also advises against gender-neutral language. The authors argue that such language "remains ambiguous and could lend itself to interpretations that are not based on an understanding of rights" (UNIFEM 2009:15). The report warns against consequences in the enforcement of dual protection orders that put unnecessary "restrictions on both parties because these could be used by a male perpetrator against a female survivor" (UNIFEM 2009: 16).

The ASEAN report recommends a detailed definition of what acts are to be included in the term "domestic violence" and to ensure that laws or policies capture women's experiences of violence in all its manifestations. It is advisable, the authors argue, to domesticate the definitions by "outlawing specific cultural manifestations of violence" (UNIFEM 2009: 17). An example of a cultural practice to be outlawed is forced child marriage that is included in the Vietnamese Domestic Violence Law.

The anti-feminist backlash against the "genderization" of DV is paired with the growing influence of fundamentalism in many countries, wherein the heterosexual family is sacralized and attempts are made to exercise sexual control on women and to push women out of the public sphere. In these discourses, women are positioned as carriers of religious and cultural authenticity and as bearers of family honour. In this view, women's sexuality needs to be controlled and guarded by their male family members, justifying the use of violence to this end.

The role of culture: the family unmasked

The insistence on "harmonious Asian families", as Wieringa analyzes in this volume, produces gendered expectations of women's behaviour. If a woman is considered not submissive, she is seen to provoke the violence enacted upon her (Burton 2011). All over Asia, women are stereotyped as either naturally or religiously ordained to be subservient, dutiful, passive and demure. The result is that women harbour feelings of guilt and self-blame if they have been abused. These attitudes also allow for women's reputations to be slandered in court by husbands and sexist lawyers. Men who kill their wives are often justified in court — they may have been provoked or may suffer from depression because of their partner's "unwifely" behaviour. If men defend themselves by invoking honour or upholding masculine dignity, their wrongs are usually excused, while such attenuating circumstances are never used in the case of wives killing their husbands.

Globally, patriarchal gender norms are a key factor in the prevalence of intimate partner violence (Garcia–Moreno et al. 2005). These norms are largely internalized by women, who agree, for instance, that women should obey their husbands, not refuse them sex and complete housework on time. The result is self-blame, shame, loyalty to the abusive partner or outright fear of retaliation if the victim seeks help. Religion is often used as a pretext for violence. This book includes examples from various religions (Catholicism, Islam, Hinduism).

Certain customs or beliefs that are prevalent in Asia reinforce the general climate in which VAW is condoned. These include the emphasis on pre-marital virginity, arranged marriages, early marriages for girls, polygyny, the dowry system and the joint family. Together, they are part of the different heteronormative structures that inform gender and kinship relations, as Wieringa analyzes. The emphasis on the "harmonious Asian family", based as it is on women's subordination, trivializes VAW and justifies it. As Amirthalingam (2005) stresses, Asian values propagated in this way are not compatible with international human rights law, ratified by the governments of the same states that propagate these values. In a similar vein, Aziz (in this volume) maintains that the cultural relativism under which the discourse of Asian values takes refuge is problematic, as masculine privilege is not challenged. Attendant conceptions of women's economic dependence (sometimes anchored in family or marriage laws, such as in Indonesia) and misogynous, patriarchal interpretations in religion help to keep women in subordinate positions. As Nandy demonstrates (in this volume), the patriarchal family structure in India is protected by both secular state laws and religious personal laws. In Indonesia, the newly promulgated regional bylaws often include articles that restrict women's mobility, impose dress codes on women, criminalize homosexuality and enshrine women's subservience (Katjasungkana in this volume). Heteronormativity imposes binary patterns of sex and gender and strengthens intolerance for intermediate categories, such as transgender or intersex.

The entrenched patriarchal biases in many countries are accompanied by a "double morality", with men allowed sexual freedoms that are denied to women (such as polygyny, tolerance for extramarital sex); this results in mistrust between spouses and a lack of communication. It is often difficult for women who have experienced violence in such cultures to come forward and fight for their rights. They may lose the support of their kin, while the state is unable (or unwilling) to protect them. Patriarchal biases related to women's sexuality and behaviour are often internalized by the law enforcers themselves. In the Philippines, as Alipio demonstrates, legal officers who should protect women, based on the anti-VAW law, are instead partial towards the perpetrators.

As Merry concludes, only if vulnerable women experience a positive reaction to their claims for rights, can they see themselves as "rights-bearing subjects and claim rights in the next crisis" (2006: 215). Thus, the transformation from a culture in which patriarchal leaders (religious teachers, village heads and family patriarchs) are the major power holders and thus, the most important sources of resources, to a modern community based on legal certainty requires the active involvement of local NGOs that can translate grievances and violence into rights language.

As noted above, definitions of what constitutes DV are not always consistent. Marital rape is often not included in anti-VAW legislation (see Nandy and Mohamad in this volume). In fact, where it is included, it is ignored by lawmakers. Women tend not to report it, police officials and judges trivialize it and religious officials condemn women who complain about non-consensual sex. Coupled with the anti-feminist backlash discussed above, women complaining of DV are often accused of causing the disintegration of the family. This victim-blaming is widespread and may extend to women's organizations supporting victims of DV or lobbying for anti-VAW legislation.

Other factors that support tolerance or prevalence of VAW are the low education levels and poverty of many women and early marriages of girls. Coupled with the public silence on sexual matters and the absence of sexual education in school curricula, young women in particular are vulnerable (Jejeebhoy, Shah and Thapa 2005). They suffer most from shame and fear, leading to serious underreporting of DV. Young women often lack persons they can trust and with whom they can share their trauma. Fear of stigma exacerbates their silence. Schoolchildren in urban environments may fall victim to economic blackmail by sugar daddies who feel entitled to force sex upon young girls in exchange for material favours.

To help fight for their rights, girls and young women need sexual literacy. The Special Rapporteur on the right to education stressed the right to sexual education in his 2010 report to the United Nations, placing it in the context of patriarchy and control of sexuality.[5] He explained the interdependence of sexuality, health and education and the relationship of this right to other rights.

The role of law: empowering but limited

An important concern in domestic violence debates is the efficacy of the law itself. Feminist organizations have invested much time, energy and resources in mobilizing a campaign to enact laws that can help reduce or deter domestic violence. However, in almost all experiences, whether in developed or developing countries, in a Western (for example, Bailey 2010) or Asian (for example, Amirthalingam 2005) context, the law has been found to be only one of many institutional structures that should be deployed towards the resolution of the problem. Many studies have emerged to assess the aftermath of a legislative victory, not just to measure the success of domestic violence law in its implementation, but also to revisit some conceptual flaws of the law itself (see Mohamad and Katjasungkana in this volume).

These emerging difficulties are related chiefly to the peculiar nature of regulating the family. It has been suggested that, (1) domestic violence law is about regulating power and control in intimate relationships and, therefore, lacks a clear divide between the adversarial parties; (2) criminalizing domestic violence involves making the private public, hence entailing different positions among states on this matter; (3) the trauma of victimization among intimate family members raises dilemmas about how the public could also remain private; (4) considerable gaps exist between cultural, religious and social realities in the intention and substance of the law itself and (5) there are legal ambivalences that treat domestic violence as both a civil and a quasi-criminal offence, or in many cases as a "wrong" that straddles crime and moral transgression.

The Protection Order is the first line of defence against more violence. This has been found to be intimidating and uncertain, as "credible" hurt is subject to the evaluation of the police (see Ganapathy and Mohamad in this volume). Criminalizing the offence is the next stage, which is again at the discretion of the police and the will of the victim. Many women withdraw their complaints out of fear of losing their children and their source of support, their offenders. Using the law is not always helpful;

instead, it could be dangerous in the long run for women who might not have the ability to see the prosecution process through to the end. Thus, while a law on domestic violence is conceptually powerful, the legal method is inherently filled with obstacles (Douglas 2012: 123). The legal method claims to be neutral but is actually biased against those who cannot use legal language and legal structures (such as the courts) properly. Other practical impediments include the lengthy litigious process before any results can be expected out of a criminal procedure.

Recent studies have shown that the criminal justice system is a limited tool when it comes to addressing domestic violence, a complex issue with social, political, and economic implications (Bailey 2010). The present criminal justice system focuses on punishment and conviction and may not suit the nature of the offence. While feminists believe mandatory punishment would have a deterrence value, if not a symbolic message, to would-be offenders, victims may be ambivalent about choosing this route. A major dilemma (see Ganapathy and Mohamad in this volume) is also whether victims should have autonomy to proceed or withdraw their complaint or should this be left entirely to the state?

On a more optimistic note, studies are also emerging that show the power of using law, not so much for its outcomes, but for the process itself. Douglass maintains that "going to law" is like "doing feminism" and eventually leads towards empowerment (2012: 130). Lazarus-Black states that the critical issue is that a DV law has an ideological impact on the nation (2001:399). Merry (2003: 973) writes that the importance of a DV law lies not so much in texts being used for enforcement but for the production of new cultural meanings and norms. Many women have had their rights-consciousness raised in the process of using the law, especially in getting access to support, advice, trust and faith provided by women's advocacy groups and service centres (see Mohamad in this volume and studies by Lazarus-Black 2001 and Douglas 2012).

Other conceptual contestations

As discussed above, the women's movement in the 1970s successfully revealed VAW and, in particular, DV to be a public issue. Yet, the debate continues in relation to law: should DV be dealt with as an issue better resolved between the parties in a civil court, as many family affairs are, or should it be seen as a criminal offence? As Burton (2011) argues, on the basis of developments in England and Wales, DV can be treated as a public issue and could acquire public attention both in a civil and in a criminal justice system. She stresses, however, that to effectively do so, traditional gender roles must be challenged.

VAW must also be seen as a form of structural violence, even when it takes place within a family setting. It is by emphasizing the structural underpinnings of VAW that it can be brought into the open and transformed from a "hidden" problem to a political cause. As long as VAW remains hidden, the suffering of victims remains hidden and perpetrators remain protected.

Another contention is the issue of consensuality. It is not a criterion in all cases to determine whether a sexual act is criminalized or not. In heterosexual marriages, non-consensual sex is criminalized, while in many Asian countries, consensual sex in LGBT relations is criminalized. The right to privacy in both cases is invoked differently. In a heterosexual marriage, women claim the right to privacy to avoid unwelcome sexual contact. LGBT people, on the other hand, are not accorded the right to privacy to protect them from state interference, in cases where homosexuality is criminalized. The right to privacy is clearly of critical concern, but it should also be applied universally in relation to premarital and extramarital relationships and to LGBT people. The basic premise should be that violence is simply not acceptable, just as racism is no longer tolerated under any circumstance.

Human rights are indispensable, indivisible and universal, but their application is not universal or unproblematic. Nor are they sufficient to protect women and sexual minorities, as Corrêa et al. (2008) argue.[6] It is, thus, important to insist that human rights apply to all persons under all circumstances and to insist on maximum applicability of human rights instruments in individual countries. Attempts to invoke religious or cultural arguments to limit the applicability of human rights must be resisted.[7]

The triangle of women's empowerment

Finally, it has to be recognized that the successful lobbying for anti-VAW legislation often takes place within the so-called triangle of women's empowerment (Wieringa and Vargas 1997). In this model, autonomous women's organizations, femocrats and politicians, and researchers collaborate, each in their different ways to get legislation passed (see Mohamad and Katjasungkana in this volume). At the first level, women's organizations call attention to the severity of the problem and lobby for an anti-VAW law. In the case of anti-VAW legislation feminist mobilization has been the motor of the triangle. Using data from 70 countries Htun and Weldon (2012) conclude that feminist mobilization in civil society in relation to VAW is the major factor impacting policy development. This variable has a larger impact than GDP, or legislative efforts stimulated by progressive parties or femocrats. Autonomous women's movements also produced an enduring impact on VAW policy as they influenced the international language on VAW policies.

Femocrats and feminist politicians enter the second stage of this collaboration to get the law passed. Research is important at various stages of the process, first in detailing the prevalence and seriousness of VAW as well as the human and economic costs, then in making an academic draft of legislation and finally in analysing the implementation of the new law. Qualitative research to assess the psychological impact and traumas of VAW must also complement other forms of investigation. Researchers can then equip themselves to participate in policies and strategies. Ultimately, a more focused policy research can help in producing more effective lobbying instruments By using such an approach, Katjasungkana argues, the Indonesian women's movement gained some victories in its fight for an anti-VAW law. This same approach can help pinpoint shortcomings in the implementation of the law as discussed in Mohamad and Katjasungkana (in this volume).

Conclusion

In view of the seriousness of VAW and DV, as a breach of human rights and a public health concern, it is critical that an agreement on definitions and research tools be reached. The anti-women's backlash spurred by the family violence approach may lead to the continuation of practices that put women's health and safety in jeopardy. For laws and policies to be effective, we believe that they must be based on grounded research and a compelling and reliable database that is context-specific and nationally and internationally comparable, as well as guided by a gender-sensitive epistemic framework. VAW is a global phenomenon, rooted in the unequal balance of power between women and men, in which women suffer severe forms of physical, emotional, sexual and economic harm. Laws and policies must reflect this recognition. International tools such as the MDGs and other human rights instruments, particularly CEDAW and the Beijing Platform For Action, should continue to be the basis of social advocacy, law-making and policy-generation for VAW. Sexual literacy, legal awareness among women and gender awareness among law enforcers must be given special attention, as should education for girls and a ban on early marriages. As DV takes place in the home and is often justified by patriarchal biases that stipulate that women should be demure, dependent and submissive, the fallacy of the harmonious Asian family must be exposed. That the home is not necessarily a safe place for women should be uncovered, so that women no longer have to suffer in shame and guilt but are instead empowered to report the violence they experience.

In redoubling efforts in the fight against VAW, a triangle of empowerment involving the collaboration of women's organizations, law enforcers and researchers is crucial. Not only because the bane of domestic violence carries with it enormous social and economic costs, but also because it is unequivocally unacceptable to leave in place conditions that allow for millions of women and girls worldwide to be subjected to the threat of battery, rape, molestation and assaults in their own homes.

Notes

1 Only in countries that have ratified the "Optional Protocol", can civil society actors lodge complaints with the CEDAW Committee. Until 2012, very few cases were brought up by civil society actors.
2 Petition circulating on aseancats@googlegroups.com, accessed 15 October 2012.
3 Over 24,000 women completed interviews in 15 sites in ten countries between 2000 and 2003.
4 Foucault elaborated this concept in several of his writings. He first discussed it in the Will to Knowledge (1976).
5 Report of the United Nations Special Rapporteur on the right to education; A/65/162, July 23 2010.
6 See also Adams and Pigg (2005) for a discussion on sexuality and morality in the global South.
7 The Indonesian Home Minister recently asserted that human rights must bow to religious values (http://www.thejakartapost.com/news/2012/09/24).

References

Adams, Vinçanne and Stacy Leigh Pigg, eds. (2005). *Sex in Development: Science, sexuality and morality in global perspective*. Durham and London: Duke University Press.

Amirthalingam, Kumaralingam. (2005). Women's rights, international norms and domestic violence: Asian perspectives. *Human Rights Quarterly* 27(2): pp. 683–708.

Ashworth, Georgina. (1986). *Of Violence and Violation: Women and human rights*. London: Change.

Bailey, Kimberly D. (2010). "Lost in translation: Domestic violence, 'the personal is political,' and the criminal justice system", *Journal of Criminal Law and Criminology*, Vol. 100(4): pp. 1255–1300.

Bates, Lisa M., Sidney Ruth Schuler, Farzana Islam and Md. Khairul Islam (2004). Socioeconomic Factors and Processes Associated with Domestic Violence in Rural Bangladesh, *International Family Planning Perspectives*, Vol. 30(4), on Gender-Based Violence and Reproductive Health, pp. 190–199.

Brah, A. and Phoenix, A. (2004). Ain't I a woman? Revisiting intersectionality. *Journal of International Women's Studies* 5 (3), pp. 75–86.

Brownmiller, Susan (1975). *Against our Will: Men, women and rape*. Middlesex: Penguin Books.

Bunch Charlotte (1991). Women's rights as human rights: towards a re-vision of human rights. In Charlotte Bunch and Roxanna Carrillo (eds), *Gender Violence: A development and human rights issue*. New Brunswick: The State University of New Jersey, The Center for Women's Global Leadership, pp. 3–18.

Burton, Mandy (2011). The legal construction of domestic violence: 'unmasking' a private problem. In Jackie Jones, Anna Grear, Rachel Ann Fenton and Kim Stevenson, eds., *Gender, Sexualities and Law*. New York and Abingdon: Routledge. pp. 161–173.

Collins, Paula, H. (2000). *Black Feminist Thought: Knowledge, consciousness and the politics of empowerment*. New York: Routledge.

Corrêa, Sonia, Rosalind Petchesky and Richard Parker (2008). *Sexuality, Health and Human Rights*. London and New York: Routledge.

Crenshaw, K.W. (1991). Mapping the margins: intersectionality, identity politics and violence against women of color. *Stanford Law Review*, Vol. 43 (6): pp. 1241–1299.

Devries, Karen, Charlotte Watts, Mieko Yoshihama, Ligia Kiss, Lilia Blima Schraiber, Negussie Deyessa, Lori Heise, Julia Durand, Jessie Mbwambo, Henrica Jansen, Yemane Berhane, Mary Ellsberg, Claudia Garcia-Moreno (2011). Violence against women is strongly associated with suicide attempts: Evidence from the WHO multi-country study on women's health and domestic violence against women. *Social Science & Medicine* 73(1): pp. 79–86.

Douglas, H. (2012). Battered Women's Experiences of the Criminal Justice System: Decentring the Law, *Feminist Legal Studies*, 20: 121–134.

Ellsberg, Mary, Henrica A.F.M. Jansen, Lori Heise, Charlotte H. Watts, Claudia Garcia-Moreno (2008). Intimate partner violence and women's physical and mental health in the WHO multi-country study on women's health and domestic violence: an observational study. *The Lancet* 371(9619): pp. 1165–72.

Esquivel-Santoveña, Esteban Eugenio and Louise Dixon. (2012). Investigating the true rate of physical intimate partner violence: a review of nationally representative surveys. *Agression and Violent Behavior*, 17(3): pp. 208–219.

Foucault, Michel. (1976). *La volonté de savoir*. Paris: Gallimard.

Garcia-Moreno, Lori Heise, Henrica A.F.M. Jansen, Mary Ellsberg and Charlotte Watts (2005). Violence against Women. *Science*, Vol. 310(5752): 25 November 2005, pp 1282–3.

Heise, Lori L., Alanagh Raikes, Charlotte H. Watts and Anthony B. Zwi (1994). Violence against Women: A neglected publish health issue in less developed countries. *Soc. Sci. Med*, vol. 39(9): pp. 1165–1179.

Htun, Mala and S. Laurel Weldon. (2012). The Civic origins of progressive policy change: combating violence against women in global perspective, 1975–2005. In *American Political Science Review*, Vol. 106, No. 3, August: pp. 548–567.

Jejeebhoy, Shireen J. Iqbal Shah and Shyam Tapa (2005). *Sex Without Consent; young people in developing countries*. London: Zed Books.

Jewkes, R. (2002) "Intimate partner violence: Causes and Prevention", *Lancet*, 359 (9315): pp. 1423–1429.

Koenig, Michael A., Saifuddin Ahmed, Mian Bazle Hossain and A. B. M. Khorshed Alam Mozumder (2003). Women's Status and Domestic Violence in Rural Bangladesh: Individual- and Community-Level Effects, *Demography*, Vol. 40, No. 2: pp. 269–288.

Kozlovski, Mary (2012) "ASEAN rights declaration meets with opposition", in *Deutsche Welle (DW)* , 19 November, *http://www.dw.de/asean-rights-declaration-meets-with-opposition/a-16390554* (last accessed 25 November 2012).

Manderson, Lenore and Linda Rae Bennett (2003). Introduction: Gender inequality and. technologies of violence. In Leonore Manderson and Linda Rae Bennett (eds), *Violence against Women in Asian societies*. London: RoutledgeCurzon, pp. 1–20

Merry, Sally Engle (2003) "Constructing a Global Law-Violence against Women and the Human Rights System", *Law & Social Inquiry*, Vol. 28, No. 4: pp. 941–977

Merry, Sally Engle. (2006). *Human Rights & Gender Violence: Translating international law into local justice.* London: University of Chicago Press.

Lazarus-Black, Mindy. (2001). "Law and Pragmatics of Inclusion: Governing Domestic Violence in Trinidad and Tobago", *American Ethnologist*, 28 (2): 388–416.

Lockhart, Lettie L. and Jacquelyn Mitchell (2010). 'Cultural competence and intersectionality: emerging frameworks and practical approaches'. In Lettie L. Lockhart and Fran S. Danis (eds.), *Domestic Violence: Intersectionality and culturally competent practice.* New York: Columbia University Press, pp. 1–29.

Meyersfeld, Bonita. (2010). *Domestic Violence and International Law.* Oxford and Portland: Hart.

Moracco, Kathryn E., Carol W. Runyan, J. Michael Bowling, Jo Anne L. Earp. (2007). Women's experiences with violence: a national study. *Women's Health Issues* 17: pp. 3–12.

UNIFEM (2009). *Domestic Violence Legislation and its Implementation: An analysis for ASEAN countries based on internationals standards and good practices.* Bangkok: UNIFEM East and Southeast Asia regional office.

Watts, Charlotte and Cathy Zimmerman. (2002). Violence against women: global scope and magnitude. *The Lancet*, Vol. 359(9313), April 6: pp. 1232–37.

Wieringa, Saskia E. (1994). Women's Interests and Empowerment; Gender Planning Reconsidered. *Development & Change*, Vol. 25/4: October, pp. 829–849.

Wieringa, Saskia E. (2009). From Solidarity to Affinity and Feminist Communal Identities. In: Wieringa et al., *A Herstory (2004–2008). The European Feminist Forum.* Amsterdam: Aletta Institute for Women's History, pp. 29–39

Wieringa Saskia E. and Virginia Vargas (1997). 'The Triangle of Empowerment: Processes and Actors in the Making of Public Policy for Women' in Wieringa and Vargas (eds), *The Women's Movement and Public Policy in Europe, Latin America and the Caribbean.* New York: Garland, pp. 3–25

Wies, Jennifer R. and Hilary J. Haldane. (2011). *Anthropology at the Front Lines of Gender-based Violence.* Nashville: Vanderbilt University Press.

Yount, Kathryn M. and Carrera, Jennifer S. (2006). Domestic Violence against Married Women in Cambodia. *Social Forces*, Vol. 85, No. 1: pp. 355–387

Yudelman, S. (1987). *Hopeful Openings: A Study of Five Development Organizations in Latin America and the Caribbean.* West Hartford, Conn.: Kumarian Press.

CHAPTER 2

Cultures of Violence and Silence

Amrita Nandy

Among all social institutions, the family enjoys a unique and special place in the social imagination as an ideal unit. It has come to be seen as a cultural trope with an ahistoric, "natural" and, most crucially, private existence. Therefore, any scrutiny into its intimate and sacrosanct space has often faced doubt, apprehension and resistance. India's engagement with the regulation of domestic violence has not been exceptional either. The long-standing struggle against the family's firm defence of privacy is replete with tussles among religious jurisprudence, cultural norms, modern legislation, notions of community identity and individual autonomy, justice and human rights' discourse.

This chapter traces the trajectory of family regulation vis-à-vis domestic violence in India and recounts crucial shifts, continuities and milestones in legislation and discourse. Through an outline ranging from the ancient Indian family's attempts at self-regulation to modern state-based regulation, it notes different ideologies and turn of events that have buttressed the notion of family privacy. The fence of privacy around the family was legally challenged in India only when dowry-related violence in the family laid bare a range of hidden domestic violence and abuse. Culturally, however, the family remains cocooned. This is true especially for the heteronormative family that has been institutionalized by the state, thus enjoying an iconic social status of sorts. (To a large extent, this explains why while rape in marriage has not been legally recognized *per se* and consensual homosexual relations were criminalized till 2009 and thus, bereft of any right to privacy all along.) Despite high-pitched and long-term mass campaigns to end the silence around domestic violence, women themselves continue to justify it amidst tacit public sanction and ironically, "Protection Officers" believe that domestic violence is a private matter. The chapter highlights, inter alia, such conundrums, polarized debates, backlash, judicial notions of chastity, morality and honour, experiments with "regulation", the state's shifting response to the family subject to its class, sexuality, religious orientation and so on. As the epicenter of these conflicts, the family has been exposed and rendered permeable, to some degree.

The chapter posits that while privacy of the family is valuable, it needs re-imagining within the framework of justice and human rights. Privacy has never been totally inviolate especially because its boundaries have constantly been adjusted by the state. Although law in India does not view domestic violence as a "private" matter, the cultural ideology that obliquely permits it, does. It contends that since law can subterraneously embody and perpetuate cultural codes, it cannot be expected to regulate, counter or undo prevalent socio-cultural notions and values, at least not single-handedly. The chapter, therefore, argues for a holistic formulation of the concept of privacy that lies both inside and outside the legislative arena.

Family and culture, an overview

To discuss the ambiguities of dealing with the family in India and place them in perspective, it will be useful to begin with a brief historical outline of how the family has been conceptualized in various socio-political discourses. Such an appraisal will highlight traditional attitudes towards the family, its private–public dimensions and attempts, if any, at its regulation.

Across most societies, the family is often singled out as a pre-political, privileged social body that deserves seclusion. In the West, for example, liberal theorists such as Locke offered "natural" explanations (often couched in religious idiom) to defend the private-ness of the family. In the *Second Treatise*, he drew sharp differences between paternal and political power, yet likened the man in the house to the ruler of a kingdom (2003: 318–320). Mentioning disputes in marriages, he dropped a covert hint at the role of the civil magistrate, while also conferring the last word upon the husband whom he saw as "naturally . . . abler and stronger" (2003: 321–322). The hierarchy within the private sphere was seen as prearranged and thus, normative — the husband was superior to the wife, children, servants and slaves (and in this order). Thus, in the eighteenth and early nineteenth centuries, common English law permitted a man to beat his wife with a stick as thick as his thumb, also called the "thumb rule" (Vindhya 2003: 334). This was seen as a way to discipline a junior, in this case the wife. Generations later, Frederick Engels turned the tables on the Lockeian stance by revealing economic inter-linkages between the rise of the monogamous family, private property and the state. In his critique of the bourgeois family, he asserted that the family was kept off-limits for outsiders because individual property — including the wife and children — had to be secured.

Engels claimed that the patriarchal family was a " . . . private service (where) the wife became the first domestic servant, pushed out of participation in social production" (1948: 105). It may be said that earlier Western liberals defended and sustained the private domain of the family while oddly charging the Marxists with invading the privacy of the family by stripping women of their "nurturing roles". Such beliefs and practices in the West inevitably triggered an antithesis and an antidote — feminism, a movement that primarily and strongly challenged this artificial private–public dichotomy with its slogan "personal is political". Western commitment to values of individualism and human rights eventually transformed their views on privacy with the result that all men, women and children are seen first as individuals and then as members of a family. Thus, while domestic violence is seen as a rather serious crime there, the idealization of the traditional family and familial ideologies continues unabated.

In India, on the other hand, the family has traditionally occupied a central social position: "if there is one 'ism' that governs Indian society, it is familyism" (Kakar and Poggendorf-Kakar 2007: 20). The emotive power and legitimacy of the family (albeit gendered and patriarchal) has been evoked extensively to frame the nation-state as a cultural family and Motherland; Indian cinema, among other popular art forms, has successfully established the currency of the family in nation-building narratives. Such is the sanctity allotted to the family in India that the case of the Indian children's custody row in Norway (Hjermann 2012) fuelled a huge national debate in India. The two siblings were taken away from their Norway-resident Indian parents on charges of serious parental neglect and care by Norwegian state authorities in May 2011. The matter was raised at the highest diplomatic level between the two countries and even by the Indian Prime Minister, thus prompting a Norwegian ombudsman to say "in our culture, the family is less a private matter". Unlike the Western emphasis on the individual, in India, the individual's identity is subsumed under and reflected from his/her family and community umbrella comprising caste, clan, religious and cultural affiliations. Hence, it will be useful to trace the evolution of family regulation in India. This trail will reveal the presence of and shifts in socio-legal attitudes towards family privacy. It must be noted here that the family that the following accounts refer to is generally the idealized patrilineal one since most other indigenous familial forms were marginalized. Importantly, ancient India was Aryan and later Hindu, and so it is inevitable to talk about the Hindu family. As Flavia Agnes cautions, the "Hindu" society of those times comprised a vast array of communities whose heterogeneous customs and practices were at best similar and "amorphous". Hence, despite the variety of regional and cultural variations, the views of most Indians vis-à-vis the family, its significance and/or privacy are more or less alike. Sudhir Kakar even refers to the ideology of the family as one of the "key building blocks of the spirit of India . . . and Indian-ness" (Kakar and Poggendorf-Kakar 2007: 4).

In ancient Aryan times (1500 BCE to 500 BCE), "law", as we know it today, was so enmeshed with religion and culture that it was difficult to distinguish one from the other. Personal life (and inter-spousal concerns) were governed by the credo of order through individual self-control or *sadacara* (Menski 2003: 435). The principle of *dharma* (roughly translated as moral righteousness) regulated human affairs and social order, not formal legal mechanisms. Werner Menski, an authority on ancient Indian law, warns that it will be "[. . .] a fundamental mistake to start with the presumption that in Hindu law it is the state that is central as a lawmaker, or even law enforcer" (2003: 10). Social norms regarding family life gradually emerged out of diverse and differing sources of scriptural tradition and customary practices and thus, were inherently ambiguous at source. For example, while scriptures saw divorce as a violation of the "union-of-souls" Hindu marriage, customary laws permitted termination of seriously flawed marriages. Or, even as the wife was expected to tolerate everything her "divine" husband did, she could leave a particularly bad marriage for life with another man. Nonetheless, most ancient Aryan and Hindu texts support the notion of the "divine" family with women as its moral guardians (Poggendorf-Kakar 2003: 193) who were kept out of "any histories that deal with 'public' spaces" (Tyagi 2008: 47).

Eventually, when classic Hindu "law"[1] *per se* emerged (in the form of *dharamasutras,* a collection of codes on ethics, rituals, philosophy and so on), it endorsed physical punishment to discipline a misbehaving wife (Agnes 2008: 256). This was in tandem with the well-accepted norm that the husband had power over his wife. Settlements were guided by the ideal of conjugal indivisibility; the family was kept intact by the husband's authority, the wife's sacrifice and endurance, and the community's intervention, if needed.

Centuries later, as the Indian subcontinent became home to an increasing number of religious and cultural communities and their various, pluralistic and ambiguous norms, each regulated its familial affairs through its own unique religious or customary "laws". By the time of British rule, the notion of family privacy intensified manifold as nationalists tried to insulate the family from the moral corruptions of English culture:

> The conception of the family as an 'isolated' private domain, as a refuge from a competitive and brutal outside world [. . .] generated a radical separation between work and leisure, public life and private life, childhood and adulthood. In this private world, husband and wife were to find solace and spiritual renewal in each other's company. (Bose 1995: 118)

The more significant development that occurred at the advent of the British was the "gradual process of homogenizing the local customs and practices which could be regulated through the state machinery" (Agnes 1999: 41). Despite their initial policy of non-interference in the "personal" laws of Indians, in their role as administrators the British were unable to deal with the plurality and diversity of laws, customs and non-state legal structures. With diffidence and little understanding of the complexities at hand, they set out to codify indigenous laws as per people's religion — "The system of dividing the communities on the basis of their religion and applying to them their own 'divine law' disregarding their caste, tribe and race differences is of recent origin, introduced by the British" (Agnes 1999: 24). The socio-legal paradigm changed from non-state to state arbitration.

Though both Hindu and Islamic laws made no distinction between personal and public and all aspects of human life were tied to the respective religion, the British created the simplistic category of "religious personal laws" ostensibly to avoid tampering with personal matters. They did so by selectively collating disparate ancient laws, patriarchal customs with "anti-women bias and English norms of Victorian prudity" (Agnes 1999: 58). Archana Parashar describes how British judges applied their rules of procedure and evidence to Hindu and Islamic law, thus "transforming them in unforeseen directions" (1992: 72). This was a turning point in the history of India when the "state" made its formal, albeit ambiguous entry in the Indian family's private domain. It had a particularly drastic impact on women's rights. Earlier held under different local, customary practices, women's rights then got politicized and remain so till date.

Making private violence public

Despite the substantive transition from ancient *dharma* to modern family law, it was not until "dowry deaths" grabbed international headlines that the veil of the private family was forcibly lifted. The argument that there are some totally private spaces that ought not to be invaded by the state became difficult to defend from this juncture.

In the 1980s, dowry-related violence triggered a high-pitched women's movement that pushed the Indian government to amend existing laws and protect women from violence. The 1961 Dowry Prohibition Act that had already banned the practice of dowry went through two amendments (one in 1984 and another in 1986). Criminal law was amended to include physical and mental cruelty to a married woman (Section 498 A of the Indian Penal Code) and dowry-related death (Section 304B). Women's activists and legislators saw dowry as the root cause of all violence against married women. (Domestic violence and dowry, though related, are rather distinct.

Dowry is a specific symptom of domestic violence practiced in India and other South Asian countries. It is a vulgar and corrupted version of *streedhan*, an old practice of giving gifts to the newlywed girl that would "exclusively" belong to her.) Some feminists are of the opinion that dowry is "not so much the cause of violence as a specific and virulent manifestation of a pervasive culture of gendered violence" (Ghosh 2004: 61). Ironically, the punitive amendments to dowry law caused inadvertent collateral damage — all other forms of domestic violence got trivialized to an extent that it "obfuscated the issue of the more banal and everyday forms of abuse that women are subjected to within the home" (Ghosh 2004: 51). The definitions of "cruelty" — "grave injury or danger to life, limb or death" — were interpreted to exclude a whole range of physical and non-physical violence. As a result, the legal approach to domestic violence became lackadaisical and neglectful —

> the judge considers 'stray domestic quarrels, perfunctory abuses by mother-in-law to her daughter-in-law in the Indian society, crude and uncultured behaviour by the in-laws or husband towards his wife [. . .] mundane matters of normal occurrence in the traditional joint Hindu families' (decision in *Padmabai versus State of Madhya Pradesh*). The response of the criminal justice system [. . .] reflects the dominant view that actions, such as harassment of the woman in her marital home, are within the ambit of normal social relations and functions. (Vindhya 2003: 343)

Cases of domestic violence suffered because of a poor law and tardy litigation. The police saw domestic violence as a private family affair instead of a crime and often used their "Special Cells" as mere means for mediation and compromise. Such indifference towards domestic violence at times forced some women to file false or exaggerated charges of dowry (occasionally, even on the advice of police officers) mostly because stringent anti-dowry laws promised legal action against abusive husbands. (However, proving dowry charges has often been difficult as transactions are not recorded and witnesses are difficult to find.) This led to a vociferous backlash by husbands accusing women of "misuse" of the law, also referred to as "legal terrorism" (Venkatesan 2005) by a Supreme Court bench.

The dowry phenomenon presents one of the most exceptional and unfortunate socio-legal commentaries on the predicaments of legislating complex issues such as violence against women. Despite so-called "draconian" laws, dowry has grown exponentially and is currently practiced in its most ubiquitous form across classes, among tribals (where bride price was common) and even among Muslims[2] (Sharma 2002). As a status symbol, dowry has been culturally institutionalized in the Indian society with ostentatious weddings as the norm among the elite. No less astonishing is the fact that the cacophonic protests against dowry in the 1980s (when dowry was modest and limited to few communities) have disappeared. Perhaps it signals a certain cynical acceptance by women's groups in India that dowry cannot be tackled as a custom or violence *per se* but as a reflection of women's social and economic devaluation amidst the growing clout of consumerist values.

All these developments ruptured the general assumption that all domestic violence in the Indian family was dowry-related. Although the family was still imagined as a private enclave, violence came to be seen as the tipping point at which its privacy could be transgressed. A general consensus for better legislation as a tool for social change began to build up; hence, a law dealing specifically with domestic violence was seen as the most obvious and much-needed solution.

Laws against violence or violence by the law?

As the judiciary equipped itself to specifically tackle domestic violence in the sanctum sanctorum of the Indian family, the intervening years gave rise to some relevant issues and confrontations between the private family and the state. This time, however, the state had to deal with a more potent "layer" of privacy that wrapped the family — religion. The conceptual binary of the private and public is also deployed between religion and state (respectively), thus making the family doubly guarded and private. Although domestic violence in India falls under secular state laws, other "personal" matters that have profound links with domestic violence (such as marriage, divorce, inheritance and so on) are covered by religious personal laws and these could be beyond state regulation. It, therefore, becomes imperative to examine the overlap between religious laws and constitutional rights vis-à-vis women.

In 1986, the Shah Bano case presented a vexing challenge as it pitted religion, gender and state against each other. The 60-year-old Shah Bano went to court to demand maintenance from her husband who had divorced her. The Indian Supreme Court ruled in her favour, asking the husband to pay her maintenance, similar to alimony. (As per secular state law, a deserted wife can claim maintenance under Section 125, Code of Criminal Procedure 1973, regardless of caste, creed or religion.) A section of Muslims saw this judgement as an anti-Islamic encroachment on Muslim personal law. The then-ruling government, afraid of a Muslim backlash and under pressure from the Muslim community, enacted the Muslim Women (Protection of Rights on Divorce) Act, 1986 (henceforth Muslim Women Act 1986). The Act was fashioned on religious personal law that offered Muslim women maintenance only for the period of *iddat* (about three months) after the divorce, and subsequently shifted her maintenance to her relatives or the Wakf Board. Many saw the act as unfair as it denied divorced Muslim women the right to basic maintenance, which women of other faiths had recourse to under secular law. Right-wing parties accused the government of being held hostage by the minority vote bank. Some Muslims defended their right to follow their "own" religious personal laws; others claimed that patriarchal prejudice of the Muslim clerics, not Islamic laws, had made Islam unjust towards women. The subject touched a political and communal raw nerve and led to the demand for a Uniform Civil Code[3] for all Indians (irrespective of their religious identities) but that has been in cold storage ever since.

Evidently, the private–public divide proved more difficult to bridge in the case of religious personal laws. This cannot be discussed in detail here without losing focus but what is relevant to the argument at hand is how "privacy" can become more inaccessible when seen through the prism of religion, especially in an environment laden with communal politics. Interestingly, although religious laws claim to be divine and therefore beyond human intrusion, they had already been tweaked by colonial jurists in India. The existing "Muslim Personal Law" in India too emerged out of the Anglo-Mohammedan law that was drawn and codified by the British. While many Muslim organizations (such as Muslims for Secular Democracy, the *Bhartiya Muslim Mahila Andolan* or Indian Muslim Women's Movement) continue to call for reforms in Muslim personal laws, Hindu personal law has been extensively reformed over the years[4]. Yet to assume that reform in personal laws turns them gender-just could be erroneous —

> The state meant to improve the position of women as a component of its plan of modernization, but it did not intend to upset or alter, in any substantial manner, the power structure of the family [. . .] reformed Hindu law provisions were mainly meant to unify and modernize the law, rather than 'liberate' Hindu women. (Parashar 1992: 77)

As divorced Indian Muslim women continue to fight for their rights, there are concurrent examples of courts ruling in women's favour, charges of state interference into the privacy of Muslim families[5] as well as Muslim women's organizations offering gender-just interpretations of Quranic verses. Newer secular legislation often runs into trouble — the Maharashtra Matrimonial Property (Rights of Women upon Marriage) Bill 2012 argues for division of joint matrimonial property at the time of divorce but is being opposed by members of the Muslim Personal Law Board on grounds of violation of Shariat (Wajihuddin 2012).

In India's baffling heterogeneity, not just religious but even customary laws can pose as "private" territories where the presence of state law is questioned. The Indian government was forced to intervene when *khap panchayats*[6] (caste councils) legitimized brutal murders of youngsters who married against customary diktats. Community leaders vociferously demanded that the Hindu Marriage Act 1955 be amended to include a ban on intra-lineage and intra-village marriages which, as per their "customs", are incestuous. It is noteworthy that while the community bypasses the authority of the state to run parallel systems of "justice", it also seeks the state's stamp of legal approval for a ban on relationships it considers prohibitory. In other words, the state's jurisprudence is both negated (through cold-blooded murders) and sought (in expecting tolerance of killings), when convenient. The councils threatened to disrupt public life through mass strikes if their demands were not met (Khatry 2010). The government has so far refused any amendments in law and promised stringent legal measures (under the Indian Penal Code) against these extra-legal bodies (Pandey 2010). Despite Indian courts granting death sentences for "honour" killers, the *khap panchayats* retain their local communities' sanction and respect for their ancient role in preserving social norms. Worse, local politicians and leaders representing these communities have pledged their support to save customary marriage laws.

The examples cited above demonstrate how "private" itself is tightly intertwined with other identities such as caste and religion in India's kaleidoscopic social fabric. Apparently, boundaries between private and public have been blurred repeatedly. Parashar and Dhanda (2008: xxi) wrote "which issues are raised in the public domain and which are relegated to the private arena, are political decisions which continually show the artificial nature of the categorization (of private and public)". In fact, the Indian legislature and state are clearly implicated in the maintenance/creation of laws — religious and secular — as well as the continuities and discontinuities of various hybrid privacies.

Private versus public, the jury is out

The debate over privacy and rights has raised its head in Indian courtrooms and left the judiciary divided on the issue. Some judgements reveal the varied stance that judges have taken on the subject. In 1983, a High Court judge struck down a Restitution of Conjugal Rights suit, where a man had appealed to have his wife return to the matrimonial home, by stating, "The remedy of restitution of conjugal rights is violative of the right to privacy and human dignity guaranteed by Article 21 of the Constitution. A decree of restitution of conjugal rights constitutes the grossest form of violation of an individual's right to privacy." (Agnes 2008: 244) This became a landmark judgement as it flagged the woman's rights of privacy as an individual over conjugal rights. On the other hand, in 1984, the Delhi High Court passed a judgment on a similar case but said the contrary —

> *Introduction of constitutional law in the home . . . is like introducing a*

> *bull in a China shop . . . in the privacy of the home neither Article 21 nor Article 14 have any place* (emphasis mine). In a sensitive sphere which is most intimate and delicate, the introduction of the cold principles of constitutional law will have the effect of weakening the marriage bond. The introduction of constitutional law into the very ordinary domestic relationship of husband and wife will strike as its very root and will be a fruitful source of dissent and quarrelling. (Agnes 2008: 245)

The Supreme Court endorsed the second judgement — the rights of conjugality superseded those of the individual. Judgements like these made the patriarchal character of the state apparent, thus shaking the faith that the women's movement had invested in it. Moreover, very poor conviction rates in domestic violence cases, lengthy court proceedings and so on contributed to women's disillusionment with legal remedies. Therefore, in the early 1990s, when rising divorce rates and the state's fear of the disintegration of the marital unit had grown manifold, a few innovative, extra-judicial alternatives to formal judiciary were created. These were projected as less "public" than the adversarial and formal civil courts and emphasized conciliation. The *nari adalats* or women's courts[7], for example, are women-run, rural arbitration fora that deal largely with domestic violence complaints. They are based on the belief that the community has rights to enter the family's privacy, while also shaming the perpetrator (Bhatla and Rajan 2008). The "judges" use their knowledge of local practices, formal laws and social networks to gather evidence, negotiate agreements, and even call the police, if needed. Most importantly, they help loosen the grip of shame and silence around domestic violence. Yet, with their limited roles and powers, the women's courts could not totally replace civil courts.

To deal with the many pending cases in city-based courts, "Family Courts" were set up in some parts of the country ostensibly to expedite cases by attempting mediation and conciliation, prior to trials in regular courts. With simplified procedures and informal mechanisms, this was seen as a speedy alternative to intimidating and congested civil courts. With their restrictive power, jurisdiction and limited numbers in India, the Family Courts too could not serve the intended purpose.

Adoption of 'Prevention of Women from Domestic Violence Act 2005'

Thanks to increasing pressure by the women's movement in India and rising international concern on the subject of domestic violence[8], the Indian government could not afford to neglect the issue of legislation on domestic violence anymore. Although Section 498A addressed cruelty and domestic violence, its vague definitions of violence (often excluding sexual violence), difficult implementation, low rate of conviction, lack of civil relief provisions to women and, as described earlier, the overarching conception of violence-as-dowry, made it quite ineffective. It also did not protect women from harassment and cruelty in natal, live-in or other non-marital relationships. The unease and angst around dealing with issues of privacy and rights within the family, especially women's rights, also delayed the arrival of a specific law —

> The intimacy of such violence requires us to adopt a special cognitive frame for understanding it as crime. Similarly, when *rights* are extended to individuals in familial relations and situations, we are led to ask *if* or how rights operate — whether identically with its 'public' exercise, or with mutations — within the intimate confines of the family. If violence in the family is problematized by the family's self-representation as benign, rights are problematized by its claims to privacy and autonomy. (Sunder Rajan 2005: 279)

After years of lobbying, revisions and re-drafting (by state and civil society agencies), the arrival of the Protection of Women from Domestic Violence Act (PWDVA) 2005 finally put all legal debates over regulating the family to rest. For the first time, a clear definition of domestic violence emerged, based on the UN Framework for Model Legislation on Domestic Violence and the United Nations Declaration on Elimination of Violence against Women[9]. Besides covering a gamut of physical, verbal, economic and mental abuses, the act also includes sexual abuse, especially forced, non-consensual sexual intercourse. Although rape begets severe punishment in Indian law, it is not recognized in marriage, unless committed with a minor or separated wife. The husband cannot be prosecuted for rape, but only be seen guilty of cruelty, if there is excessive and unreasonable demand for sex or some kind of unnatural sex. Section 375 of the Indian Penal Code makes an exception to the offence of rape in marriage as sexual intercourse is seen as a right of the husband and a natural implication of the marriage. Yet, the PWDVA does not recognize Section 375, and thus, takes a radical step towards acknowledging sexual violence as "one of the most common yet invisibilized forms of violence against women" (Jaising et al. 2009: 155). By conceptually including marital rape in the PWDVA (through the euphemistic term "sexual abuse"), yet another dimension of violence in the family has been challenged. Whether women will report such intimate abuse is a moot point, especially when male "Protection Officers" refuse to recognize rape in marriage (Lawyer's Collective Women's Rights Initiative and ICRW 2009: 92). The 2012 monitoring and evaluation report states that while there have been some complaints of sexual abuse by married women, "courts do not specifically note the existence of sexual violence in the orders passed" (Lawyer's Collective Women's Rights Initiative and ICRW 2012: 160). Even women are reported to "not even view forced/coercive sexual acts by their husbands/male partners as a form of violence" (Lawyer's Collective Women's Rights Initiative and ICRW 2005: 132). While the legal silence on the subject of marital rape has been disrupted, court judgements continue to belie its existence by endorsing sexual obligations of partners and admonishing abstinence (Agnes 2012).

To deal with gendered violence in various private domestic relationships, the act has taken the unprecedented step of including "any relationship in the nature of marriage", thus including women in live-in relationships, legally void/voidable marriages and common law marriages. It can also be used in natal family relationships by mothers, daughters, widows and so on. Unlike in the pre-PWDVA days when a woman had to visit a number of courts to seek different kinds of relief, the new law offers her a "single-window clearance" — one court for a number of supposedly immediate relief measures such as protection from violence, monetary relief and compensation, temporary custodial rights and the right to the "shared household"[10]. The right to reside in the shared household is one of the highlights of the act as it addresses a major lacuna in the system — dispossession from the house. Since women usually do not have any ownership or rights over property, they are very susceptible to dispossession in times of violence. All these comprise the civil orientation of the law; the focus is no longer on penalizing the perpetrator but on securing civil compensation and support for the victim. The earlier legal provision against domestic violence (Section 498 A) was driven by a criminal law. It made the complainant heavily dependent upon state bodies; the procedure could only begin with a complaint to the police. The PWDVA, on the other hand, lessens this dependence and instead allows women direct access to the court through new support structures in the form of Protection Officers, Service Providers[11] and even Counselors.

The bill, seen as the state's first comprehensive response to domestic violence, is very significant to the discussion in this chapter. It clearly implants the concept of human rights straight in the heart of different gendered relationships and the family. Its radical conceptual framework re-defines the contours of privacy and the extent of public intervention. Whether this conceptual clarity has cleared the *de facto* ambiguity of regulating the family and had a transformative impact on socio-cultural norms is another matter of debate that the following section explores.

New law, old culture, familiar ambiguities

Although the legislation is still relatively young, monitoring reports[12] of the post-PWDVA scenario indicate an increase in the number of cases filed under the act but a mixed response vis-à-vis the outlook towards privacy and violence. There has been greater visibility of the issue and even many pro-women judgements since the implementation of the PWDVA 2005, but cultural stereotypes and biased interpretations continue. An example —

> No Hindu lady will dare to take such an extreme step of filing complaints against the husband and his relatives [. . .] in Indian culture, the wife does not go to the extent of leaving her matrimonial home unless and until the ill-treatment becomes unbearable. (Lawyer's Collective Women's Rights Initiative and ICRW 2005: 152)

The notion of family privacy, however, continues to feature prominently among attitudes and perceptions on the subject. The 2009 monitoring and evaluation report reveals that over 86 percent of Protection Officers in Rajasthan and over 50 percent in Delhi agreed with the statement "domestic violence is a family affair" (Lawyer's Collective Women's Rights Initiative and ICRW 2005: 152). In 2012, after nearly half a decade of the implementation of the act, this view has seen little change — more than half of the Protection Officers interviewed in Delhi still agreed with the statement (Lawyer's Collective Women's Rights Initiative and ICRW 2012: 53). Protection Officers also believe that the aim of counseling under the PWDVA is to "save families from breaking down" and "to strike a compromise" despite the fact that the act clearly states that "if, and only if, the court feels that counselling could lead to an end in violence and empower the woman should the court direct counseling" (Jaising et al. 2009: 83). Although counseling is optional and certainly not the mandate of the Protection Officer, most of them agreed to the statement — "Counselling the woman is the PO's [Protection Officers'] duty under the PWDVA". A majority of Protection Officers also believed that counseling should be suggested before the court is approached and before the Domestic Incident Report[13] is filed. This again reveals the popular perception that all private mechanisms should be exhausted before the (private) family goes to the (public) court, and private matters should best be kept invisible. In a candid statement about the regulation of domestic violence, a (woman) Joint Commissioner of Delhi Police, asserted —

> Counselling is the first response of the Crime against Women Cell in domestic matters [. . .] in the conditions prevailing in India, it can be said to be the most suitable way of dealing with domestic discord. . . . it strikes a balance between *unnecessarily criminalizing the domestic arena* (emphasis mine) on the one hand, and totally screening it from intervention on the other. (Deol 2005)

The above-mentioned quote reflects a sort of reluctance at engaging with family life. As Vindhya argues, "Law [. . .] treated domestic violence differently from other assaults hesitating to interfere in the private relationship of the husband and wife" (2003: 334). It is no surprise then that in India's domestic violence discourse — legal and popular — counseling has emerged as the closest "private" solution to the issue. An early draft version of the domestic violence act (circulated by the Government of India under the title 'The Protection from Domestic Violence Bill 2001') included "mandatory counselling of the woman with the abuser". In the Family Courts Act 1984, counseling was the "first step to see if their differences could be settled through negotiation . . . rather than taking them straight for legal remedies which have adversarial processes inbuilt into them" (Kishwar 2008: 230). Women's activists objected to forcing the woman to be counseled, especially when its purpose was to convince her to accept violence as a normal part of marriage — "counselling has remained at best a mere formality and at worst a system that forces women to accept unfavourable settlements because no serious effort has been made to train and orient the required number of social workers to support women claimants" (Kishwar 2008: 230). It is apparent that legal reforms have hardly dented the notion of the divine family, the sacred conjugal bond and, therefore, of violence as normal and private. Yet, while married women remain its primary users, unmarried women too have started making use of it to seek protection from the violence of the natal family. Moreover, courts have started to recognize the rights and entitlements of women in non-marital and non-normative relationships that have long been seen as deviant. This has subverted the exclusivist focus of law on "legitimate" families and relationships, thus holistically challenging patriarchy in the private arena.

That the police or judiciary too can embody traditional cultural codes only points to the omnipotent presence and influence of a culture that produces, reiterates and authorizes norms. The construction of ideal femininity is based on traditional beliefs and practices that emphasize her sacrifice, suffering and endurance for the "honour" of the family (and nation, in case of the nationalist). The Hindu right wing invokes traditional values to preserve the private sphere of the family and guard it from the "other" —

> By emphasizing role models and values of the traditional Indian family, and pointing to the breaking up of families and the high divorce rates in the West, politicized Hindu movements have tried to win over the urban middle class — a class torn between its traditional outlook and an increasingly Americanized, modern lifestyle imported from the West. (Poggendorf-Kakar 2003: 180)

Marriage and children are central to the projected image of the ideal woman. Her role promises to be empowering and beyond the drudgeries and violence of home — "Her identity is determined not by her interest as an individual, but her function in the family and in society" (Poggendorf-Kakar 2003: 192). Thoughts of "emancipation", within and outside the marriage are decried — "Hindu marriages are considered sacrosanct [. . .] there could be separation of the couple but no dissolution of their marriage. Yet the element of divorce was introduced in Hindu marriages which caused a dent in Hindu family life" (Poggendorf-Kakar 2003: 193). The good woman's most valued attribute is her silence. This sentiment is even reflected in several court rulings on rape — "no self respecting woman would come forward in a court just to make a humiliating statement *against her honour* (emphasis mine) such as is involved in the commission of rape on her" or "the rapist degrades the very soul of the helpless female" (Goonesekere 2004: 113).

The link between these deeply entrenched norms of womanhood and the culture of silence around domestic violence is *a posteriori* — a majority of women interviewed during the last National Family Health Survey justified violence against them by their husbands[14]. As many as 54 percent women and 51 percent men agreed that it is justifiable for a husband to beat his wife (for example, when she disrespects her in-laws or neglects the house or children). The survey revealed that most women (two out of every three interviewed) had never told anyone about the violence they faced at home. Only one in four abused women had ever sought help (and that too only from their families) and only two percent had reported matters to the police. Other surveys establish that the "educational level of women is one of the main determinants of (women) justifying at least one reason for the husband beating his wife" (Sahoo and Pradhan 1999: 7). UNICEF's *The State of the World's Children* 2012 reported that among 15- to 19-year-olds in India, 57 percent boys and 53 percent girls believed that a husband was justified in beating his wife under certain circumstances (UNICEF, 2012). It seems that notions of self identity, shame and honour exert more pressure and influence on the collective consciousness of women than laws that promise them redressal.

With such stiff cultural resistance to making private matters public, a backlash against legislation was inevitable. Since the early years of anti-dowry and anti-domestic violence legislation, there have been massive public campaigns and propaganda against these laws. Men's groups (comprising husbands, mothers-in-law and sisters-in-law) across the country have facilitated a large and active country-wide network of different organizations such as the *Bharat Bachao Sangathan* (Save India Organisation), *Pariwarik Suraksha Samiti* (Family Protection Group) and the *Pati Pariwar Kalyan Samiti* (Husband Family Welfare Group). Their umbrella network (cleverly titled *Save the Indian Family*)[15] claims to rescue the institution of the family from the state. The ideological premise of these groups is the right of privacy that fundamentally belongs to the family —

> Any cohesive social unit which empowers its members to take care of each other based on mutual trust and friendship is a family. And in such a family *the government has no business interfering* (emphasis mine).[16]

By appropriating the symbolic, cultural idiom of the perfect Indian family, the group attempts to appeal to traditional and popular notions —

> Homes and relationships cannot be run by state terrorism and force [. . .] women cannot both obtain 'relief' and also retain relationships by taking recourse to these legislations [. . .] There appears to be a sinister plot to finish Indian society and its family unit and thus India's advantage.[17]

According to *Save the Indian Family*, empowerment of women may prove to be as fatal to India's national security as the other grave threats faced by it:

> crime and extremist activities in India may go to a whole new level if India's age old family system is broken with the excuse of empowering women.[18]

Through their own websites (www.498a.org), active presence on social networking sites such as Facebook, Twitter and a large network of helplines within India and outside, these groups demand amendments in dowry and domestic violence laws by inexplicably accusing women of "misuse". Although the contentious debate about misuse is outside the scope of this chapter, statistics,[19] however, establish the counterview — despite the increase in crimes of dowry and domestic violence, few women seek legal remedies. The high-pitched backlash is intended to deter women from using the law; however, it has reinforced prevalent misogynism where any demand by women for their rights in the family is labeled as anti-family.

Sophisticated feminist analyses have even problematized women's roles as not just victims of violence but sometimes also as its agents, for example, in the larger complexity of conflict related to various ethnic or communal identities. Despite the discursive and critical feminist analyses of the family as a site of violence and its privacy as anachronistic, the family's idealized traditional image as secure and private continues to obfuscate violence and ensure women's silence. The heightened presence of law in family matters has become a mere chink in the armor of the private family, as proven by the rise in the practice of dowry and dowry-related crime, the prevalence of honour killing, persistent domestic violence and so on. The irony is that women continue to carry the cross of the family, community and nation's honour in India's patriarchal regime.

Conclusion

In the Indian socio-cultural imagination, the domestic space continues to be seen as an exclusive territory that is incompatible with "laws", albeit legally "the philosophical rug has been pulled out from under the [. . . .] defenses of fundamental privacy rights" (Cohen 2002: 9). Years of consistent campaigning by women's groups has led to a sharp piece of domestic violence legislation that is theoretically influenced by feminist consciousness and legally by human rights discourse. Yet, "public" regulations can simultaneously be rendered ineffective by omnipotent notions of privacy that promote silence around and tacit acceptance of domestic violence. The notion of the private family and its sanctity has even overwhelmed the judiciary — "the conduct of marital relations and conjugal duty allow domestic violence to be selectively tolerated by the judicial system" (Vindhya 2003: 344). It may not be an exaggeration to say that while law tries to bring order in the family, law itself can be mediated by and enmeshed in culture.

A significant reason for the much-valued notion of family privacy is the high moral, cultural and political stature allotted to the heteronormative family, the only "natural" looking model validated by law and religion. The heteronormative family's reproductive, child-centered structure and system suits the state and the market. As a model of Indian-ness, it has been useful for nationalists — on it, they pitch their battle against the lack of "family values" of the "other". This monogamous, patrilineal and patrilocal family cannot represent the myriad other family forms such as single-parent, adoptive and same sex families, among others. The state too has contributed to the socio-cultural upkeep of this type of family so as to morally police non-normative sexualities. In fact, the immense zeal of the Indian state to criminalize consensual homosexual relations[20] vis-à-vis its protracted reluctance to criminalize violence in heterosexual private relations speaks volumes about its attitudes. Although feminists have long argued and denounced the private–public divide, their challenge to and critique of the position of the heterosexual family has not been as forthcoming. Perhaps this confrontation with the heterosexual family could unsettle both its patriarchal order and privacy.

Central to the exercise of unpacking the theoretical private–public divide will be a compelling re-conceptualization of privacy. Although a feminist articulation on these lines has long been done, it needs reiteration in the changing contemporary context. Feminists have often found privacy problematic as it turns the family into a sanctuary of gendered hierarchies, male domination and violence. Catherine MacKinnon sneered at what she called "the ideology of privacy", arguing that it is only "a right of men 'to be left alone' to oppress women one at a time" (1984: 53). Others such as Anita Allen have argued in favour of "meaningful and adequate individual forms of personal privacy" for women as a "way of exposing the myth that God, nature, morality, and the family require that women lead cloistered lives in the private sphere of the home [...]" (1996: 193–212). Allen imagines this sort of privacy as pro-woman as it will allow her the right to control her sexual and reproductive life.

Nonetheless, as exemplified in the chapter, the private–public divide in the state's discourse is particularly artificial and flimsy because the state itself draws these boundaries. Besides, the decision to regulate the family, and to what extent, has always been the state's prerogative. For example, in the mid-1970s, the then-ruling government dissolved this divide to coercively sterilize poor women and men during its intense national family planning drive. In fact, India's National Population Policy 1976 asked state governments to "pass suitable legislation to make family planning compulsory for citizens" and to stop childbearing after three children, if the "state so desires" (Srinivasan 1998: 1–22). Yet another example of the state's interference in an arena that should solely be the family's prerogative is the Government of India's Child Care Leave *only* for its women employees. It offers mothers up to two years break from work "for rearing or to look after any of their needs like examination, sickness etc."[21], besides the six-month maternity leave and other entitled holidays. While for years women have asked for equal opportunity and greater participation outside the domestic space, this leave not only perpetuates women's familial, care-giving roles, it also creates a systemic glass ceiling. Absence from work for years can boomerang on women's participation, learning, productivity and chances at professional advancement. Women anyway tend to crowd the public sector precisely for benefits such as generous leave while settling for wages lower than those offered by the private sector.

On the other hand, there have been shifts in the judiciary's stance towards "private" matters. In July 2009, the Delhi High Court ruled[22] that the state's act of criminalizing homosexuality (through Section 377 of the Indian Penal Code) was "violative of the Constitution of India in so far as it criminalizes consensual sexual acts of adults in private" and stated that —

> it is not within the constitutional competence of the state to invade the privacy of citizens' lives or regulate conduct to which the citizen alone is concerned solely on the basis of public morals. The criminalisation of private sexual relations between consenting adults in the absence of any evidence of serious harm deems the provision's objective both arbitrary and unreasonable. (Ibid.: 76)

The quote affirms that only "serious harm" or violence should make the state "invade privacy". (It is ironical that the state refused to "invade" marriages where "serious harm" such as rape has been committed for the longest time possible.) This ruling claims that the right to privacy is part of the Indian Constitution through various provisions such as Article 19 (freedom of speech, expression and so on) and Article 21 (right to life and liberty) (ibid.: p. 28). In a rare example that upholds the value of privacy, it said —

> privacy allows persons to develop human relations without interference from the outside community or from the state. The exercise of autonomy enables an individual to attain fulfillment, grow in self-esteem, build relationships of his or her choice and fulfill all legitimate goals that he or she may set. In the Indian Constitution, the right to live with dignity and the right of privacy both are recognized as dimensions of Article 21. (ibid. 39–40)

Perhaps Frances E. Olsen is right when he asserts that "non-intervention (of the state) is a false ideal because it has no coherent meaning [. . . .] the state is continuously affecting the family by influencing the distribution of power among individuals" (1994: 842). Olsen strongly disagrees with the popular view that the state should intervene only when necessary because it "presupposes that non-intervention is a possible choice; and second, it usually accepts non-intervention as a norm or as an ideal" (1994: 863).

Another useful strategy may be to lessen the dependence on law as the solitary or most sought-after tool to deal with family ambiguity. Since law is inextricably involved in the very acts that it condones, controls and penalizes, it becomes a site of ambiguity instead of a force against these acts. (The chapter has already exemplified how judges reinforce notions of morality, chastity and honour.) As Nivedita Menon cautions, "our attempts to transform power relations through the law tend rather to re-sediment them and to assert dominant values" (Menon 2004: 206). It may, therefore, be useful to go along with feminist legal scholars such as Margaret Davies (2011: 1–7) who emphasize the necessity to re-conceptualize law as "horizontal" or plural, open-ended, self-reflexive and inclusive instead of "vertical" or hierarchical, positivist, autonomous and exclusive. This may create newer and alternative legal meanings that do not devalue subjectivities and imagine moving the "subject" from a passive recipient of law to an active agent of its creation.

Feminists and the women's movement in India have had a difficult and paradoxical relationship with law. While some of their most crucial battles were fought on legal sites, on other occasions they have rejected law as a strategy. While legal reform can lead to a change in social practice/behaviour (the legal ban on Sati helped end the practice), sometimes it is civil society-led campaigns and mobilization that force the state towards legal reform (such as in the case of the de-criminalization of homosexuality). The peculiar case of dowry reform through legislation however offers wider and critical lessons. If the accent on law is moderated, it may open up other disparate sites for simultaneous negotiations on a number of related issues. The threads of the issue of domestic violence, for example, lie in the economic rights of women in personal and secular laws, socio-cultural notions of honour and shame, patriarchy, nationalism, fundamentalism, popular media, masculinities and so on. Nothing less than a concerted push that unsettles age-old notions of identity, power, hierarchy and so on may start a process of change.

This chapter has no sparklingly new recommendations to offer to tackle the conundrum of the private–public family. The intent has been to explore intractable knots up close and examine possibilities at unraveling those. It still begs the question that though the violent family needs protection from the state, what if the family needs protection from the violent state? Self-regulation by the family seldom works. On the other hand, the state tends to become panoptic. Given the complex and competing undercurrents of power play between the family and the state, a balancing act between a reconstructed form of privacy, intense socio-cultural campaigns with cautious regulation may ease the ambiguities and paradoxes.

Notes

1 The later Vedic period from 500 BCE saw a transition towards literature comprising socio-legal recommendations. Yet, this was not "law" but a loose assortment of complex, diverse and even contradictory socio-legal systems. In fact, scholars have termed it postmodern because of its "internal dynamism and perennial capacity for flexibility and realignment in conjunction with the societies to and in which it applies" (Menski 2003: xi).

2 A 16-state survey by the All India Democratic Women's Association found that dowry has become a common practice among the Muslims in India. Traditionally, the Muslim groom would give *mehr*, the marriage gift (in cash or kind), to the bride. For details, see http://www.indiatogether.org/opinions/kalpana/dowvict.htm

3 The Uniform Civil Code is part of Article 44 of the Indian Constitution, which provides a Directive Principle that, "The state shall endeavour to secure for the citizens a uniform civil code throughout the territory of India". However, the same Constitution also guarantees the Fundamental Right to be governed by one's religious personal law. The juxtaposition of these two seemingly dissonant principles has been a political tightrope for ruling governments.

4 The Personal Laws (Amendment) Bill 2010 amended the Guardians and Wards Act, 1890, and the Hindu Adoptions and Maintenance Act, 1956. Earlier, in a Hindu family, only the father was considered the natural guardian of the child for adoption and guardianship, and only unmarried or divorced women and widows were allowed to adopt a child. The amendment makes adoption gender-friendly by giving women equal rights in guardianship and adoption of children. It allows the mother along with the father to be appointed as a natural guardian and also aims to remove adoption hurdles for married women.

5 In May 2002, the Bombay High Court ruled that divorces between Muslim couples would have to be "convincingly proved in a court of law under the

civil procedure court and the Indian Evidence Act". A mere statement, written or oral, by a man divorcing his wife would not be accepted. The ruling is now binding for Maharashtra. Source: Soma Wadhwa (20 May 2002) "Talaq to Unreason", *Outlook*.

A Delhi High Court judge has ruled that irrespective of Muslim personal law, under which a Muslim man is bound to maintain his wife only during the *iddat* period (around three months after divorce), his wife is entitled to maintenance under Criminal Procedure Code till she remarries. (Source: "Court boost for Muslim women", *The Statesman,* 13 August 2010) <http://thestatesman.net/index.php?option=com_content&view=article&id=338094&catid=35>

6 *Khap panchayats* are traditional, area-based, self-styled caste councils whose rulings have no legal sanction. In keeping with tradition, they oppose marriages within the same lineage and are known to mete out harsh punishments to "erring" youngsters.

7 Organized under the state-sponsored Mahila Samakhya programme, an empowerment initiative for rural women, the *nari adalats* are informal, community-based legal structures run by poor rural women.

8 The Congress on Human Rights (held in Vienna in 1994) and the Fourth World Conference on Women (held in Beijing in 1995) were some of the most influential international conferences that decisively defined domestic violence and pushed for rights-based legislation.

9 The 85th plenary meeting of the United Nations General Assembly on the Declaration of the Elimination of Violence Against Women on 20th December 1993; GA Res. 48/104 of 1993. Source: <http://www.un.org/documents/ga/res/48/a48r104.htm>

10 The Right to Reside (Section 17, PWDVA 2005) ensures that the aggrieved woman shall have the right to reside in the shared household, whether or not she has any title or beneficial interest in the same. A woman shall have the right not to be evicted or excluded from the shared household or any part of it by the respondent *save in accordance with the procedure established by law.*

11 The act orders the appointment of Protection Officers (Chapter III, Section 8 and 9, pp. 4–5) as the interface between women facing domestic violence and the courts. They work under the supervision of the Magistrate and have both pre-and-post litigation duties seeking to facilitate the woman's access to the court, provide support services and protect her from violence. The act also created the role of Service Provider (Chapter III, Section 10, pp. 5–6), a civil society organization registered under the act to provide local support services (such as legal, medical, counseling or even shelter) to women in distress.

12 *Monitoring and Evaluation Reports, Parts I to V* (Lawyer's Collective Women's Rights Initiative and ICRW); Rakhi Lahiri, *The Protection of Women From Domestic Violence Act: The Current Situation* (Human Rights Law Network; 2009); and Making *the PWDVA Successful,* Report of the Second National Women's Conference (Delhi: February 2009)

13 The Domestic Incident Report is a record of the woman's complaint that is noted by the Protection Officer and submitted to the local magistrate. The report is the first administrative step towards filing a domestic violence case.

14 The National Family Health Survey is the most comprehensive survey and the only one of its kind conducted in India under the stewardship of the Ministry

of Health and Family Welfare, Government of India. The 2005–6 survey comprised interviews with more than 230,000 women (between the age group of 15 and 49 years) and men (aged 15–54 years) throughout India.
Source: http://www.nfhsindia.org/NFHS-3%20Data/Press%20Briefing%20Kit/Domestic%20 Violence.pdf

15 Save Indian Family Foundation; www.saveindianfamily.org

16 Save Indian Family Foundation; http://www.saveindianfamily.org/articles/blogs/1049-hey-you-stay-away-from-my-family.html

17 Save Indian Family Foundation; http://www.saveindianfamily.org/articles/blogs/1030-indias-new-domestic-violence-act-a-study-report.html

18 Save Indian Family Foundation;<http://www.saveindianfamily. org/articles/views/1044-family-breaking-is-an-issue-of-national-security.html

19 Crime records from the National Crime Records Bureau (NCRB), National Commission for Women (NCW) and several research studies on domestic violence show that, if anything, cruelty towards women in India on account of dowry demands has gone up in the past two decades. The increasing desire for a male child is related to female foeticide and the rising demand for dowry. As per the NCRB website (http://ncrb.nic.in/cii2007/cii-2007/CHAP5.pdf), the proportion of reported female deaths by suicide was considerably higher under causes like dowry dispute (98.8 percent) and physical abuse (60.3 percent).

20 For decades, Section 377 of the Indian Penal Code, known as the anti-sodomy law, criminalized male sexual behavior, irrespective of the consent of the people involved as it was considered "against the order of nature". On 2 July 2009, the Delhi High Court pronounced that it should be read down to exclude consensual sex between adults.

21 Circular by Ministry of Personnel, Government of India: http://india.gov.in/govt/studies/estt.(l).pdf

22 Naz Foundation vs Govt of NCT of Delhi and others (2009) WP(C) No.7455/2001, Delhi High Court Judgement; 2nd July, 2009 http://www.nazindia.org/judgement_377.pdf

References

Agnes, F. (2008) 'Hindu Conjugality' in Archana Parasher and Amita Dhanda (eds.) *Redefining Family Law in India*, Routledge, Delhi, pp. 236–257.

Agnes, F. (1999) *Law and Gender Equality, the Politics of Women's Rights in India*. Oxford University Press, Delhi.

Agnes, F. (2012) 'New family laws are divorced from reality', *Tehelka*, Vol. 9 (14), 7 April 2012 Source: http://www.tehelka.com/story_main52.asp?filename=Op070412proscons.asp

Allen, A. (1996) 'Privacy at Home: The Twofold Problem' in Nancy Hirshmann and Christine Di Stefano (eds.), *Revisioning the Political: Feminist Reconstructions of Traditional Concepts in Western Political Theory*, Westview Press, Boulder Colorado, pp. 193–212.

Bhatla, N. and Rajan, A. (2008) 'Private concerns in public discourse, women initiated community responses to domestic violence' in *Democracy in the Family, Insights from India* by Joy Ranadive-Deshmukh, Sage, Delhi, pp. 128–150.

Bose, Pradip K. (1995) 'Sons of the Nation: Child Rearing in the New Family' in *Texts of Power: Emerging Disciplines in Colonial Bengal* (ed.) Partha Chatterjee, University of Minnesota, Minnesota, pp. 118–142.

Cohen, Jean L. (2002) *Regulating Intimacy: A New Legal Paradigm,* Princeton University Press, Princeton and Oxford.

Davies, M. (2011) 'Feminism and the Idea of Law' in *Feminists@Law* Vol. 1(1), pp. 1–7.

Deol, K. (2005) *Crime Against Women Cell, The Delhi Police Experience,* 130th International Training Course: Integrated Strategies to Confront Domestic Violence and Child Abuse, May 16 - Jun. 24, 2005, Visiting Experts Paper, Resource Material Series No. 69, Source: http://www.unafei.or.jp/english/pdf/PDF_rms/no69/05_P77-84.pdf

Engels, F. (1948) *The Origin of the Family, Private Property and the State,* Foreign Languages Publishing House, Moscow.

Ghosh, Sobha V. (2004) 'Contextualising Domestic Violence: Family, Community, State' in Rinki Bhattacharya (ed.) *Behind Closed Doors* Sage, Delhi, pp. 51–64.

Goonesekere, S. (2004) *Violence, Law and Women's Rights in South Asia,* Sage, Delhi.

Hjermann, R. (2012) 'Protecting the vulnerable', *The Times of India,* 21 March 2012 Source: http://timesofindia.indiatimes.com/home/opinion/edit-page/Protecting-the-vulnerable/articleshow/12344951.cms

Jaising, I., Basu, A. and Dutta, B. (2009) *Handbook on Law of Domestic Violence,* LexisNexis Butterworths Wadhwa, Delhi.

Kakar, S. and Poggendorf-Kakar, K. (2007) *The Indians: Portrait of a People,* Penguin, Delhi.

Khatry, R. (2010) 'Khap Panchayat puts Haryana, Centre on Notice', *The Indian Express* 2 August 2010 Source: http://www.indianexpress.com/news/khap-panchayat-puts-haryana-centre-on-notic/654772/

Kishwar, M. (2008) *Zealous Reformers, Deadly Laws,* Sage, Delhi.

Locke, J. (2003) *Two Treatises of Government* (ed.) Peter Laslett, Cambridge University Press, Cambridge.

MacKinnon, C. (1984) 'Roe v. Wade: A Study in Male Ideology', in *Abortion: Moral and Legal Perspectives* (ed.) Jay L. Garfield and Patricia Hennessey, University of Massachusetts Press, Amherst, pp. 45–54.

Menon, N. (2004) *Recovering Subversion: Feminist Politics beyond Law,* Permanent Black, Delhi.

Menski, W. (2003) *Hindu Law: Beyond Tradition and Modernity,* Oxford University Press, Delhi.

Olsen, Frances E. (1994) 'The Myth of State Intervention in the Family' in *Feminism* (eds.) Susan Moller Okin and Jane Mansbridge, Schools of thought in Politics Series; No. 6, University Press, Cambridge, pp. 835– 864.

Pandey, V. (2010) 'Government Plans to Tighten Noose on Khap Panchayats' *Daily News Analysis,* 25 June 2010 Source: http://www.dnaindia.com/print710.php?cid=1400914

Parashar A. and Dhanda, A. eds. (2008) *Redefining Family Law in India* Routledge, Delhi.

Parashar, A. (1992) *Women and Family Law Reform in India,* Sage, Delhi.

Poggendorf-Kakar, K. (2003) 'Virtuous Mother, Virile Hero and Warrior Queen: The Conception of Gender and Family in Hindutva', in Pernau M., Ahmad I.

and Reifeld H. (eds.), *Family and Gender, Changing Values in Germany and India*, Sage, Delhi, pp. 179–194.

Sahoo, H. and Pradhan, Manas R. (1999) *Domestic Violence in India: An Empirical Study*, Centre for the Study of Regional Development, Jawaharlal Nehru University and International Institute for Population Sciences.

Sharma, K. (2002) 'Rooted Custom', *India Together*, November 2002 Source: http://www.indiatogether.org/opinions/kalpana/dowvict.htm

Srinivasan, K. (1998) 'Population Policies and Programmes since Independence: A saga of Great Expectations and Poor Performance', *Demography India* 27 (1), pp. 1–22.

Lawyer's Collective Women's Rights Initiative and ICRW (2009) *Staying Alive, Third Monitoring and Evaluation Report 2009 on the protection of Women from Domestic Violence Act 2005*, Lawyer's Collective Women's Rights Initiative and ICRW, Delhi.

Lawyer's Collective Women's Rights Initiative and ICRW (2010) *Staying Alive, Fourth Monitoring and Evaluation Report 2010 on the protection of Women from Domestic Violence Act 2005*, Lawyer's Collective Women's Rights Initiative and ICRW, Delhi.

Lawyer's Collective Women's Rights Initiative and ICRW (2012) *Staying Alive, Fifth Monitoring and Evaluation Report 2012 on the protection of Women from Domestic Violence Act 2005*, Lawyer's Collective Women's Rights Initiative and ICRW, Delhi.

Sunder Rajan, R. (2005) 'Rethinking law and violence: the Domestic violence (prevention) bill in India, 2002' in Shani D'Cruze and Anupama Rao (eds.), *Violence, Vulnerability and Embodiment: Gender and History*, Blackwell, UK, pp. 276–300.

Tyagi, J. (2008) *Engendering the Early Household: Brahmanical Precepts in the Early Grhyasutras, Middle of the First Millenium* B.C.E., Orient Longman, Delhi.

UNICEF (2012) The State of the World's Children 2012, UNICEF, New York

Venkatesan, J. (2005) 'Dowry law is a shield, not an assassin's weapon: court', *The Hindu*, 22 July 2005 *Source:* http://www.hindu.com/2005/07/22/stories/2005072202631500.htm

Vindhya, U. (2003) 'Private Crimes and Public Sanction: Violence against Women in the Family' in Pernau M., Ahmad I., Reifeld H. (eds.) *Family and Gender, Changing Values in Germany and India*, Sage, Delhi, pp. 322 – 348.

Wadhwa, S. (2002) 'Talaq to Unreason', *Outlook*. (20 May) http://www.outlookindia.com/article.aspx?215693

Wajihuddin, M. (2012) 'It's a potential flashpoint', *The Times of India*, 26 March 2012 Source: http://lite.epaper.timesofindia.com/mobile.aspx?article=yes&pageid=9&edlabel=TOIM&mydateHid=26-03-2012&pubname=&edname=&articleid=Ar00900&format=&publabel=TOI

All internet sources were last checked on 3 October 2012.

CHAPTER
3
Culture, Power and Narratives in Domestic Violence Law

ZARIZANA ABDUL AZIZ

In November 2009, singer and actress Rihanna admitted that going back to her boyfriend Chris Brown after having been brutalised by him was a mistake and sent the wrong message to many young girls. "That's not what I want to teach people" (Rihanna 2009). In *Town of Castle Rock v. Gonzales* (2005) 545 US 748, the Supreme Court was placed in a position to shape the legal-cultural narrative on domestic violence.[1] Instead of seizing the opportunity, the Supreme Court rejected the argument that would have obligated the police to intervene in cases of domestic violence and thus send a strong signal that domestic violence is unacceptable, a decision that elicited recommendations to the contrary from the Inter-American Commission in *Jessica Lenahan (Gonzales) v. United States of America* (2011).[2]

This chapter postulates that the acceptance or rejection of domestic violence is shaped by those who are in positions of power and influence. While celebrities like Rihanna are capable of influencing the cultural narrative of domestic violence, it is the state, more than any other entity or individual, that is particularly invested with the power to shape public perception. States legitimize ethos, values and practices through their legal and political machinations as well as through their actions and more so, their inaction and are in positions to politically determine cultural narratives. They are thus imbued with the responsibility to encourage and create a culture free of domestic violence. When power is invested in the state, as it is in the modern conception of the Westphalian state, states must mediate the cultural narrative.

Part I of this chapter looks at narratives of cultural discourse and examines how and by whom these narratives are formulated. Assertions that domestic violence is embedded in any one culture must be challenged to expose it as a practice supported and re-enacted through cultural narratives. It is more constructive, rather than essentializing domestic violence as culturally embedded, to acknowledge that domestic violence is a culture in and of itself. In this latter construction, culture is looked upon as a socio-political symbolic discourse that changes over time with the state playing a role in its incarnation. Consequently, even if domestic violence exists as an oppressive and reprehensible practice within cultures, it should not be preserved, respected and perpetuated.

Part II examines how and why domestic violence continues to be erroneously placed within culture and the difficulty in confronting it due to the intersecting issues of privacy, culture and honour. In Part III, the chapter explores the contestation of rights and argues that the contest between the right to privacy within the family and the rights of victims of domestic violence cannot today be resolved in favour of the former.

Part IV then examines patterns of state action and inaction that tolerate if not encourage domestic violence arguing that the state is not only responsible but is best positioned to eliminate domestic violence. The chapter concludes by reiterating the primacy of eradication of violence in the construction of society and the nation state. In the endeavour to eliminate domestic violence, culture needs to be deconstructed. Instead of justifying domestic violence in the name of culture, culture should be enlisted to create a non-violent society.

The narrative of cultural discourse: Conceptual understanding of culture and domestic violence

This part challenges cultural narratives that demand social and legal acceptance of domestic violence and assertions that all cultural practices should be preserved. When conservative forces claim ownership over an "authentic" interpretation of culture, tradition and/or religion that includes domestic violence, women are not only told to accept violence, they are denied any role as equal and active contributors to the development and production of culture (Ertürk 2007).[3] Thus, normative laws and rights are not only intrinsic to cultural formations, the formulation of the cultural narrative is itself bound to law making, power and privilege.

There are two meanings of culture that are separate and distinct but commonly misunderstood (Sewell 1999). Firstly, culture as contrasted with other complex studies of human existence and secondly culture as an abstraction that provides symbolic meaning. The common idea that domestic violence is embedded in cultural practices coincides with the meaning of culture as concrete and bounded beliefs and practices specific to a community or society. In this instance, culture is understood as a system of practice that is distinct to a society or group, for example, American culture or Brazilian culture. This is an erroneous understanding of the relationship between domestic violence and culture that has resulted in the isolation of domestic violence as intrinsic within certain cultures but extrinsic to others, as illustrated through the following cases.

The first case occurred in Germany and involved a Moroccan couple. In March 2007, a German judge cited verses from the Quran which, she said, sanctioned physical abuse of a woman by her husband (Landler 2007). In the Moroccan cultural milieu, she added, it was common for husbands to beat their wives.[4] The second case occurred in the United States in 2010 during the trial of a man of Iraqi descent who was charged with the murder of his daughter for "being too westernised" because she had left her husband in Iraq and was living with her boyfriend in Arizona. At the trial, defence counsel asked the judge to take special precautions to ensure that the accused should not be prosecuted for his "racial, political, religious or cultural beliefs" (Gardiner 2010).

The proponents of recognizing domestic violence as embedded within Moroccan and Iraqi culture would likely reject that these centuries-old traditional and cultural beliefs of male authority in the family are justifications for domestic violence in the context of German and American societies. Clearly, the essentialization of domestic violence is more easily undertaken when applied to "other" cultures, resulting in states' acceptance and tolerance of domestic violence as a traditional manifestation of "other" cultures. These same cultural arguments would not usually be invoked against women not from "other" cultures, thus conceptualizing only women from certain communities as victims of culture.

Today, just as no one can imagine defending domestic violence as culturally embedded in American culture, no one should defend domestic violence as culturally embedded in any culture. The confusion originates from the conflation of acknowledging the prevalence of domestic violence with accepting and tolerating domestic violence as a traditional manifestation of culture deserving of preservation. It is this mistaken reasoning that allows culture to be invoked as an explanation, if not a justification, for domestic violence, thus conceptualizing women not as victims of violence but transgressors of culture (Davidson 2009). The reasoning sets up a false contestation between domestic violence and culture, compelling society and states to choose between honouring and preserving culture and eradicating domestic violence.

Furthermore, incidences of domestic violence within a certain culture do not constitute proof that they form part of that cultural milieu, be it Moroccan, Iraqi, American or European. What they do prove, however, is that domestic violence is as pervasive a problem within Moroccan and Iraqi cultures as within American and European cultures. If domestic violence is embedded only in certain cultures, how do we explain the global and pervasive nature of domestic violence? The US Department of Justice estimates that 960,000 to 3,000,000 women are physically abused by their husbands or boyfriends each year (Greenfeld, 1998). The US

Centers for Disease Control (CDC) reported in 2003 that violence against women is the leading cause of injury among women with 5,300,000 cases of intimate partner violence taking place each year (CDC, 2003). Approximately one-third of female murder victims and five percent of male murder victims are killed by an intimate partner (Bureau of Justice Statistics, 2006). Further, in 2007, seventy percent of victims killed by intimate partners were women, a statistic that has changed little since 1993 (US Bureau of Justice Statistics cited in UN Office of the High Commissioner for Human Rights, 2011). The socio-economic cost of violence against women in the United States for example is estimated to be between US$5,000,000,000 and US$10,000,000,000 annually (Laurence and Spalter-Roth 1996). According to MacManus and Van Hightower (1989: 269), battering is the "single largest cause of injury to women in the United States." (Thirty percent of abused women in the United States lost their jobs due to the abuse (Morrison et al. 1999). Meanwhile, the European Women's Lobby estimates that forty-five percent of all women in Europe have been subjected to and suffered from men's violence, with every fifth woman in Europe estimated to have been subjected to domestic violence (2007).

Victims of domestic violence are not limited to certain cultural backgrounds. In the United States, not only are women of different cultural backgrounds vulnerable to violence by an intimate partner, economic factors rather than cultural factors appear to play more pertinent roles in the frequency and level of domestic violence (Catlano et al., 2009).[5] Shelters across the United States have seen an increase in domestic violence incidents, because financial constraints are forcing people to stay with their abusive partners and leading to heightened stress within the home resulting in an increase in the frequency and severity of domestic violence (Davidson, 2009). The financial crisis that continues to see unemployment maintained between nine and ten percent bears out the connection between socio-economic factors and domestic violence, challenging the idea that domestic violence is embedded in culture (US Bureau of Labor Statistics, 2011).

If domestic violence is prevalent in all our cultures, what we are experiencing as culture here is not the concrete and bounded beliefs and practices specific to a community or society. What we are dealing with is domestic violence that exists as an abstraction and finds expression in ideas, beliefs, customs and rules. In this instance, the meaning of culture as it relates to domestic violence should be that of culture as contrasted with other complex studies of human existence. In this instance, culture refers to an abstraction that provides symbolic meaning. Among other aspects, culture is expressed in language, ideas, beliefs, customs, rules, institutions, rites and rituals that provide symbolic meaning for our existence and shape our actions (Rupesinghe 1994). Seen through this lens, domestic violence becomes a culture in and of itself.

Domestic violence manifests itself through illiberal norms and oppressive practices in every society. However, societal or customary practices need not always be preserved. Other practices, even those that privileged powerful members of society once defended in the name of culture, have long been delegitimized or abandoned due to evolving values and ethos. Slavery and torture have evolved over time from acceptable practices to prohibited norms internationally.[6] Like domestic violence, tradition and customs, religious precepts, social order and national interest were arguments used to justify slavery and torture. Unlike slavery and torture, however, these justifications continue to have traction in domestic violence.

> Local customs, however hardened by time, are not decreed in heaven. Habits and feelings they engender may be counteracted and moderated. Experience attests that such local habits and feelings will yield, gradually though this be, to law and education. And educational influences are exerted not only by explicit teaching. They vigorously flow from the fruitful exercise of the responsibility of those charged with political official power and from the almost unconsciously transforming actualities of living under law. (*Cooper v. Aaron*, 1958)

The discussion on the important and extensive role of cultural factors has often been focused on the need for unquestioned cultural conservatism. The danger of encouraging and preserving conservative customs in cultural groups solely on the basis that they have been practiced over the ages is that it necessarily implicates culture's paralysis and strips it of dynamism. For culture to maintain its dynamism, we need to provide persons within the cultural group with cultural freedom, which includes the liberty to question the automatic endorsement of past traditions when people see reason for changing their ways of living (Sen 2007).

It is also imperative that we discern the interrelationship between culture, power and privilege. Power and the use of power to protect privilege, not only leads to the defeat of the voices of the powerless but, over time, to their silence altogether (Gaventa, 2006). Thus, culture as a practice is reflected in wilful action, power relations, struggle, contestations and contradictions (see also Raz 1994). Questioning the narrative of culture and domestic violence puts power back at the centre of our understanding of culture and allows us to interrogate the terms of engagement and the interests that determine the narration of culture. The political strategy of powerful members of a group who prefer their narratives of culture to legitimize domestic violence, promotes the idea that there is an inherent cultural right that allows some persons in certain communities to execute violence against women. Consequently, the upholding of these cultural practices tends to be represented without reference to and emptied of the actual injuries to women.

One way to accommodate concerns on essentializing oppressive elements in cultural groups is to exclude illiberal norms and practices in our cultural narratives so that what is essential for cultural survival does not overlap with what is oppressive and reprehensible (Song, 1995). While culture may be the locus of certain ethos and virtues, protection of these should only be granted if they provide value to individuals (ibid.). This is because not all cultural practices contain universal goodness that needs preservation and continued and continuous everyday choreographed enactments.

An example of these contestations can be seen in the gang-rape of Mukhtar Mai, ordered by a Pakistani tribal council (Tohid, 2002). As the international community sought to understand this outrage, it was tempting to invoke the equally incomprehensible Pakistani culture as the cause for the gang-rape (Merry, 2003). The case, however, is better understood in the context of local political struggles rather than Pakistani culture. Mukhtar Mai, like others before and after her, was raped as revenge. The Mastoi tribal leaders who ordered the gang-rape of Mukhtar Mai were powerful members of a remote community (Tohid, 2002). In the case of Mukhtar Mai, the revenge was for the alleged audacity of a male member of her family to socially liaise with a woman from a higher caste (Massod, 2006).

Many Pakistanis condemned the rape and the Chief Justice of Pakistan ordered the provincial police chief along with other senior provincial officials to appear before the Supreme Court in connection with the incident (Massod, 2006). It is important to note that all cultures are open to historical change and no culture should be "regarded as entities paralyzed by tradition, cast either as static or inert or in the 'process of decline'" (Narayan, 1997). Mukhtar Mai herself sought to create an alternative cultural narrative. She used her compensation money to build two schools, one for girls and one for boys. "Education will play a very, very important role in changing the minds of men," she said (O'Shea, 2004).

The contestations within Pakistani society over the Mukhtar Mai case demonstrate that the leap from acknowledging the occurrence of these incidences to justifying it in the name of Pakistani culture can only happen if we adopt and legitimize the narratives of the powerful and vengeful male Mastoi tribal members. The role of the State of Pakistan must be to mediate between these contesting narratives. Should the State of Pakistan incarnate and perpetuate the narratives and reprehensible acts of these tribal leaders as part of Pakistani culture, to be enacted and re-enacted over time or should it favour the narratives of those who condemned the gang-rape of Mukhtar Mai and found it deserving of punishment, thus rejecting the reprehensible acts of the tribal leaders as part of Pakistani culture? Choosing on the side of the tribal leaders would constitute the state as not only participating in a culture of sexual violence against women but incarnating sexual violence as part of Pakistani culture. On the other hand, choosing on the side of those who condemned the gang-rape and punishing the tribal leaders as well as providing reparation for Mukhtar Mai sends a powerful signal that — the state not only does not tolerate sexual violence against women but it is determined to root out sexual violence from society and its institutional and cultural structures, thus creating a Pakistani culture free of sexual violence. Clearly, the state has a pivotal and definitive role in the creation, perpetuation and incarnation of culture. Consequently, it is not the state that is held at the whims and mercy of culture but it is the state that moulds culture and with it, cultural identity.

Uncovering why domestic violence is erroneously essentialized as culture

Arguments positing a clash between traditional cultures and modernization in the discourse of domestic violence are misplaced. Domestic violence is a systemic global practice embedded in masculinities, patriarchy and the domination of women that is then justified in the name of honour, culture and religion, in the process, re-conceptualizing women not as victims of violence but violators of culture and family (or more correctly male) honour. This justification of domestic violence obscures the fact that it is steeped not in culture, honour or religion but in practices of violence. The dominant notions of manhood in society have built into it the idea that men are superior to women and are entitled to govern them. Clearly the ideology of subordination of women is not particular to any culture.[7]

A state that abdicates its duty to confront and eradicate domestic violence expects a wife and other female members of the family to accept violence as a part of marital and family life. The state's conceptualization of the family as situated within the private realm under a husband's stewardship, away from state scrutiny and intrusion, serves to maintain status quo even in cases of domestic violence.[8] In this instance, remaining neutral does not equate to being neutral. Through its inaction, the state perpetuates a culture of domestic violence.

Even states that eschew discrimination on the grounds of gender or sex do not see their acceptance of the unequal treatment of women within the family as a contradiction.[9] However, so long as men's "conjugal mastery" over women can be rationalized as rooted in tradition and culture, the right to maintain and enforce this mastery through domestic violence will remain unquestioned.[10] Cocooning domestic violence within tradition and culture deceptively increases the appearance of the naturalness of and necessity for domestic violence even as it appeals to the justice of maintaining the status quo.

Ironically, the state's inaction in the face of domestic violence is an aberration as the state has an interest and a duty in confronting and eradicating all forms of violence. Rules against violence and use of force is the reason societies are built in the first place, with the objective of overcoming the Hobbesian "state of nature" where each person has a right, or license, to everything in the world that inevitably leads to conflict — a "war of all against all" (*bellum omnium contra omnes*) (Hobbes, 1660). Confronting violence is and must be the primary duty of the nation state. It is imperative that we critically examine how cultural discourses are created, reproduced and instrumentalized to challenge women's human rights (Ertürk, 2012). Eradicating structural and institutional violence presupposes solving the contest between the right to family and privacy and the rights of a woman to be free of and protected from violence in favour of the latter as well as transforming structures.

To analyze the practice and prevalence of domestic violence, it is important to inquire not only into the subordination of women but the relationships between men.[11] The continuous competition for social status and hierarchy with other men has given rise, in some circumstances, to what anthropologists call a "culture-of-honour" stance. This stance embraces the notion that a man's honour is tied up with physical prowess, toughness and courage, and requires men to define themselves as dominant over women, using violence if necessary.

In a study among men in northern and southern United States, Cohen and Vandello (1998) deduce that an affront, no matter minor or imagined, must be understood in the context of reputation, face, relative social status and enduring relationships. Provocations carry a great deal of meaning about status and social position and letting infractions to honour go unanswered amounts to announcing that one can be walked over with impunity (ibid.). The historical roots of the culture-as-honour stance can be traced to the nature of economic activity in an era of little law enforcement, where any encroachment to livelihoods, as in a herding economy can be fiercely guarded against potential predators, by giving a warning of not interfering in the affairs of the community.

> Anthropologists note that herdsmen the world over tend to be quite vigilant against threats and encroachments because they are in a very precarious situation — that is, their livelihood can be rustled away from them instantly. Thus, to deter potential predators they adopt a tough, 'don't mess with me' stance. (Cohen and Vandello 1998: 570)

Second, such a posture becomes all the more important in places where people have to protect themselves and cannot rely on the state or effective law enforcement for their protection. And this was especially true of the frontier Southwhich lacked adequate law enforcement and had in many areas a herding economy. Consistent with this, the West today also shows residuals of a culture-of-honour ideology (Cohen and Vandello 1998: 570)

While culture-of-honour may explain why men believe an affront must be redeemed by violence to restore their masculine standing, it does not explain why states are willing to enforce its regulatory mechanisms with regards to violence occurring amongst men but are reluctant to punish perpetrators of violence against women, particularly domestic violence.[12] Consequently, while other expressions of culture-of-honour are circumscribed by the state, the main surviving expressions of culture-of-honour violence remain violence against women generally and domestic violence specifically. This disinclination not only translates into impunity for perpetrators of domestic violence, it points to a breakdown of societal order and failure of states in discharging their guarantee to protect women from violence, appearing to abdicate altogether their responsibilities toward women. Paradoxically, the state is required to exercise a higher, and not a lower, degree of vigilance in relation to domestic violence because violence in the home can so easily be rendered invisible.

The links to violence as a means of redeeming affronts in culture-of-honour societies must be checked by the state. When the state assumes the right to punish transgressors in the name of society, the individual simultaneously gives up his right to do so. In which case, the culture-of-honour stance no longer has the significance reserved for it in herdsman societies. If the state allows a husband to commit domestic violence with impunity or accepts his honour defence, it is representing that it will support domestic violence as providing symbolic meaning and shaping our actions at the expense of women's security and lives. The state represents that it is willing to incarnate domestic violence as a culture in and of itself.

Domestic violence excused in the name of culture erases from view the injury to women, and actively redescribes it as injury to male and family honour. The reluctance of law to punish such loss of self-control is also expressive of an attitude that regards women as the property of their families. Legitimizing the commission of a category of violence in the name of honour circumscribes the boundaries of "honour". In this instance, legal rules not only influence the development of the "honour" norm, they create it. The law, in espousing a norm that the ordinary man can lose his self-control and commit violence against his wife and other women in his (or her) family, removes the constraint on men to control their behaviour. When law provides domestic violence with an excusatory dimension, men are wont to practice it whenever an affront is perceived (see also Reilly 1997).

Opuz v. Turkey, a case decided by the European Court of Human Rights in 2009, is illustrative of how the honour defence is used by a perpetrator. In this case, the applicant claimed that the Turkish state authorities had failed to protect her and her mother from domestic violence by H.O., her husband. H.O. had beaten the applicant severely, including injuring the applicant and her mother with a knife and later running over the applicant and her mother with his car as well as issuing death threats against the applicant and her mother. While the applicant and her mother were preparing to leave for another town, H.O. fatally shot the applicant's mother. In defence, he claimed that he had killed his mother-in-law for the sake of his honour and the children (he blamed his mother-in-law for his marital problems when she intervened to protect her daughter, the applicant).[13] The honour defence is not unique to Turkey. In Brazil, for example, although the Supreme Court of Brazil has struck down the archaic "honour defence" as a justification for wife-killing, many courts remain reluctant to prosecute and punish perpetrators of domestic violence (*Maria Da Penha v. Brazil 2000*).

The "honour defence" is pursued by the accused because it has proven to be a successful strategy resulting in criminal courts imposing lenient punishments or no punishment at all on the perpetrators of such crimes. Argued and created in the courtroom setting, the "honour defence" is conceptualized, developed and approved by the state. It is the state's failure, as the representative of society, to take effective action to sanction against domestic violence that has resulted in society associating honour as a defence for domestic violence and incorporating the "honour defence" as part of its cultural identity.

In law, the defence of honour and provocation are often used interchangeably (see also Torri 2001). The defence of provocation is premised on the loss of self-control due to sudden and grave provocation. Historically, the defence of provocation was potentially available to a man who responded with homicidal violence upon discovering his wife in the act of adultery (Reilly 1997). The availability of the defence was indicative of a particular understanding of the marriage relationship and of the comparative social positions of women and men within that relationship (Reilly 1997). Over this century, however, what is a socially acceptable emotional response has arguably changed. Yet, states continue to accept these emotional responses as justifiable. Indeed, Opuz presents an example of when the defence of provocation should not succeed as the final act of murder was neither grave nor sudden. Even the State of Turkey in Opuz was held by the European Court to have been capable of foreseeing the lethal attack by H.O. (*Opuz v. Turkey 2009*). Consequently, H.O.'s actions could not have been sudden or grave and H.O. should not have been able to avail of the defence of "severe provocation".

Like self-defence, a defence of provocation must be premised on an absence of opportunity to avert violence, in the sense that the provocation must have been grave and sudden. Honour crimes, however, are often seen as punishment for moral transgressions against family and male honour. Therefore, acknowledging that honour crimes are crimes of revenge more correctly reflects the responsibility law expects of the individual. It is instructive at this juncture to compare the treatment of the "honour defence" to that of self-defence, which is more commonly raised by victims of domestic violence when they are prosecuted for attacking or killing the perpetrators of violence. One such case is *State v. Stewart*, a decision by the Supreme Court of Kansas (1988). The court held that Peggy Stewart could not avail of a self-defence instruction to the jury because there was an absence of imminent danger. The facts disclose that Peggy Stewart had suffered long years of abuse. She had been hospitalized with broken ribs, had run away from home, had been threatened with death and had witnessed her husband abusing her children. All this put her in fear for her life to the extent that she was convinced that she had to kill or be killed. Yet the court found Peggy Stewart to have "voluntarily agreed to return home" and showed no inclination to leave even after her partner, Mike, threatened her. After being abused, she went to bed and lay there for two hours, then retrieved the gun she had earlier hidden and shot Mike while he slept. The court also found that as she had access to the keys of the cars parked in the driveway, she could have driven away. "Under such circumstances," said the Court, "a battered woman cannot reasonably fear imminent life-threatening danger from her sleeping spouse" (*State v. Stewart 1988: 648*).

In a clear demonstration of double standards, the availability of escape, even though escape (running away) had proven futile in an earlier attempt as Mike had pursued her and brought her home, became a determining factor in the dismissal of Peggy Stewart's claim of self-defence, while in Opuz, time and opportunity did not deny H.O. the defence of provocation although he had doggedly pursued his wife and stalked her for months before killing her mother. Why was a Kansas Court unable to rationalize the sense of futility of escape that Peggy Stewart experienced? Why was a Turkish court not moved to demand strict accountability from H.O. when he continued to stalk his wife and mother-in-law, eventually killing his mother-in-law? These cases demonstrate that it was not domestic violence per se that formed the basis of the courts' rationalization; it was violence by a man against a woman in the name of male honour that the courts were willing to rationalize and, to a greater or lesser extent, accept and forgive, thus encouraging and perpetuating a culture of domestic violence.

Contestation of rights

Rights do not exist outside of the structures of political discourse. The recognition and preservation of rights are subject to and informed by the political aspirations of the state in shaping its culture. Cultures are shaped by states, either through its affirmative action in promoting certain values, ethos, customs and practices or its inaction in allowing them to be enacted and re-enacted without state interference. By extension, cultures, therefore, are not above reproach. Duncan Kennedy argues that rights reasoning allows us to measure political and cultural aspirations and values (1998). Rights are mediators between the domain of pure value judgments and the domain of factual judgments and allow us to be right about our value judgments (Kennedy 1998).[14] The reason for an appeal to a right is that a right cannot be reduced to a mere "value judgment". How then do we resolve rights of different individuals when they conflict with each other? In weighing costs and benefits, our aspirations should be focused on distribution of power and status and the means of achieving them (Kennedy 2005).

The state and society generally have a deep interest in the institution of the family, which in domestic violence cases, translates into prioritizing the perpetrator's right to family over that of the victims's human rights to life and to physical and mental integrity, preserving the family institution through varied and often inflexible rules and taboos. Positing the institution of the family within the private sphere and removing the private sphere from scrutiny of the law and the community, the state was able to divest itself of all responsibility over the supervision of behaviour within the family. In so doing, the state cloaks itself in an aura of neutrality while turning a blind eye to injustices and violence within the family. Even where the family is regulated by law, its regulation is unobtrusive and leaves behaviour within the marriage beyond the pale of state regulation. The consequence of this apparent "neutrality" is disastrous on the weaker members of the family, namely, women and children, particularly when the family is wreaked with violence.

In *Opuz v. Turkey* (2009 European Court of Human Rights) the state relied on this contestation of rights to justify its non-interference with the family and H.O.'s rights to privacy. The state argued that it was justified in not taking adequate action to intervene as "the authorities could not be expected to separate the applicant and her husband and convict the latter while they were living together as a family, as this would amount to a breach of their rights under Article 8 of the Convention" (*Opuz v. Turkey 2009*).[15] The European Court was, however, critical of the state's having given exclusive weight to the need to refrain from interfering in what they perceived to be "family matters" and held that the argument was incompatible with the positive obligations of states to secure to the victims enjoyment of their rights (*K.A. and A.D. v. Belgium, 1998 and 1999* cited in *Opuz v. Turkey*).

Inevitably, conflicts between rights are unavoidable. At its most basic, rights are claims that have achieved general endorsements and acceptance and conflict between rights as well as the traditions, institutions and authorities that endorse a right is logical (Kamenka 1988). It is the state's duty to intervene in the commission of violence against another person

(Hobbes 1660). This duty, however, embraces different notions of responsibility. Implicit in this, for example, is the state's positive obligation to promote and protect the right to security of every person. In considering contesting rights, states must, therefore, resolve the contest in favour of protecting the safety and security of every person. In some instances, the national authorities' interference with the private or family life of individuals is necessary not only to prevent the commission of criminal acts but to promote and protect the health and security of others.

Role of the state in shaping culture

Culture is a social construct entrenched and maintained through state and non-state institutions that the state is invested in creating and maintaining in its attempt to define a cultural identity. Eagleton (2000) notes that the state incarnates culture, which, in turn, embodies our common humanity. The condoning of domestic violence by the entire system serves to perpetuate the alleged basis and factors that sustain and encourage domestic violence.

Yet the meaning of symbols may change over time and place, which makes for autonomy in the cultural dimension. For signs to have meaning, there must be systematic relationships among signs and a group of people who recognize those relationships (Eagleton 2000). When we take the meaningful aspect of human action out of the flow of concrete interactions, we are able to disentangle the semiotic influences on action from other sorts of influences (Preis 1996). In this sense, culture may be thought of as a network of relationships.

Every society . . . possesses, or is part of, a socio-political imaginaire, that is an ensemble of symbolic discourses. This imaginaire can function as a rupture or reaffirmation. As reaffirmation, the imaginaire operates as an 'ideology' which can positively repeat and represent the founding discourse in society, what I call its 'foundational' symbols, thus preserving its sense of identity. After all, cultures create themselves by telling stories of their own past (quoting Ricouer in R. Kearney, 1984 cited in Kapferer 1994).

Through its legal and political machinations, states create and perpetuate a culture of domestic violence.[16] If society sees no evidence of willingness by the states, as representatives of society, to take effective action to sanction against domestic violence, society will more readily associate domestic violence with its cultural identity. Failure to prevent and prosecute domestic violence raises the spectre of impunity. When states fail to prevent or prosecute domestic violence, it is the state and not traditional practice or ethos that should be the focus of our inquiry. Examining domestic violence from the perspective of the state's role exposes domestic violence as a culture in and of itself.

In the United States, the same pattern of tolerance and, in fact, encouragement, was evinced in the 2009 case of *Okin v. Cornwall-on-Hudson Police Department* (2nd Circuit Court of Appeal). Michele Okin made several police complaints from December 2001 alleging that Sears had punched her, choked her and kicked her as well as threatened to kill her. Okin alleged that the police endangered her by emboldening Sears and that the police officer's dismissive and inappropriate behaviour witnessed by Sears affirmatively increased the danger she faced. Okin alleged that during these incidences, one officer laughed at her while others refused to take her complaints and yet another police officer took to discussing football with Sears when summoned to investigate a complaint of domestic violence (*Okin v. Cornwall-on-Hudson P.D* 2009: 430). Sears even told another police officer that he sometimes smacked Michele Okin around and the officer made no arrest (*Okin v. Cornwall-on-Hudson P.D* 2009). The court held that a reasonable view of the evidence supported the inference that police action rose to the level of affirmative conduct that created or increased the risk of violence to the victim.

> The officers' conduct, both in response to that first complaint and thereafter, could be viewed as ratcheting up the threat of danger to Okin. Okin would be more vulnerable once Sears was aware of the officers' dismissive and indifferent attitude toward Okin's complaints, as such awareness nullifies the deterrent capacity of police response. The implied message of the officers' conduct may have galvanized Sears to persist in violent encounters with Okin. A reasonable factfinder undoubtedly could conclude that defendants, by their affirmative conduct, enhanced the danger to Okin because they conveyed to Sears that he could continue to engage in domestic violence with impunity, and that defendants thus violated Okin's due process rights. (*Okin v. Cornwall-on-Hudson P.D* 2009: 430)

Jessica Lenahan (Gonzales) made similar claims — that the police failed to respond to her calls and to protect her children who were identified as at-risk in a restraining order. Referring to various information received, the Inter-American Commission in the Jessica Lenahan case noted:

> [T]he problem of domestic violence in the United States was considered a 'private matter,' and therefore, undeserving of protection measures by law enforcement agencies and the justice system. Once domestic violence was finally recognized as a crime, women were still very unlikely to gain protection in the United States because of law enforcement's widespread under-enforcement of domestic violence laws. Very often, the police responded to domestic violence calls either by not taking any action, by purposefully delaying their response in the hope of avoiding confronta-

tion, or, by merely attempting to mediate the situation and separate the parties so they could 'cool off'. (*Jessica Lenahan (Gonzales) v. United States of America 2011*)[17]

These cases illustrate the state's political and cultural attitude towards domestic violence. Domestic violence is shaped by ideological orientations of power wielded by the state. It is simultaneously personal and direct, yet made up of social rules of the game that have an economic, social, cultural or ideological content (Rupesinghe 1994). Tolerance of domestic violence by state organs exposes domestic violence as a pattern (*Jessica Lenahan (Gonzales) v. United States of America 2011*).[18] The state's inaction in enforcing the letter of the law coupled with the signals given by the legal and judicial officers that domestic violence was tolerated, implicitly sanction the continued practice of domestic violence, if not provide a fertile terrain for a thriving culture of domestic violence.

Where a culture of domestic violence exists, domestic violence is transformed into institutional and structural violence that is found formally or truly embedded in society. It becomes accepted, or at least tolerated, with the complicity of the people and generally accepted by both the beneficiaries and the victims (MacGregor and Rubio 1994). Further, the state supports and maintains this structural violence by granting husbands and male partners impunity for domestic violence, and even where the perpetrator has committed severely violent acts, the state appears reluctant to take "invasive measures" against him.

In international law, states are required to act with due diligence to eliminate violence against women (*Jessica Lenahan (Gonzales) v. United States of America 2011*).[19] The Fourth World Conference on Women in Beijing in 1995 acknowledged that violence against women "derives essentially from cultural practices".[20] Despite this and international and regional instruments investing states with the responsibility to eliminate violence against women, many states specifically lodged reservations on the grounds of culture against their otherwise legally binding international obligations to eliminate violence against women[21] and continue to view their duty to act with due diligence to end domestic violence as circumscribed by cultural practices and to regard their duty as derogable.[22]

These reservations, in so far as they apply to domestic violence, are made all the more serious in view of "the argument that domestic violence should be understood and treated as a form of torture and, when less severe, ill-treatment" (Coomaraswarmy 1996, see also Copelon 1994). In 2000, the Human Rights Committee indicated that domestic violence can give rise to violations of the right not to be subjected to torture or ill-treatment under Article 7 of the International Covenant of Civil and Political Rights.[23] Similarly, the United Nations Special Rapporteur on Torture and Other Cruel Inhuman and Degrading Treatment or Punishment reported that a parallel between torture and domestic violence in the form of intimate partner violence should be drawn to raise awareness with regard to the level of atrocity that they can reach.

> Domestic violence, as well as torture, tends to escalate over time, sometimes resulting in death or leaving women's bodies mutilated or permanently disfigured. Women who experience such violence, whether in their homes or in a prison, suffer depression, anxiety, loss of self-esteem and a feeling of isolation. Indeed, battered women may suffer from the same intense symptoms that comprise the post-traumatic stress disorder identified in victims of official torture as well as by victims of rape. Another parallel between privately battering women and torture, which refers back to the element of powerlessness, is the intention to keep the victim in a permanent state of fear based on unpredictable violence by seeking to reduce the person to submission and destroy his/her capacity for resistance and autonomy with the ultimate aim of achieving total control. (Nowak 2008)[24]

Illustrating the parallels between torture and domestic violence facilitates holding states accountable for their failure to act with due diligence. Similarly, in a few cases, such as Opuz it was observed that domestic violence could be sufficiently serious to amount to ill-treatment (*Opuz v. Turkey* 2009). These are significant findings as there are no major legal differences in the qualification of a behaviour as torture or cruel, inhuman or degrading, treatment from a practical standpoint except for the severity of the action and how the same affects the victim.

The prohibition of torture as a whole is a *jus cogens* that violates the demands of humanity and dictates of public conscience.[25] In this regard, as there can be no "cultural defence" against torture, there can be no cultural defence against domestic violence. Jeremy Waldron posits that torture is *malum in se*, namely that torture is just wrong and would be wrong whether positive law prohibits it or not (Waldron 2005). Acknowledging that domestic violence can be torture, or at the very least ill-treatment, elevates it into *jus cogens* prohibition in international law, which necessarily means that states are not able to derogate from their obligation to intervene to prevent, stop, sanction and provide remedies in cases of domestic violence.

Conclusion

Traditional practices, ethos and values that form the "cultural excuse" for domestic violence must be interrogated. Memories and histories of a time when men had to fend for themselves without the state's intervention are no longer legitimate nor deserving of preservation. Domestic violence cannot be justified in the name of the family, society or national/traditional culture. Neither can perpetrators be given impunity under any guise. States should be held accountable for complicity in domestic violence, whenever they create and implement laws that directly or indirectly trap women in abusive circumstances. This includes accepting, justifying and excusing domestic violence on cultural grounds. The state's sanction of domestic violence in the name of culture on the one hand and its refusal to intervene into family life in the name of right to privacy and family on the other has created a fertile terrain for the perpetuation of domestic violence. It is essential that we remove the culture of violence from the family, eliminate state tolerance (and implicit encouragement) of domestic violence and emphasize the message that domestic violence has no part to play in the cultural identity of society.

The avoidance and prevention of violence constitute the basic purpose of lawmaking. The rule is so fundamental that "if a legal system did not have them there would be no point in having any other rules at all" (Hart 1958). The predominant model of addressing domestic violence both as discrimination and through the formal judicial system has borne limited success. Hence, it is essential that we now broaden our understanding of domestic violence to emphasize the harm it causes. Domestic violence is an assault on human dignity, often seeking to reduce or eradicate a person's autonomy, destroy her self-esteem and compel her into subjugation. There is no society that does not prohibit arbitrary acts of force and habitual and pervasive acts of cruelty (see also Weiss and Hubert 2001). To understand domestic violence we must look at its personal aspect as committed by a perpetrator and the harm to the victim on the one hand and the structural aspects of domestic violence including its legitimization by the state on the other.

> When all women, regardless of their background, fear the threat of male violence (and modify their behavior so as to avoid it), this violence is not some private affair but a societal practice — with a point. The violence expresses — and helps to realize — the view that men are entitled to dominate over women . . . Where violence against women is common, every woman is victimized by the reality of this practice, insofar as where she lives, what she does, what activities she undertakes, and what her family life is like, are all affected either by the threat of such violence, or by the fact of it. (Hampton 1998)

If domestic violence can constitute torture and torture is *malum in se* as well as a peremptory norm, any formulation of the family that harbours the culture of domestic violence at its very foundations is unacceptable and cannot be normalized within our respective national imaginations and aspirations. If we as society allow ourselves to be enlisted to rationalize domestic violence, all that society treasures of families is evacuated and what is left is an empty shell incapable of maintaining and fulfilling its function.

Domestic violence has decivilized us as a human race. Its practice is normalized in our imagination; its defence bound in the name of culture, honour and religion. Clearly, domestic violence is embedded within society's structures "which are shaped, maintained, and eventually transformed with margins of plasticity by human beings, and in many cases this also includes the victims, all of whom are shaped by the same structures" (MacGregor and Rubio 1994). The cases described in this chapter disclose a clear pattern of state-legitimated domestic violence, whether expressly or implicitly. Reproduced and replicated in this manner, domestic violence graduates from violence sanctioned by specific cultures to a state perpetuated culture of violence in and of itself.

Culture is thus formalized into a conventional mode of perceiving domestic violence as a socially sanctioned punishment of hallowed values visited upon women violators, thereby rendering women active agents of their own injury. Cultural practices have become exercises of power because culture is often used in competing ways to fulfil diverse political agendas. Therefore, the aim should be clearing a passage towards a non-violent society, which is the ultimate goal of being human (Arendt 1970). In this analysis, structural violence flows inside social structures and stems out into interpersonal relationships, simultaneously existing from and within structures, constituting the victim as part of the structure, both in a position of acquiescence and confrontation where culture is used to legitimize violence. Deconstructing culture in the context of domestic violence, therefore, involves examining the identities of those claiming their rights to culture, the authorities that sanction these rights, and in the event culture is used to claim legal rights, the role of the state as the final arbiter in recognizing and perpetuating these claims. In this regard, it is more accurate to construct domestic violence as a culture in and of itself, rather than embedded in culture, and to scrutinize the role of the state in alternatively creating, tolerating, developing and encouraging a culture of domestic violence as well as the state's role and responsibility in its eradication.

Notes

1 Despite her complaints to the police throughout the ordeal, the police did not take action to investigate the disappearance of Jessica Lenahan's (formerly Gonzales) three daughters, who were taken by her husband in contravention of a court restraining order. The children were later found dead in Simon Gonzales' truck. The Supreme Court rejected the argument that the authorities could be held responsible for failure to enforce a restraining order in a domestic violence situation.

2 Having failed at the highest court domestically, Jessica Lenahan then took her case to the Inter-American Commission. The commission underscored that "the entire State structure — including the State's legislative framework, public policies, law enforcement machinery and judicial system" must "adequately and effectively prevent and respond" to domestic violence. The

commission also recommended the US adopt "public policies and institutional programs aimed at restructuring the stereotypes of domestic violence victims, and promote the eradication of discriminatory socio-cultural patterns that impede women and children's full protection from domestic violence acts".

3 In her 2007 report, the United Nations Special Rapporteur on Violence against Women, its Causes and Consequence likewise challenged the dominant culture-based paradigms that justify or explain violations of women's rights. The report critically examines how cultural discourses are created, reproduced and instrumentalized. It also traces the trends in the development of the international normative framework on violence against women, warns against cultural essentialism that ignores the agency of women in the developing world and the trajectories of their resistance to violence and oppression and underlines the primacy of women's right to live a life free of gender-based violence over any cultural considerations (Ertürk, 2007).

4 The judge was subsequently removed from the case on the grounds that her reasoning could not be justified.

5 Annual rates of domestic violence between 1994 and 2004 indicate that non-Hispanic and Hispanic females and males are equally subjected to domestic violence.

6 Slavery was declared a crime against humanity. See the Slavery Convention 1926 and the Supplementary Convention on the Abolition of Slavery, the Slave Trade, and Institutions and Practices Similar to Slavery 1957, 226 UNTS 3, (30 April 1957). See also Convention against Torture and Other Cruel, Inhuman or Degrading Treatment or Punishment A/RES/39/46 dated 10 December 1984.

7 Domestic violence, though a culture by and of itself, may manifest itself differently in each society. See also Kimberle Crenshaw's discussions on intersectionality between domestic violence, poverty and race (Crenshaw, 1991). Similarly, the United Nations Special Rapporteur on Violence against Women, its Causes and Consequences, in noting the high incidences of violence against Native American women identified causes of violence as reflected in the socioeconomic realities faced by Native American communities, coupled with the historical discrimination they have experienced (Manjoo, 2011 citing the Bureau of Justice Statistics, 2009).

8 On another level, the state's interest in protecting the status quo in the family may lie, in part, in the family's efficiency in assuming responsibility over the care of the young, the old and the weak. Where the family is unable to fulfill its function, the state may be compelled to take over the care of the young, the old and the weak, a role which, understandably calls for expanded state services and benefits. This clearly juxtaposes the interest of the family against the interest of victim-survivor, a juxtaposition that is almost always raised in the prosecution of perpetrators of domestic violence but almost never raised in the state's decision whether to prosecute the perpetrator of other crimes, like theft or drunk driving.

9 For example, the Prime Minister of Singapore viewed not according equal treatment to women as "traditional areas of differential treatment" (Kong & Yeoh 2003).

10 The assumption being that a woman always agrees to subordinate herself as a wife (Pateman 1998).

11 Critically examining relationships between men allows us to challenge the legitimacy of such power expectations by exposing their dysfunctional and debilitating effect on women and families (Dowd 2008).

12 "So that in the nature of man, we find three principal causes of quarrel. First, competition; secondly, diffidence; thirdly, glory. The first maketh men invade for gain; the second, for safety; and the third, for reputation. The first use violence, to make themselves masters of other men's persons, wives, children, and cattle; the second, to defend them; the third, for trifles, as a word, a smile, a different opinion, and any other sign of undervalue, either direct in their persons or by reflection in their kindred, their friends, their nation, their profession, or their name." (Hobbes 1660)

13 Since H.O. was found to have had acted on provocation, the Turkish Court shortened his sentence of life imprisonment to fifteen years, ten months and a fine. H.O. was released pending appeal.

14 Duncan Kennedy uses rights as mediators to resolve this dichotomy. In this mediation, rights are confined to those that are universal. They are neither arbitrary nor subjective but derive from needs, values or preferences that every person shares or ought to share. Once the existence of the right is acknowledged, then we all have to agree to its observance. In this way, we can reason whether a value judgment is correct.

15 Article 8 of the European Convention For The Protection Of Human Rights And Fundamental Freedoms provides that a person has a right to respect for his private and family life, his home and his correspondence ¶ 144.

16 Culture, in this instance, is to be understood as the study of a category of social life conceptualized as "learned behavior" that is concerned with meaning and not culture as a system of practice that is distinct to a society or group (Sewell 1999).

17 In *Thurman v. City of Torrington*, 595 F. Supp. 1521 (D. Conn. 1984), the police watched as the estranged husband stabbed and kicked the victim in her neck, throat and chest, paralyzing her from the neck down and causing permanent disfigurement, cited in Supplemental Amicus Curiae Brief submitted by Maya Raghu from Legal Momentum and others on behalf of petitioners on 15 October 2008, p. 40, note 22.

18 The Commission was presented uncontested statistics indicating that half of the murders in the State of Colorado, USA, are committed by an intimate or former partner and the victims are disproportionately female. On average, the abuse had taken place over a period of three years. Forty-five percent of female homicide victims statewide were killed by an intimate partner.

19 See also *González and Others* ("Campo Algodonero") v. Mexico, Case Nos. 12.496, 12.497, & 12.498, Inter-Am. Ct.H.R., § 310 (16 November 2009).

20 "Violence against women throughout the life cycle derives essentially from cultural patterns, in particular the harmful effects of certain traditional or customary practices and all acts of extremism linked to race, sex, language or religion that perpetuate the lower status accorded to women in the family, the workplace, the community and society". Beijing Declaration and Platform for Action, Fourth World Conference on Women, 15 September 1995, A/CONF.177/20 (1995) and A/CONF.177/20/Add.1 (1995) ¶ 119.

21 See CEDAW and Reservations: Culture, Religion and Tradition and the

Implementation of CEDAW Principles (International Women's Rights Action Watch Asia Pacific, 2007, unpublished). These reservations affect violence against women as CEDAW General Recommendation 19 emphatically declared that the "full implementation of the Convention required States to take positive measures to eliminate all forms of violence against women". CEDAW General Recommendation 19, Violence against Women (Eleventh session, 1992), UN Doc. A/47/38 at 1 (1993), reprinted in Compilation of General Comments and General Recommendations Adopted by Human Rights Treaty Bodies, UN Doc. HRI/GEN/1/Rev.6 at 243 (2003) at ¶ 4.

22 Specifically States have a duty to prevent violations, protect victims/survivors, investigate and prosecute incidences of violations, punish perpetrators and provide redress and reparation to victims/survivors. See Convention on the Elimination of All Forms of Discrimination against Women, GA res. 34/180, 34 UN GAOR Supp (No. 46) at 193, UN Doc A/34/46, entered into force 3 September, 198; Articles 2, 3 and 5 of the European Convention of Human Rights and Fundamental Freedoms, ETS No. 005, November 4, 1950 also available at http://conventions.coe.int/treaty/EN/Treaties/html/005.htm (accessed 22 August 2011); Protocol to the African Charter on Human and Peoples' Rights on the Rights of Women in Africa, 13 September 2000 adopted by the 2nd Ordinary Session of the Assembly of the Union, Maputo, CAB/LEG/66.6; reprinted in 1 Afr Hum Rts LJ 40 (25 November 2005). Also available at http://www.africa-union.org/root/au/Documents/Treaties/Text/Protocol%20on%20the%20Rights%20of%20Women.pdf (accessed 22 August 2011).

23 International Covenant on Civil and Political Rights, GA Res 2200A (XXI), 21 UN GAOR Supp (No. 16) ¶ 52, UN Doc. A/6316 (1966), 999 UNTS 171 (Mac 23, 1976). General Comment No. 28 Equality of rights between men and women (article 3), (Sixty-eighth session, 2000), UN Doc CCPR/C/21/Rev.1/Add.10 (2000), reprinted in Compilation of General Comments and General Recommendations Adopted by Human Rights Treaty Bodies, UN Doc HRI/GEN/1/Rev 6 at 179 (29 Mac 2000). Also available at http://www.unhchr.ch/tbs/doc.nsf/(Symbol)/13b02776122d4838802568b900360e80?Opendocument (accessed 8 October 2011).

24 Committee against Torture and Other Cruel Inhuman and Degrading Treatment or Punishment (CAT Committee) similarly said that protection of victims of torture include protection of victims of gender based violence including domestic violence. Committee Against Torture, General Comment 2, Implementation of article 2 by States Parties, U.N. Doc. CAT/C/GC/2/CRP.1/Rev.4 (2007).

25 See *Prosecutor v Furundžija* Case No. IT-95-17/1-T, ICTY Trial Chamber, Judgment, § 154 IT75-19-1 (10 Dec. 1998). *Jus cogens* is a body of peremptory principles of international law that are universal and non-derogable, for example, torture, genocide and slavery.

References

Arendt, H. (1970) *On Violence*, Harvest Books, New York.

BBC (2005) History of a rape case, 28 June, available at http://news.bbc.co.uk/2/hi/4620065.stm [accessed 26 October 2012]

Catlano, S., Smith E., Snyder H., & Rand M. (2009) *Female Victims of Violence*, Bureau of Justice Statistics.

Centers for Disease Control and Prevention (2003) *Costs of Intimate Partner Violence Against Women in the United States*, National Center for Injury Prevention and Control Publication, Atlanta Georgia.

Cohen, D. & Vandello J. (1998) 'Meanings of violence', *Journal of Legal Studies*, Vol. 27(44), pp. 567–69.

Coomaraswarmy, R (1996) *Report of the Special Rapporteur on violence against women, its causes and consequences*, UN Economic and Social Council [online] Available at: <http://www.unhchr.ch/Huridocda/Huridoca.nsf/estFrame/c41d8f479a2e9757802566d6004c72ab?Opendocument> [Accessed 14 October 2012].

Copelon, R (1994) 'Recognizing the egregious in the everyday, domestic violence as torture' *Colum. Hum. Rts. L Rev.* Vol. 25(2) (Spring 1994), pp. 291–367.

Crenshaw, K. (1991) 'Mapping the Margins: Intersectionality, identity politics, and violence against women', *Stan. L. Rev.,* Vol. 43(6), pp. 1241–1219.

Davidson, C, (2009) 'Recession increasing domestic violence, decreasing victim options, *The Atlantic Monthly*, [online] Available at:<http://www.theatlantic.com/national/archive/2009/12/recession-increasing-domestic-violence-decreasing-victim-options/32205/ >[Accessed 4 February 2011].

Dowd, N.E. (2008) 'Masculinities and feminist legal theory', *Wisconsin Journal of Law, Gender and Society,* Vol. 23(2), pp. 201–48.

Eagleton, T. (2000) *The idea of culture*, Blackwell Publishers, Oxford, England

Ertürk, Y. (2007) *Intersections between culture and violence against women*, 4th Session of Human Rights Council 17 January 2007, United Nations: New York.

European's Women's Lobby (2007) *Reality check: When women's NGOs map policies and legislation on violence against women in Europe*, [online] Available at: http://www.ewlcentreonviolence.org/IMG/pdf/Copy_of_NAP-final-feb07.pdf [Accessed Jan. 19, 2011].

Gardiner, D. (2010) 'Dad accused in 'honor killing' will not face death penalty', *The Arizona Republic* 19 February 2010, [online] Available at:<http://www.azcentral.com/community/glendale/articles/2010/02/19/20100219honor-killing.html > [Accessed 28 June 2010].

Gaventa, J. (2006) 'Finding the spaces for change: A power analysis', *IDS Bulletin* Vol. 37(6), pp. 23–33.

Greenfeld, L. (1998) 'Violence by intimates: Analysis of data on crimes by current or former spouses, Boyfriends, and Girlfriends', U.S Department of Justice Bureau of Justice Statistics.

Hampton, J. (1998) 'Punishment, feminism and political identity: A case study in the expressive meaning of the law', *Canadian Journal of Law & Jurisprudence,* Vol. 11(1), pp. 23–45.

Hart, HLA (1958) 'Positivism and the separation of law and morals' *Harvard Law Review,* Vol. 71(4) (February 1958), pp. 593–629.

Hobbes, T. (1660) *The Leviathan,* Chapter XIII. [online] Available at: <http://oregonstate.edu/instruct/phl302/texts/hobbes/leviathan-c.html# CHAPTERXIII > [Accessed 8 February 2011].

Kamenka, E. (1988) 'Human rights, people's rights' in P. Alston (ed.), *The Rights of Peoples,* Oxford University Press, Oxford, p. 127.

Kapferer, B. (1994) 'Remythologizations of power and identity: Nationalism and violence in Sri Lanka' in *The Culture of Violence*, Rupesinghe (ed.), United Nations University Press, New York, pp. 60–61.

Kearney, R. (1984) Dialogues with Paul Ricoeur, R. Kearney, *Dialogues with Contemporary Continental Thinkers: The phenomenological heritage*, Manchester, Manchester University Press.

Kennedy, D. (2005) *The Dark Sides of Virtue: Assessing international humanitarianism*, Princeton University Press, Princeton, New Jersey.

Kennedy, D. (1998) *Critique of Adjudication*, Harvard University Press, Cambridge, MA.

Kong & Yeoh (2003) *The Politics of Landscapes in Singapore: Construction of 'nation'*, Syracuse University Press, Syracuse.

Landler, M. (2007) 'German judge stirs protest by citing Koran', *New York Times* 22 March 2007, [online] Available at: <http://www.nytimes.com/2007/03/22/world/europe/22iht-germany.4995843.html> [Accessed 28 January 2011].

Laurence and Spalter-Roth (1996) 'Measuring the costs of domestic violence against women and the cost-effectiveness of interventions: an initial assessment and proposals for further research,' Institute for Women's Policy Research, Washington DC.

MacGregor and Rubio (1994) 'Rejoinder to the theory of structural violence', in *The Culture of Violence,* Rupesinghe, ed. United Nations University Press, New York, pp. 42–57.

MacManus, Susan A., and Nikki R. Van Hightower (1989) 'Limits of State Constitutional Guarantees: Lessons from Efforts to Implement Domestic Violence Policies,' *Pub. Admin. Review* 49(3), pp. 269–277

Manjoo, R. (2011) UN Human Rights Council, *Report of the Special Rapporteur on violence against Women, its causes and consequences, Ms. Rashida Manjoo — Addendum — Mission to the United States of America*, 6 June 2011, A/HRC/17/26/Add.5, available at: http://www.unhcr.org/refworld/docid/4ef1ad5d2.html [accessed 14 October 2012].

Massod, S. (2006) 'Vendetta rapes continue as Pakistan resists change', *New York Times,* 14 September 2006, [online] Available at: <http://www.nytimes.com/2006/10/14/world/asia/14pakistan.html> [Accessed 22 January 2011].

Merry, S.E. (2003) Human Rights and the Demonization of Culture, *Political and Legal Anthropology Review,* Vol. 26, Issue 1, pp. 55–76.

Morrison A.R. and Orlando M.B. (1999) 'Social and Economic Costs of Domestic Violence: Chile and Nicaragua' in *Too Close to Home: Domestic Violence in the Americas*, Inter-American Development Bank Washington DC, pp. 51–80.

Narayan, U. (1997) *Dislocating Cultures: Identities, Traditions, and Third-World Feminism,* New York, Routledge.

Nowak, M. (2008) *Report of the Special Rapporteur on torture and other cruel, inhuman or degrading treatment or punishment*, U.N Human Rights Council 15 January 2008, ¶ 44. [online] Available at: http://daccess-dds-ny.un.org/doc/UNDOC/GEN/G08/101/61/PDF/G0810161.pdf?OpenElement (Accessed 8 February 2011).

Pateman, C .(1998) *The Sexual Contract*. Stanford University Press, Stanford.

Preis, A. (1996) 'Human rights as cultural practice: An anthropological critique', *Human Rights Quarterly*, Vol. 18(2) (May 1996), pp. 286–315.

O'Shea, Chiade (2004) 'School hope for rape victim', *BBC News*, 7 December 2004, [online] Available at: http://news.bbc.co.uk/2/hi/4042941.stm [Accessed 22, 2011].

Raz, J. (1994) 'Multiculturalism: A liberal perspective' in J. Raz (ed.), *Ethics in the Public Domain: Essays in the Morality of Law and Politics*, Clarendon Press, pp. 155, 170–71.

Reilly, A. (1997) 'The heart of the matter: Emotion in criminal defenses', *Ottawa Law Review*, Vol. 29(1), pp. 117–151.

Rihanna (2009) *Interview on 20/20*, Interviewed by . . . Diana Sawyer [tv] ABC News, 2 October 2011, 9:00.

Rupesinghe, K. (1994) 'Forms of violence and its transformation' in Rupesinghe, (ed.), *The Culture of Violence*, United Nations University Press, New York, pp. 14–41.

Sen, A (2007) *Identity and violence: The illusion of destiny*, Norton, New York.

Sewell, W.H. (1999) 'The Concepts of culture' in Bonnell and Hunt (eds.), *Beyond the Cultural Turn*, University of California Press, Berkeley, pp. 35–61.

Song, S. (2007) *Justice, Gender and the Politics of Multiculturalism*, Cambridge: Cambridge University Press.

Tohid, O. (2002) 'Protests over Pakistan gang rape', *BBC News World Edition*, 3 July, 2002, [online] Available at: <http://news.bbc.co.uk/2/hi/south_asia/2089624.stm > [Accessed 22 January 2011].

Torri W. (2001) 'Social change, crime, and culture: The defense of provocation', *Crime, Law and Social Change*, Vol. 36, No. 3, pp. 309–325.

UN Office for the High Commissioner of Human Rights (2011) *Special Rapporteur on violence against women finalizes fact finding mission to the United States of America*. [press statement] 8 February 2011.

US Bureau of Labor Statistics, Labor Force Statistics from the Current Population Survey, [online] Available at: http://www.bls.gov/cps/ [Accessed Jan. 25, 2011].

US Senate Report (1990) Report No. 101–545, pp. 37

Waldron, J. (2005) 'Torture and positive law: Jurisprudence for the White House', *Columbia Law Review*, Vol. 105(6) (October 2005), pp.1681–1750.

Weiss and Hubert (2001) *The responsibility to Protect: Research Bibliography, Background: Supplementary Volume to the Report of the International Commission on Intervention and State Sovereignty*, International Development Research Centre, Ottawa, Canada.

Legal Authorities

Cooper v Aaron (1958) United States Supreme Court, 358 U.S. 1, at 25.

González and Others ("Campo Algodonero") v. Mexico (2009), Case Nos. 12.496, 12.497, & 12.498, Inter-Am. Ct.H.R., § 310.

Jessica Lenahan (Gonzales) v. United States of America (2011) Report No. 80/11, Case 12.626 Merits.

K.A. and A.D. v. Belgium, 1998 and 1999 App. No. 42758/98 and 45558/99, § 81, 17, Eur. Ct. H.R.

Maria Da Penha v Brazil (2000), Inter-American Court of Human Rights, Case 12.051 Report No. 54/01, OEA/Ser.L/V/II.111 Doc. 20 rev. 704.

Okin v. Cornwall-on-Hudson Police Department (2009), 2nd Circuit Court of Appeals, 577 F.3d 415.

Opuz v Turkey (2009), European Court of Human Rights, App. No. 33401/02.
Prosecutor v Furundžija (1998), ICTY Trial Chamber, Judgment, Case No. IT-95-17/1-T, 10 December 1998.
State v. Stewart (1988) Supreme Court, 243 Kan. 639.
Town of Castle Rock v. Gonzales (2005) United States Supreme Court, 545 U.S. 748.
Thurman v. City of Torrington (1984) 595 F. Supp. 1521 (D. Conn. 1984).

CHAPTER

4

Domestic Violence in the Harmonious Asian Family and the Enforcement of Heteronormativity in India and Indonesia

SASKIA E. WIERINGA

Heteronormativity in Asia is constructed around the claim that all its agents work towards the creation or preservation of harmonious Asian families. Yet, there is enormous violence involved in the perpetuation of this myth. This chapter is based on the life stories of widows/divorced women, sex workers and lesbians in India and Indonesia. I focus on the factors that produce domestic violence and make it intelligible within the normative patterns of Indian and Indonesian families. The emphasis is on the mechanisms, what I term the passionate aesthetics, that inform the particular construction of heteronormativity in these countries. These aesthetics are commonly classified as "private" as they are played out within the domestic unit. At the same time, the untenability of the distinction between the public and the private sphere becomes clear since heteronormativity is exposed as informed by social constructs and institutions.

The research project on which this chapter is based was conducted in the framework of the Kartini Asia Network.[1] The fieldwork was implemented between 2005 and 2007 and explored the ways in which passionate aesthetics are being constructed in India and Indonesia. Women from three categories of those excluded from the bounds of "normalcy" or orthodox heterosexuality were interviewed — widows/divorced women, sex workers and young urban lesbians. The first category includes both widows and divorced women in Indonesia, because the Indonesian word *janda* is used to classify both, emphasizing the perception that they have had heterosexual relations and must again long for it.[2] We compared their life trajectories in Jakarta and Delhi, two major cities in widely different parts of Asia. More than thirty in-depth profiles were collected; each was based on numerous research visits with intimate details about the life histories of these women, and focussed on their experiences in their families, their sexual and emotional lives and their dreams for the future. Important topics included the manner in which their identities and subjectivities are constructed, their social, economic, sexual and religious agency and the embodiment of that agency, as well as the role of the state and NGOs.

Passionate aesthetics

One of the core concepts used in this study of heteronormativity in Asia is passionate aesthetics. Aesthetics here refer not to standards of beauty but rather to a set of principles that underlie the making of distinctions in matters of morality. I use the Kantian definition of aesthetics, as I want to emphasize that heteronormativity is a system of values that, like any value judgment, is subjective, while it is at the same time considered to have universal relevance (Kant 1997). Any aesthetic distinction is based on subjective views, yet acquires a hegemonic power in a given context. The adjective passionate is added to stress that we deal with a system that regulates erotic desires and sexuality.

Passionate aesthetics is defined as the institutions, dynamics, motivations, codes of behaviour and (re)presentation, as well as the subjectivities and identities that together make up the complex structure of desires, erotic attractions, sexual relations, kinship and partnership patterns that are salient in a given context. Passionate aesthetics thus underlie particular regimes of heteronormativity and of sexual subcultures. Although the passionate aesthetics informing erotic desires and love have many ennobling characteristics, they may also have effects of violence, both in the physical and symbolic sense.[3] One of the effects of passionate aesthetics is maintaining the internal cohesion of heteronormativity; in constant processes of expulsion and repulsion, a category of abject others is created while the inner core group is silenced or seduced into subjection.[4]

Heteronormativity is more than a reference to a normalized sexual practice; it informs the normativity of daily life, including institutions, laws and regulations that impact the sexual and reproductive lives of members of society as well as the moral imperatives that influence people's personal lives. Heteronormativity refers to practices, norms governing those practices, institutions that uphold them and effects produced by those norms within individuals. These effects can be seen in behaviours and feelings as well as in the aspirations for the future that the narrators nourish for themselves and their children. As Butler reminds us, we are constantly performing our gender, dancing around the norms that govern a particular social and historical context. A norm "renders the social field intelligible and normalizes the field for us" (2004:42). However, norms are not stable; in the repeated performance of sexual and social norms lies the possibility for revision. Norms can best be understood by the effects they produce. Norms help us navigate our daily lives; they constitute a moral compass to guide us in the myriad decisions that must be taken. The more invisible they are, the more effective they can be, since the less they can be contested.

The life stories collected in this project provide rich examples of the effects these often-invisible norms produce in the lives of those who are positioned both within and outside the institution of normative sex. The passionate aesthetics displayed in these life stories demonstrate how heteronormativity is continuously produced, reproduced and also how change is possible, by displacement, partial adherence, fusion, subversion or downright rejection of dominant norms.[5] Heteronormativity is not homogeneous nor does it produce uniform effects. Gender and age differences are important intersecting variables, as are ethnicity, caste, religion and socio-economic conditions. Not all heterosexual practices or lifestyles have similar status; there are hegemonic and subordinate forms of heterosexualities (Seidman 2005, ref in Jackson 2006, see also Rubin 1989). Violence, as I will explore in this chapter, is an intrinsic part of the passionate aesthetics that underlie heteronormativity.

The harmonious Asian family

The passionate aesthetics by which the present day heterosexual patriarchal family in Asia is represented as the ideal of a harmonious family — the repository of marital bliss composed of dutiful, virtuous wives and responsible husbands — are multiple. The glorification of this family model hides its underlying symbolic and physical violence. In India and in Indonesia, numerous reports spell out the ubiquity of violence and the cruelty women and (girl) children are subjected to.[6]

In India and in Indonesia, for women the normative family model is based on pre-marital virginity, chastity during marriage and motherhood. Self-sacrifice and dependence upon males is glorified for women. These norms are anchored in religious values. The Indian "divine family" (see Nandy in this volume) should not be ruptured by divorce; in Indonesia too, marriage, particularly a woman's sexual obligation to her husband, is seen as a service to God. In both countries, divorced women are heavily stigmatized; this stigma even extends to organizations that attempt to empower those women. In both countries, the divine nature of the relationship implies women's sexual service to their husbands. Ideals of purity and self-sacrifice in India are often enforced by in-laws; in Indonesia, these ideals are more directly tied to social control over sexual behaviour by husbands. Women are taught the lessons of subservience and subordination to men from an early age. Asian families are supposed to be heterosexual. The two major studies on Indian family life do not even mention homosexuality (Patel 2005, Uberoi 1994). The dominant Asian family is not only heterosexual, it is also supposed to be within caste lines (India) or religious systems. Women's control over their own lives is denied in the public realm; there they are seen as victims, to be "protected" rather than "empowered" by the state (see Ganapathy in this volume).

The family is not always the safe haven, the model of harmonious life, that its proponents would like it to be. It can, in fact, be a very violent place, particularly for young girls. The cloak of family values has hidden from public view the physical and sexual abuse taking place within homes. Childhood sexual abuse was only acknowledged through the second wave feminist movement (Kaye 2003). The two major studies on the Indian family system referred to above (Patel 2005 and Uberoi 1994) do not mention incest, other than referring to it as a category of marriage avoidance. Yet, when we (coordinators of the sexuality theme of the Kartini Asia Network) conducted a training on sexual rights with Indian activists in Khajurao in 2007, almost all female participants recounted stories of incest and sexual violence by family friends (or the family priest). Most were detailing their experiences for the first time. In Indonesia too, talking of incest is taboo. Our narrators suffer the pain, guilt and shame in silence. They initially tried to hide these traumatic experiences and paint a rosy picture of their childhood. Particularly the fathers, in many cases the perpetrators, were spoken about with apparent affection. The following story portrays the ways in which a family can be a dangerous place for a young woman:

> Susi, a sex worker from Cirebon, Indonesia, initially spoke of having had a wonderful childhood and of her father as a kind and caring parent. However, she ran away from her home in Bandung when she was sixteen and is now a very troubled young woman. Her father worked in an airline company and recently became elected as a member of the regional council (DPRD). In Susi's mind, her father was a warm-hearted man, the best father in the world. If he was rude at times, that was, she said, because he used to take drugs when he was young and kept bad company. Yet she was unable to share with this 'best father in the world' the great trauma of her life — that she was frequently raped by her uncle, his brother. She could only disclose this to an elder sister. In fact, she was afraid that her father would kill his own brother for she knew very well that he was ill-tempered.

> Later in the interview process, it transpired that this excellent father was somewhat less of an ideal husband. For years, he had a relationship with a singer, a *pesinden*.[7] However, Susi didn't blame her father. It must have been the *pesinden* herself, she thinks, who practised *guna-guna* or *susuk* (black magic) on him. The only way she could share her secret was by writing her family a very circumspect letter, explaining she was leaving for Cirebon and that her father's family should not be blamed. Bewildered, her father started hunting for the truth. It turned out that his brother had not only repeatedly raped Susi but another daughter as well. He reported the case, but uncle had taken precautions. He had mortgaged their house without their being aware of it and threatened not to pay the debt, so they would lose their house. Susi's father withdrew his complaint. Susi, who had hoped she would finally be vindicated, became desperate. She traces her addiction to drugs, nightlife and free sex to that moment.

One of our Indonesian lesbian narrators, Lee, also initially presented her family as an ordinary entity and her parents as hardworking entrepreneurs. Yet, in her case too, her experiences in this family were painful.

> Lee was raped by her uncle, who was very close to her and she was deeply traumatized by that. Like Susi, she was unable to share this with her parents. She is still very emotional about it and wants revenge. She only contains her rage towards him as she doesn't want to be sent to prison. This was not the only violence she experienced in her own family. When it transpired that she was having a same-sex relationship with her present partner, Annisa, she was beaten up by male kin. She fled from her family five years before the interview process and never went back. Yet, in spite of these traumatic events, she longs for the intimacy of family life. Particularly at the end of the fasting month, when it is the custom in Indonesia for families to gather, she misses them deeply.

The above vignettes indicate the lure of the harmonious heterosexual family, an ideal that remains intact even when psychic and sexual violence occurs. Instead of blaming the perpetrators or those who shield them, most of our narrators have internalized the shame and guilt, thus attesting to the power of the symbolic violence of heteronormativity. Many feel it is their own fault that their "loving" parents behaved so callously towards them (Tal 1995). If only they had been more loveable it might never have happened. Strikingly, the violence girls and their mothers experience does not lead to bonding between them. Rather, the girls feel estranged from their mothers and idolize their fathers. In the following sections, I look in some more detail at the passionate aesthetics upholding the heteronormative family.

1. *Maintaining the binary*

In most present day cultures, the core of heteronormativity is formed by sexual difference — the assumption that humanity is neatly and "naturally" divided into biological females and biological males who demonstrate feminine and masculine behaviours linked to their biological identities. Any variation from the two categories is not acceptable. A second binary is the split between "normal" and "abnormal". The supposed naturalness of these divisions supports the hierarchy between sexes and genders. A third, less commonly noted, characteristic is that the "abnormal" category is further subdivided into various types of abjection, while their shared origin has become blurred. The three categories of marginalized women we researched are similarly constructed as "abject" by their heteronormative societies, while they are each set apart as distinct categories. So, widows deplored their social marginalization but were happy they were not sex workers or lesbians who they considered immoral. Sex workers felt dejected because of their degraded status but were proud independent income earners, unlike widows whom they despised for their poverty. The lesbian activists suffered many forms of abjection, but experienced satisfaction in fighting for sexual rights, unlike the "meek" widows and "rejected" prostitutes.

This makes it difficult to see through the barriers that keep them apart from each other. They do not see each other as allies but as differently abjected others and constantly weigh their relative distance from the socially valued "normal". Their point of reference remains the heterosexual patriarchal family, not the commonality of their positions as falling outside its boundaries. The Indonesian *janda* can become "normal" again when they marry, even if they become secondary wives. Sex workers with a stable boyfriend in Jakarta expect that at some time in the future they will be able to leave sex work and live "normal" lives. For (middle class, Hindu) widows and for sex workers in India, these routes seem closed (see also Menon and Bhasin 2001). Most lesbians do not want to create "normal" heterosexual families, but some of them replicate certain aspects of it in their same-sex relationships (see Blackwood 1999, Sharma and Nath 2005 and Wieringa 2007). Most of our narrators dream of future happiness for themselves and/or their children in circumstances resembling those of the "harmonious nuclear family" that created such havoc in their lives in the first place, either through their parental families or in their married lives. The widows and sex workers do not blame the heteronormative construct for their current state of abjection, but rather their own bad luck. The lesbian activists see through the myth, but not all of our narrators were activists and even the activists structure their private lives along at least some major aspects of the "heterosexual matrix" (Butler 1990).

2. *Importance of pre-marital virginity*

Pre-marital virginity remains important in India; for instance, in Madhya Pradesh in 2009, it became known that virginity tests were conducted before a government-conducted mass wedding of rural women on 30 June (Singh 2009). Activists protested, but it is unlikely they made a dent in the underlying enforcement of virginity. In Bollywood films, sexually explicit scenes are taboo. When film actress Khushboo voiced her views on pre-marital sex in November 2005, a media uproar followed. Her remark that girls should take precautions when engaging in sex was considered irresponsible; it was feared that "far flung implications, like spread of AIDS, degeneration of the family system and the society as a whole" might be the result (Mitta 2005).

In Indonesia too, the media carry many stories extolling the merits of virginity. In its March 2005 issue, the popular monthly *Male Emporium* reported the following conversation between Lusi, a sex worker, and a regular client of hers, Roy.

> Roy once asked Lusi to become his housewife. Lusi refused, explaining that she was not clean anymore. As she was no longer a virgin and [had been] used for men's sexual release, she felt that she was a dirty woman and that it was improper for her to be married, as marriage was something holy and virtuous.

3. *Arranged marriages*

Parental control over the marriages of girls extends to the choice of a marriage partner. Many of our narrators, particularly Indians, said their marriages had been arranged by their parents, often without them having had much say in the matter. The pressure to remain a virgin until the marriage date leads to early marriages, particularly for girls in poor households who cannot afford to attend secondary school (Patel 2005, Uberoi 1994, Geertz 1961). Again and again, our narrators told us stories of being married off forcibly at a very early age.

> Hemali was married at the age of fourteen to a trader. He used to walk through remote villages to sell bed sheets and other materials. Once, he asked Hemali's mother if she was looking for a groom for her daughter. Negotiations went on for some months, Hemali being unaware of them. However, she did notice that he was coming more regularly to her village. All of a sudden, her father had fixed her marriage to this strange man. Her husband brought her to a town in the plains and took her to a small room inside a narrow lane. She was raped that very night. She knew nothing about sex. She hated his smell, his body, his organ. It was too big and ugly. She bled a lot as he had sex with her three times that night. Her entire body was sore.

Another story comes from Indonesia.

> At sixteen, Tina was forced to marry a much older man, maybe around fifty; she doesn't remember his age. He was a widower at the time, with the reputation of being a womanizer. Tina found him ugly and resisted the marriage as much as she could. However, her mother and grandmother insisted. She remembered that she screamed and that her mother threw a pail of soap water at her. She still doesn't know why they were so keen on her accepting the marriage. She suspects that her grandmother owed him money, as he was a trader, and he wanted one of her granddaughters in exchange. She was the youngest granddaughter and the most vulnerable one. The others all managed to refuse. Another reason probably was that they were afraid of him. He had a reputation for being able to use *guna-guna* (black magic) and was known to practice *santet* (a particularly dangerous form of black magic).

4. Polygyny in Indonesia

The 1974 Indonesian marriage law recognizes polygyny, although it sets certain conditions. A man can only marry four wives and the consent of the first wife is needed. However, many men either do not present a letter of consent to the registrar or marry in front of a religious official only, the so-called *kawin siri* or unregistered marriage. Needless to say, the new wife can be divorced without any difficulty by the husband. Children born in these unions cannot get a birth certificate and often find it difficult to enrol in schools (for which a valid birth certificate is needed). First wives are often unaware of their husbands marrying this way.

Not only do the various wives feel the pain of their husbands' philandering, the children in polygynous marriages suffer too. A famous case in Indonesian history is the Letters of R.A. Kartini, the daughter of a secondary wife of the regent of Jepara, widely considered the most important feminist in Indonesia around the end of the nineteenth century. She keenly felt the humiliation of her mother in the household of her father, whom she deeply loved.[8] In spite of her vehement protestations against the injustices of polygyny, she was forced to concede to a marriage with the regent of Rembang who already had some secondary wives. Her brilliant letters have been a source of inspiration for the Indonesian women's movement.

Our narrators also have numerous stories to tell about polygynous husbands or fathers, as the following story attests.

> Heni is the daughter of an army officer who had five wives. Although she describes him as a nice man, she remembers she hated him for marrying again and again and neglecting her mother, herself and her siblings. Heni's own marriage was arranged, but she didn't mind as she

knew her husband-to-be and had been in love with him. However, after five years, when she was two months pregnant with her fourth baby, he left her to marry another woman. Thereafter, her life was one big struggle to educate her children and she got into sex work to do so.

5. India: joint families and dowry deaths

Traditionally, after marriage, Indian women live with their in-laws. Sons are dependent on their mothers, and daughters-in-law are often treated badly (Patel 2005; Uberoi 1994, 2006). The problems often centre around money. Girls have to provide a dowry upon marriage. There are many conflicts about these dowries, sometimes ending in the murder of the young wife, as Nandy explains in this volume.

The standard narrative of a dowry death is harassment of the daughter-in-law by a group of her affinal kin (comprising mother-in-law, husband, brother-in-law, sister-in-law, etc; see also Sen 2001). In the litigation that may follow, the conjugal family invariably takes the plea that the death was either due to an accident in the kitchen or suicide following mental illness (commonly subsumed under the clinical term "depression"). For instance, a small article with the title "Mother-in-law gets life term for dowry death" details the fate of Sonia who was harassed by her husband and in-laws and finally burnt to death by her mother-in-law (TNN 2005). In her dying declaration before the sub-divisional magistrate, Sonia accused her mother-in-law, husband, father-in-law and sister-in-law of harassing her for not having brought a colour TV, a scooter and a washing machine. In another case of dowry death, the police filed a case of dowry harassment against the deceased's husband and parents based on the statements of the wife's mother, who said her daughter had been repeatedly tortured for dowry by her husband and his parents.[9] The latter, however, claimed that the girl in question was depressed and committed suicide. There were ligature marks on her neck.

The combined effects of a marriage system that is unjust to girls and economic deprivation are felt most glaringly in the profiles of the Indian sex workers. The intersecting realities of class, religion, rural poverty, illiteracy and unjust family relations drove these women to sex work on Delhi's G. B. Road.[10] Almost all the women we interviewed came from a rural agrarian background. Poverty pushes women to seek employment in cities, but their vulnerability mostly derives from the deceit of one's own family members, including fathers and husbands. Three of the sex workers mentioned it as the reason they were in the sex trade. Sexual violence plays a major role in most stories. Hemali was sold into a very unhappy marriage by her own father. Anjuman was brought to a brothel by her uncle and aunt at the age of eleven. Sonali was raped by her husband after a forced marriage; to escape his hold, she fled to a brothel. Syeda arrived at a brothel immediately after her husband's death, having nowhere else to go. Dolly was raped by her employer when she was still very young. The police refused to lodge a complaint as the rapist was not only a rich but also an influential man. Dolly was badly beaten up by the police and having nowhere else to go ended up on G. B. Road.

6. *Communication between spouses*

Even where there is no mention of direct physical or sexual violence between spouses, marital relations in the heterosexual families of our narrators were not always cordial and warm. There was often a lack of communication or even downright deceit. An example of a cold, dysfunctional family is that of Putri:

> Putri grew up in what everyone considered a normal family. Her father was a sailor, her mother a housewife with many social activities. However, the lack of communication between the spouses and with their single daughter is striking. Her father, the sailor, was only at home for a few weeks during the whole year. Putri herself thinks the total time she spent with her father cannot have been more than five months. In those five months, he never once asked what she did at school or what she liked. They were usually silent, not having found any topic to discuss. Her father was quite happy to leave the upbringing of his child to her mother. Her mother was rarely at home either and brought Putri up with a heavy hand. For instance, Putri initially had difficulty reading; she couldn't differentiate between "p" and "m". As an educational tool, her mother poured ice water over her every time she mixed these consonants up. Her mother would be furious if any of her commands were not obeyed. She claimed always to know best for her child and, therefore, could never be blamed in any way. Putri realized quite early on that her mother had no clue about who her daughter was and what she felt. No wonder that in her own relationship Putri cannot find the words to express her love for her lover, Nina.

The family life of an Indonesian woman is dogged by the fear that one day she might find out her husband has another wife. There are so many stories on that theme that married women know they can never be secure. With so much deceit and adultery about, it is not surprising that jealousy is considered a normal characteristic of a good relationship. An oft-quoted saying is "*cemburu tanda cinta*", jealousy is a sign of love. A little jealousy is considered appropriate behaviour between lovers or spouses, but excessive jealousy can lead to problems. Diana's husband became very abusive due to his jealousy. Diana had a busy job and she would sometimes come home late, which her husband resented. If he had visitors when she came home he might burst out with a "she comes home late because she is having an affair", which hurt Diana very much. He would sometimes lock her out of the bedroom. When she became pregnant, she "thought to have an abortion. But my husband got mad; probably a man like him would think that I would be submissive and more subordinate if I got a child".

7. *Money matters*

Money matters are a source of much strife within the Asian households discussed here. In India and in Indonesia, men are supposed to be the breadwinners and derive social standing and power within the household if they fulfil that role well. In Indonesia, this is even formally stated in the marriage law (Katjasungkana and Wieringa 2003). In popular understanding, women provide sex to their husbands, and men give their wives money. The housewife-breadwinner ideology does not hold up in poor households, where both women and men have to work. In anticipation of a man's breadwinner's role, boys get better education than their sisters if there is not enough money to provide schooling for all siblings.

Many of our narrators, both in India and in Indonesia, report serious troubles around money in their marriages, often leading to violence. Indonesian Jenar, for instance, knew that a wife has the right to get *nafkah lahir dan batin* in her marriage, that is, money and sexual fulfilment. *Nafkah* literally means nourishment. This is what her husband was expected to provide. However, her husband did not stick to his part of the deal and "was too lazy to work". He gave the money he earned to his mother. Jenar felt very uncomfortable with this situation and looked for work herself. Her decision to divorce her husband was linked to his being such a bad provider. After speaking to a colleague of hers whose husband did provide financially for his family, she exploded:

> I told him roughly, my thing (reproductive organ) is ruined by you and yet you didn't give me money. You just want the pleasures! Well, am I a servant? If it is like this, maybe it is better to be a *cabo* (prostitute); then I get sex plus the money at the same time.

Another narrator, Rita, a widow who works as a seamstress in Jakarta, has the following story to tell:

> When her marriage was deteriorating, her mother advised her to ignore the frequent quarrels. She told her daughter that fights between husband and wife were usual and that they were actually the spice of marriage. So, Rita felt desolate - who could she turn to? She realized that she had to keep silent about her problems, that it was taboo to complain so much about your husband. In the end, people would blame her for the difficulties between them. However, her husband was not providing for her and their son anymore, and he had a woman on the side. Was she to

ignore all that? And how was she to survive anyway? She was desperate and felt her life was broken into myriad pieces. She first sold everything that she could, even clothes and underwear, and in the end filed for divorce.

8. *Acceptance of male superiority*

Although the characteristics of Indian and Indonesian heterosexual orthodox families differ in some aspects, both constructs are suffused with patriarchal values. The threat of polygyny with its accompanying deceit and jealousy in Indonesia and arranged marriages and dowry issues in Indian families are all supported by patriarchal values. Male superiority runs deep. Sometimes it is built on overt forms of violence, at other times the symbolic violence of some kind of male mental or intellectual superiority is accepted as natural by the women of the house. Women are supposed to adjust to the habits of their husbands. Fathers or husbands are the obvious sources of power, but brothers and sons assume their roles in the patriarchal household hierarchy quickly if a vacuum arises. The imposition and maintenance of patriarchal values is one of the major expressions of the passionate aesthetics of heteronormativity. These values include that men are superior, earn more money and have more power.

9. *Expulsion and repulsion*

Two imbricating processes form the basis of the passionate aesthetics of "othering" — expulsion and repulsion. While expulsion has to do with the construction of physical, material and social barriers and taboos, with invisibilization and silencing, repulsion refers to the fears, desires and fantasies that are involved within the "normal" and the "abnormal". Not only is a person expelled from the boundaries of "normalcy", but all elements that may be sympathetic to that constructed "abjected" person also have to be removed from the consciousness of those within the fold of heteronormativity and those outside it. Often, the excluded others internalize the disgust, hatred and fear expressed by the "normal" population. Precisely because the "normal" and the "abnormal" are so closely intertwined, the process of its forced separation entails a lot of violence.

Widowed or divorced women in India and Indonesia are literally expelled to the margins of their societies. Kusum Didi, a character in the well-known 1952 Indian feminist novel *Aangan* (inner courtyard), exclaims "Knowing me for a widow, people avoided my shadow" (Mastur 2001: 27–8). She is widowed at a very young age and eventually commits suicide. Although avoidance taboos are no longer as strong as in this example, Indian widows still face the stigma that they are somehow responsible for their husbands's death. Faced with social ostracism, isolation and avoidance, the widows and *janda* recounted their pain and suffering as well as the ways they negotiate these daily techniques of expulsion. Many of them have internalized their fate and feel guilty or ashamed. Hindu notions of purity and the sanctity of marriage keep widowed women isolated.

Religion is an important intersecting factor. In Islamic Indonesia, there is strong pressure on widows to marry. In India too, Muslim women face fewer problems remarrying than (high caste) Hindu women. The Muslim community does not frown upon remarriage, and there is an understanding for the desire for sexuality and love. Sunita's mother, for instance, asked her to put on lipstick and kohl. Sunita herself regularly applied henna and dressed in bright colours. She was proud of her beautiful face and body.

Class differences also play an important role in how the effects of widowhood are experienced. There is a sense that widowed women are responsible for their ill luck and overall they have the image of seductresses, which can only be countered by practicing chastity. Even Indian Hindu widows, who are supposed to remain chaste all their lives, fall prey to this pornographic gaze. Indian Muslim women and Indonesian women can regain their chastity by tying themselves to a lawful husband again. Middle-class women in particular are always considered blemished, even if they have returned to the folds of a heteronormative marriage.

While in India, particularly in the middle classes, divorce is hardly acceptable, in Indonesia there is currently a surge of divorces, most of them initiated by women. This is widely attributed to two reasons: women's increased financial independence and their disappointment that men do not live up to their standards of companionship.[11]

In India, high-caste widows in particular were prohibited from remarrying. In 1856, the Hindu Widow Re-marriage Act put a formal end to this practice, but it did not lift the stigma widows live under. Rules for the remarriage of widows differ from one group to another. Generally, lower-ranking groups always allowed widow re-marriage, particularly if the woman was relatively young. The strictest adherents to the non-remarriage of widows have always been Brahmans. Almost all groups have always allowed widowers to remarry.

The shame of being a sex worker is so great that the Delhi prostitutes were reticent to talk about their experiences. The stigma of sex work experienced by our narrators in Delhi is so strong that even when trafficked girls are brought back to their natal homes, their parents do not want to take them in, as they have become impure and dirty in their eyes. The only way out for these girls then is to re-enter the trade. Some of our narrators were widows, who turned to sex work as they saw no other way to make a living. Others were raped or trafficked into G. B. Road. All of them internalized heteronormative society's repulsion of them and accepted to some degree the violence and violations meted out to them.

Conclusion

This study of the private lives of sex workers, widows/*janda* and women in same-sex relationships enables us to investigate the passionate aesthetics of heteronormative relationships in India and Indonesia. The class/caste divide and religion largely determine the internalization of a "culture of morality and silence" imposed on our narrators. After studying the workings of heteronormativity in India and Indonesia, we have seen the extent of its physical and symbolic violence and the various ways its orthodoxy constrains those within its boundaries and marginalizes the abjected others. The nine forms of passionate aesthetics that I have listed in this chapter range from epistemological considerations (the stress on binaries) to marital arrangements and internalized shame and guilt. Although the study set out to collect the narratives of the private lives of three categories of abjected women in India and Indonesia, it is clear that their lives touch upon many issues that are considered public: religion, the media, laws and other institutions. The analysis of the passionate aesthetics at work in the upholding of heteronormativity reveals the untenability of the public–private divide in a discussion on violence against women.

Our narrators, all of whom as intimate outsiders lived both normative and non-normative lives whether as children in their natal families or in their adult lives, have experienced the ways in which women within this structure are policed as well as the punishment meted out to those who transgress or are expelled from the boundaries of heteronormativity. The violence they experienced ranges from physical to symbolic, from rape to shame. The basic premise underlying this chapter is to discuss conventional notions of what constitutes "normal" sexuality, to question the hegemony of heteronormative norms and to show that both the normative and non-normative are social constructs, built on embodied experiences and that violence or the threat of violence is an integral part.

Heteronormativity presents the heterosexual family as the ultimate goal in life for women, where they will attain the bliss of a "normal", "harmonious" family life. However, in reality, the family is often not the safe haven promised to them. Once cracks become apparent, women are supposed to adjust, emotionally, intellectually and financially. Passionate aesthetics involve various modes of control, abjection and violence, rendering the non-heterosexually-married space for women highly unattractive or even dangerous. However, there is danger within the "normal" heterosexual family too. The success of these aesthetics lies in the way women, even in non-heterosexual relationships, aspire to its values, while women who have experienced various forms of violence themselves continue to love or at least live with the perpetrators of that violence.

The above stories demonstrate the multiple effects of the aesthetics at work in creating abjected others. The process of expulsion may be gradual, such as with some of the lesbian women, or sudden, as the widows experienced, but it invariably leads to estrangement or psychological or physical violence from family members, friends and colleagues. The forms of repulsion they experience from "normal" society are often internalized and may lead to emotional chaos or even (attempted) suicide. They feel cast out and unwanted. Almost all women portrayed above suffer from a low self image, feelings of guilt and shame, depression and a sense of loneliness. This may in turn lead to substance abuse. Many sex workers on G. B. Road are addicted to alcohol; other narrators use drugs.

Perceiving violence against women as a private issue may have the effect of making structural factors fuelling this violence invisible. Heteronormativity is not limited to the bedroom but extends its tentacles to court rooms, board rooms and to the locations in which other societal institutions operate as well.

Notes

I am grateful for the generous grant from the Asian Research Institute at the National University of Singapore that allowed me to work for three months in 2009 on this project. I also thank my co-coordinators, Abha Bhaiya and Nursyahbani Katjasungkana, for their collaboration in the research. I am indebted to all the researchers who gathered the material for the interviews upon which this chapter is based.

1 The Kartini Asia Network was formally established in Manila in 2003. Its present headquarters are in Jakarta. It is active in 19 Asian countries and works on 5 overlapping themes — women's studies, fundamentalism, livelihood, conflict resolution and sexuality. See its website: **www.kartiniasia.org.** The coordinators of this project were Abha Bhaiya, Irwan Hidayana, Nursyahbani Katjasungkana and the author. The researchers were Ambarien Al Qadar, Bernadeth Sinta Situmorang, Bharti M. Borah, Endah Sulistyowati, Pooja Rao, Ratna Batara Munti, Renu Adhlaka, Shabnam Berar and Widjajanti Santoso.

2 A further classification can be made by adding the words *mati* (death) or *cerai* (divorce) after the word *janda*. See also Marianti (2002) for a study on widows in Indonesia.

3 See Bourdieu (1991) for a discussion on the concept of symbolic violence.

4 See Kristeva (1982) for a discussion on abjection.

5 See the monograph on the topic, entitled "Heteronormativity and passionate aesthetics in Asia", forthcoming 2013, Sussex Academic Publishers. See also the article "Passionate Aesthetics and Symbolic Subversion; Heteronormativity in India and Indonesia" in *Asian Studies Review*. December 2012.

6 In India, the lesbian group Sappho for Equality, in collaboration with the Kartini Asia Network, documented 92 kinds of violence lesbian women expe-

rienced, ranging from abuse and ridicule to murder or double suicide (Ghosh 2011). See also Nandy in this volume for references to domestic violence in India. In Indonesia, the network of offices of feminist lawyers, APIK, documents cases of domestic violence. See the chapter by Nursyahbani in this volume. The women's rights group Komnas Perempuan publishes yearly reports on violence against women, the Peta Kekerasan Pengalaman Perempuan Indonesia (map of violence experienced by Indonesian women); see www.komnasperempuan.or.id.

7 A *pesinden* sings in a very high voice and usually sings in a traditional *gamelan* orchestra, for instance, accompanying a *wayang* (shadow play with leather puppets) performance.

8 This conflict in her life only became clear after the publication of the full edition of her letters by Jaquet (1987).

9 As reported in the 4 November 2005 issue of the Hindustan Times.

10 A notorious red light district in Delhi.

11 According to the Ministry of Religious Affairs in Indonesia, over 200,000 divorces were registered in 2008. BBC world news, 22 June 2009, http://news.bbc.co.uk/go/pr/fr/-/2/hi/asia-pacific/7869813.stm.

References

Blackwood, Evelyn (1999) Tombois in West Sumatra; Constructing Masculinity and Erotic Desire. In: Evelyn Blackwood and Saskia E. Wieringa, eds, *Female Desires; Same-Sex Relations and Transgender Practices Across Cultures,* pp. 181–206 New York: Columbia University Press. pp. 181–206

Bourdieu, Pierre (1991) *Language & Symbolic Power*. Cambridge, Harvard University Press.

Butler, Judith (1990) *Gender Trouble; Feminism and the Subversion of Identity.* New York and London: Routledge.

Butler, Judith (2004) *Undoing Gender* New York and London: Routledge.

Geertz, Hildred Java (1961) *The Javanese Family; A Study of Kinship and Socialization*. New York: Free Press of Glencoe.

Ghosh, Subhagata (2011) *Vio-Map; Documenting and mapping violence and rights violations taking place in lives of sexually marginalized women*. Kolkata: Sappho for Equality.

Jackson, Stevi (2006) Gender, Sexuality and Heterosexuality; The Complexity (and Limits) of Heteronormativity. *Feminist Theory* , Vol. 7 (1): 105–121.

Jaquet, F.G.P. (1987), *Kartini, Brieven aan Mw R.M. Abendanon-Mandri en haar echtgenoot met andere documenten. (Kartini; letters to Mrs R.M. Abendanon-Mandri and her husband and other documents*). Dordrecht: Foris.

Kant, I. (1997). *Foundations of the Metaphysics of Morals, and What Is Enlightenment?* (L. W. Beck, Trans.). Upper Saddle River. New Jersey: Prentice-Hal.

Katjasungkana, Nursyahbani and Saskia Wieringa (2003) Sexual Politics and Reproductive Rights in Indonesia. In*: Development*, vol. 46, no. 2, June, pp. 63 – 68.

Kaye, Kerwin (2003) Sexual Abuse and the Wholesome Family: Feminist, Psychological and State Discourses. In: Elizabeth Bernstein and Laurie Schaffner, eds, *Regulating Sex: The Politics of Intimacy and Identity*. New York and London: Routledge, pp. 143–167.

Kristeva, Julia (1982) *Powers of Horror: An Essay on Abjection* New York: Columbia University Press.

Marianti, Ruly (2002) *Surviving Spouses; Support for Widows in Malang, East Java*. Amsterdam: University of Amsterdam.

Mastur, Khadija (2001 orig 1952*), Aangan, Inner Courtyard*, translated by Neelam Hussain. Delhi: Kali for Women.

Menon, Ritu and Kamla Bhasin (2001) Her Body and her Being: Of Widows and Abducted Women in Post-Partition India. In, Margaret Jolly and Kalpana Ram, eds, *Borders of Being. Citizenship, Fertility and Sexuality in Asia and the Pacific* Ann Arbor: University of Michigan Press, pp. 58–82.

Mitta, Manoj (2005) HC's stand: difference between law, morality, *The Times of India*, 7 December 2005, p. 5

Patel, Tulsi, ed. (2005) *The Family in India, Structure and Practice*. New Delhi: Sage.

Rubin, Gayle (1989) Thinking Sex: Notes for a Radical Theory for the Politics of Sexuality. In Carole Vance, ed, *Pleasure and Danger; Exploring Female Sexuality,* London: Pandora Press, pp. 267–320

Sen, Mala (2001) *Death by Fire; Sati, Dowry Death and Female Infanticide in Modern India*. London: Weidenfeld and Nicolson.

Sharma, Jaya and Dipika Nath (2005) Through the Prism of Intersectionality: Same Sex Sexualities in India. In: Geetanjali Misra and Radhika Chandiramani, eds, *Sexuality, Gender and Rights; Exploring Theory and Practice in South and Southeast Asia*. New Delhi: Aage. pp. 82–98

Singh, Harmeet Shah (2009) Inquiry into Indian brides 'virginity tests', July 14, 2009, CNN, Available online at edition.cnn.com/2009/WORLD/asiapcf/07/14/india.virginity

Tal, Kali. *(*1995) *Worlds of Hurt: Reading the Literatures of Trauma*. Cambridge University Press, Cambridge.

Times News Network (TNN) (2005) Mother-in-law gets lifer for dowry death, *The Times of India*, 18 December 2005, Available online at http://articles.timesofindia.indiatimes.com/2005-12-17/delhi/27866265_1_dowry-life-imprisonment-sonia

Uberoi, Patricia ed. (1994) *Family, kinship and Marriage in India*. Oxford: Oxford University Press.

Uberoi, Patricia (2006) *Freedom and Destiny: Gender, Family and Popular Culture in India*. New Delhi: Oxford University Press.

Wieringa, Saskia E. (2007) "If There is no Feeling . . . " The Dilemma Between Silence and Coming Out in a Working Class Butch/Fem Community in Jakarta. In: Mark B. Padilla, Jennifer S. Hirsch, Miguel Munoz-Laboy, Robert E. Sember and Richard G. Parker, eds, *Love and Globalisation: Transformations of Intimacy in the Contemporary World*. Nashville: Vanderbilt University Press, pp. 70–93.

CHAPTER

5

Domestic Violence and Migration in the Philippines

Transnational Sites of Struggle and Sacrifice

CHERYLL ALIPIO

In May 2010, actress, model and former beauty queen Ruffa Gutierrez donated PHP200,000 (US$4,334) to the Women's Crisis Center in Quezon City, Philippines after the centre reported that an average of thirty Filipino women suffer from domestic violence every day (Flores 2010).[1] A popular actress, Gutierrez has acted in television dramas and cinematic films that often depict scenes of domestic abuse. While disturbing stories of violence committed on women and children have become common fare in the Philippine media, Gutierrez shocked her fans by publically revealing in 2007 that she was a victim of domestic violence. After splitting up with her husband, a wealthy Turkish businessman, she gained custody of their two daughters and left Istanbul for Manila.

"Starting all over again," Gutierrez notes, "is the most difficult part. Yet, it's been three years and I have a new life. So, when you feel like giving up, continue to pray and God will always give you help" (Rosal 2010). Through her disclosure, she became the voice for Avon's domestic violence crusade in the Philippines and unwittingly provided proof that domestic violence is not the monopoly of poor families (Delfin 2008); it also affects the upper classes and famous stars.[2] Ironically, in the context of the Philippines, this may be a positive development, especially when coupled with a show of faith in God. With nearly 80 percent of the population practicing Roman Catholicism and most households in cities, villages and slums alike having access to and regularly watching television, Gutierrez's revelation became *tsismis* (gossip) and so, inadvertently, raised awareness about domestic violence.

Stories of women who courageously broke their silence to speak up about domestic violence show that despite the enactment in 2004 of Republic Act (RA) 9262 (the Anti-Violence Against Women and Their Children Act), domestic violence remains rampant in the country. This is especially true in the Southern Tagalog region and in populous areas such as Manila, Cebu City in the Visayas, and Davao City in Muslim-dominated Mindanao, where reported cases of rape and acts of lasciviousness are high (Quismundo 2009). Data from the Philippine National Police Women and Children Protection Center (PNP–WCPC) shows that the number of women physically and verbally abused in 2008 was fifty-one percent more than that in 2007, with 1,212 more cases reported by the year's end than the 2007 figure of 2,387 (Quismundo 2009). Aurora Parong, director of Amnesty International Philippines, explained that while "[t]he law (RA 9262) is considered as a significant victory for women because many of its provisions are based on the inalienable right of women not to suffer discrimination and violence most especially within an intimate relationship. . . . Protection of women's rights does not end with the enactment of a law. It needs a follow through in implementation. Six years later after the birth of RA 9262, we [still] see many loopholes in the implementation" (Amnesty International Philippines 2010).

"Domestic violence, as defined by the law, is not anymore a private matter only for the family to handle. It is a public scandal and a grave abuse to women's rights," Parong insists (Amnesty International Philippines 2010). Although the law provides that all units of society and government must act to prevent domestic violence, Parong states that "the lack of political [as well as public and private] will to implement the law has made it only [one more] piece of paper that the president signed" (Amnesty International Philippines 2010) in addition to other "pieces of paper" like the Anti-Child Abuse Law of 1992 (RA 7610), Anti-Sexual Harassment Act of 1995 (RA 7877), Anti-Rape Law of 1997 (RA 8353) and the Rape Victim Assistance and Protection Act of 1998 (RA 8505). With the inability of the law to stem domestic violence and by extension, gender-based discrimination, women have looked outside the confines of the state and family for ways to escape abuse. While a considerable amount of academic research has been done on domestic violence in recent years and research on domestic violence in immigrant communities continues to emerge (see Menjívar and Salcideo 2002; Raj and Silverman 2002; Sokoloff and Dupont 2005; Tran and Des Jardins 2000), inquiries on the implications of domestic violence on migration and religion remain minimal, often focusing on the "run away" experience of women (see Faier 2008; Parreñas 2001).

Drawing upon ethnographic fieldwork carried out between 2006 and 2007 in San Pablo City in the Southern Tagalog province of Laguna, Philippines this chapter explores the migration decisions, economic strategies and familial sacrifices that women make when faced with domestic violence. The chapter focuses, in particular, on providing an overview of the literature that has emerged on the historical and modern constructions of gender in the Philippines and its relation to state laws and colonial and religious discourses on what is permissible and impermissible in Philippine society. It then outlines how these patriarchal ideologies and institutions underlie the structural inequality found in cultural, social, and economic realms. With this gender-based discrimination governing the extent to which Filipino women and their interests are reflected in the legal system, the chapter explores women's strategies in dealing with domestic violence. The chapter uses feminist approaches to law, human rights, ethnography and poetry to "probe beyond the realm of filial piety and finances" to understand how "something wrong at home" could cause women to leave the Philippines as migrant workers (Constable 1999: 212). While labour migration provides opportunities for self-transformation and empowerment, the chapter argues that women continue to struggle transnationally as they move from one form of abuse to another. The chapter reveals that the Catholic faith which historically structured family relations and gender identity is central not only in enabling women to free themselves from violence and poverty, but is also a coping mechanism that exposes their suffering and sacrifice. In recognition that violence is not just a crime committed in private on individual bodies but also a public issue symptomatic of wider social problems, the chapter concludes in an examination of the ways in which local communities can work to resolve gender-based discrimination as a means to prevent future violence against women and children in the Philippines.

Violence and victims defined

The enactment of the Anti-Violence Against Women and Their Children Act of 2004 (RA 9262) is a result of the growing support for women's rights that developed after the end of President Ferdinand Marcos' martial rule in 1986. According to Women Working Together to Stop Violence (WWTSVAW 2009: 2), a coalition network of ten NGOs that work on the issue of violence against women (VAW), women's groups and human rights based NGOs began to incorporate advocacy against violence into their services of education and training; organizing, networking and coalition building; and legislative lobbying during the 1990s. This work influenced the ratification of several gender-specific laws protecting women and girl children from violence by the state *and* individuals, groups or corporations (RA 7610, RA 7877, RA 8353 and RA 8505) (WWTSVAW 2009: 2). With RA 9262, the Philippine government clarifies its intent to protect women and children by criminalizing and making public one of the most widespread forms of gender-based discrimination. Declaring violence against women and their children (VAWC) a public crime implied that the crime is perpetrated not only on a single individual but against society, and that any individual with public knowledge of the circumstances of an abusive act is authorized *and* responsible to file a criminal complaint.[3]

Under Section 3 of RA 9262, violence is specifically defined as "any act or a series of acts committed by any person against a woman who is his wife, former wife, or against a woman with whom the person has or had a sexual or dating relationship, or with whom he has a common child, or against her child whether legitimate or illegitimate, within or without the family abode, which result in or is likely to result in physical, sexual, psychological harm or suffering, or economic abuse, including threats of such acts, battery, assault, coercion, harassment or arbitrary deprivation of liberty."[4] The careful wording of violence shows that the law recognizes the inequality inherent in abusive relationships. However, heterosexuality is privileged since the definition specifies the gender of the abuser. With the powerful influence of the Catholic Church on Philippine society and politics and their stance against same-sex marriage, civil unions and domestic partnerships, the law repudiates the reality that intimate partner violence can also affect those in lesbian relationships. Therefore civil rights laws do not protect the lesbian, gay, bisexual and transgender (LGBT) community, as will be discussed later in the chapter.

The definition of physical, sexual, psychological and economic abuse further shows the government's understanding that VAWC often combined two or more abusive elements. As a result, the following acts are now defined as crimes: stalking; forcing the woman to witness the physical, sexual and psychological abuse of a family member; forcing the wife and mistress/lover to live in a conjugal home or sleep together in the same room with the abuser and acts that aim to make the woman financially dependent on the abuser (WWTSVAW 2009: 8). From 2004, when RA 9262 was enacted, to 2009, the Philippine National Police (PNP) found that the total cases of violence against women increased by 3,214 (see table 5.1, overleaf).

In addition to their rights under existing laws, RA 9262 gives victim-survivors the right to: (1) be treated with respect and dignity; (2) avail of legal assistance from the Public Attorney's Office, the Department of Justice or any public legal assistance office;[5] (3) be entitled to support services from the Department of Social Welfare and Development (DSWD)[6] and local government units (LGUs); (4) be entitled to all legal remedies and support as provided for under the Family Code and (5) be informed of their right to apply for a protection order. The Barangay (village) Protection Order (BPO) is the single most important, and accessible, action that can be taken to immediately protect an individual from further harm and harassment within their home and neighbourhood. Although the BPO is effective for only 15 days without extension, victim-survivors can also be issued a Temporary or Permanent Protection Order by the court; this would be effective for a longer period of time and can be enforced anywhere in the country.[7] Locating critical interventions at the LGU-level, like in the barangays, is a significant feature of RA 9262 as it accounts for the stark reality that most women cannot afford to or would not go to court to seek protection from abuse owing to lack of economic resources, awareness of their rights, knowledge of the services available to them, as well as inaccessibility to courts and other institutions due to lack of transportation or transportation fare[8] and because of fear due to social stigma and cultural shame. These reasons, and others that I will discuss later in the chapter, lead to an underreporting of cases of violence against women and children.

Table 5.1 Number of violence against women cases by type of act*

	2004	2005	2006	2007	2008	2009
Physical Injuries**	3,553	2,335	1,902	1,505	1,307	1,498
Rape	997	927	670	837	811	770
Lasciviousness	580	536	389	358	445	485
Maltreatment/Threats	319	223	204	182	220	208
Attempted Rape	194	148	186	147	204	167
Incestuous Rape	38	46	26	22	28	27
Others+	590	1,159	1,577	2,678	3,890	6,330
TOTAL	6,271	5,374	4,954	5,729	6,905	9,485

Sources: National Statistical Coordination Board 2006, 2007, 2008, 2009, and 2010.
Notes: * These are cases reported to the Philippine National Police (PNP).
** The category of "Physical Injuries" included the act of wife battering for the years 2004 and 2005.
+ The PNP does not clarify the types of acts included in the category of "Others."

Below is a data set of child abuse from the DSWD but, like the statistics for VAW, the numbers are unreliable with many abused children scared to speak out about their abuse (see table 5.2). During the fifteen months I spent in ethnographic fieldwork in a barangay of San Pablo City, the local barangay office was closed most of the time, depriving the people of any support. The rules and regulations of RA 9262 explicitly state that in addition to issuing BPOs, barangay officials have specific duties and functions pertaining to providing assistance to women and children who experience violence and abuse. In particular, barangay officials must undertake an education programme on VAWC; a family violence prevention programme, including peer counselling for men and a "one-stop, 24-hour help desk."[9,10] Tragically, in the barangay I worked in, there were at least four known cases of rape of minors, with one ending in the victim being murdered. Before I arrived, another

Table 5.2 Number of child abuse cases by type of act*

	Girls						Boys					
	2004	2005	2006	2007	2008	2009	2004	2005	2006	2007	2008	2009
Sexually Abused	3,350	2,889	2,745	2,217	2,202	1,898	66	50	58	60	24	31
Neglected	1,324	1,164	1,118	1,122	964	1,215	1,303	1,258	1,149	1,127	1,002	1,197
Physically Abused/												
Maltreated	643	563	406	404	388	296	571	446	390	459	266	291
Abandoned	448	417	445	391	446	498	578	519	594	487	540	593
Victims of Child Labour	235	199	152	223	89	55	98	69	79	62	41	28
Sexually Exploited	314	257	241	154	123	105	34	10	3	11	42	23
Others**	180	302	171	320	342	247	53	195	55	191	141	45
TOTAL	6,494	5,791	5,278	4,831	4,554	4,314	2,703	2,547	2,328	2,397	2,056	2,208

Sources: National Statistical Coordination Board 2006, 2007, 2008, 2009, and 2010.
Notes: * These are cases reported to the Department of Social Welfare and Development (DSWD).
** The DSWD does not clarify the types of acts included in the category of "Others."

researcher had found many more children, most often those of overseas Filipino workers (OFWs), being abused in the same barangay as well as in the neighbouring ones.

While it is difficult to determine whether the services of the barangay office and officers would have prevented such violent and vicious acts, these acts of violence point to the inadequate resources women and children have at home and in society, and begs for a clearer understanding of the exact sources of this lack of human rights. When faced with scarce personal, community and state resources as well as obstacles in their pursuit of justice, what can women and children do? Saba Mahmood (2005: 188) argues for the need "to analyze agency in terms of the different modalities it takes and the grammar of concepts in which its particular affect, meaning, and form reside". Accordingly, in the next section, I give a brief overview of the historical and modern constructions of gender in the Philippines and examine how they were formed in relation to colonial governments and the Catholic Church. From these very public discourses about women and their bodies, I argue that the violence and violations perpetrated against women and children stem from the structural inequality they receive in cultural, social and economic realms. At the same time, violence against women, as Charlotte Bunch (1987) asserts, is central to maintaining these asymmetrical power relations in both the public and private spheres. This gender domination and discrimination, in turn, governs the extent to which Filipino women and their needs, concerns and desires are fully reflected or their voices entirely ignored in a rights-based legal system (Edwards 2011: 44). In the reconceptualization of women and violence in the Philippines, the following section traces how patriarchal interests, ideology and institutions has been historically enacted on Filipino women's bodies.

Colonial and Catholic constructions of gender

In pre-Hispanic Philippines and other parts of Southeast Asia, gender roles and relationships were driven by principles of "human sameness and complementarity" that prevailed over structures of hierarchy and difference (Chant and McIlwaine 1995: 7). Contemporary writing on gender and the family, which has asserted egalitarianism in domestic relationships and democratic consultation between spouses on matters of household expenditure and labour allocation, often points to this pre-Hispanic pattern of gender roles and relations as its roots. However, under Spanish and American colonial rule, which lasted more than 400 years, Filipinos imbibed patriarchal influences. The roots of VAW as a form of gender-based discrimination can be traced to colonization and its introduction of the male-centred and male-dominated religion of Roman Catholicism in the country. Spanish colonizers used the religion to facilitate their rule over the local people. Laws like the institutionalization of property ownership, passed during this time, deprived women of their independence. The legal rights given to men subsequently made women dependent, even subordinate, to male figures in their lives (Rodriguez 1990: 20).

In her poem, "*Ang Pagiging Babae Ay Pamumuhay Sa Panahon ng Digma*" (To Be a Woman is to Live at a Time of War), Joi Barrios (1990), a renowned Philippine poet, scholar on women's empowerment and activist during President Marcos' dictatorship, writes: "I grew up with fear beside me, / Uncertain of a future / Hinged / To the men of my life: / Father, brother, / Husband, son."[11] Like Chandra Mohanty (1991: 74) who points out that "[w]omen are constituted as women through the complex interaction between class, culture, religion and other ideological institutions and frameworks," Barrios describes how Filipino women and their lives are defined in relation to men. Similar to Dianne Otto's (1999: 118) view that women, as depicted in the text of the International Covenant on Civil and Political Rights (ICCPR) of 1966, are constructed in "procreative and heterosexual terms as mother and wife and as inevitably subject to and dependent on 'men' in their various forms: individually as fathers and husbands and collectively as the State, the military" and I would include the Church as well, Barrios illustrates Catholicism's strong influence, that is, the "fear" it imposes in women's lives. The poem also points to the Church's protective and paternalistic ideology that places controls on women's future movements, a "hinge" that restricts their education to rudimentary reading and arithmetic, home crafts, the Christian doctrine and to any wishes and whims made by the men in their lives (Sobritchea 1990: 29).

American colonial rule in the Philippines did very little to eradicate the patriarchal norms, beliefs and practices introduced by the Spanish colonizers. The American schooling system maintained the same sexual division of labour and even encouraged women to pursue careers that were compatible with their "womanly" qualities (Sobritchea 1990: 29). "Women's work" was thus built upon women's "natural" inclination towards caring and relational thinking (Glenn 1992: 1). These were side jobs that did not interfere with women's main task of caring for the family, that is, teaching and nursing their children. The socialization of Filipina women, consequently, placed an emphasis and primacy on the female reproductive role as mother, wife and daughter. Like Michel Foucault's (1990 [1978]) account of eighteenth-century Europe, Filipino constructions of women's roles placed controls on the female body, such that women were regulated to the private sphere of the home.

Cultural beliefs further intensified the necessity for regulating the physical mobility of females (Sobritchea 1990: 32). Using physical weakness and their "dangerous" reproductive capacity as a justification for protection, rural females were disallowed from roaming freely outside or even within their village. They were expected to stay at home and restrict their social activities. Indigenous beliefs also served as a means for social and physical control as anecdotes told of places inhabited by malevolent spirits, suprahumans and black magic. Rural lore is rife with stories of sorcerers or non-human creatures preying upon young and innocent girls who stayed out late at night or wandered far from the village.

Thus, American colonial education laid great emphasis on Castilian values and norms of sexual behaviour, such that the practice of monogamy and chastity prevails in the Philippines even today (Israel-Sobritchea 1990: 29). The strong value placed on virginity until marriage and sex only for procreation reflects the Catholic upbringing of most Filipinos, who are taught to feel ashamed and guilty for any sins and taught that "staying married for the sake of the family is considered a sacrifice with heavenly rewards" (Raposas 2008).[12] The ideal Filipino wife and mother, Stella Go (1993: 26) adds:

> is expected to be religious and without major vices, a loving and loyal companion to her husband. She is supposed to be undemanding and faithful to her husband. She is expected to keep the family united. No matter what the husband does, the marriage must be kept intact. Consequently, the wife must forgive an unfaithful husband. As a mother, she is expected to sacrifice herself for the family. She is expected to suffer in silence, and to endure the husband's bad habits. . . .

Yolanda Tanigue, director of the PNP-WCPC, finds that in actual cases of domestic violence there is indeed "an element of forgiveness [for] the sake of family togetherness" and to keep private matters from becoming public (Delfin 2008). Tellingly, prior to RA 9262, rape was classified as a crime against chastity and was a private offense, which implied that the women violated became unchaste and that only the chaste could be violated. Courts, consequently, tended to treat these as crimes of lust or passion, conveniently excusing the rampant violations of women and disregarding women's basic rights in the process. RA 9262 overturned this view, and rape is now classified as a crime against persons and is considered a public offense.

Yet, findings from focus group discussions, conducted in 2006 by WWTSVAW, are very revealing. They found that the beliefs of some barangay officials effectively hindered the implementation of RA 9262 (WWTSVAW 2009: 32):

> intimate partner violence is considered a private matter; women are blamed for the violence because women, more than men, have the responsibility to make the relationship work and maintain harmony in the family; women hit by their partners will eventually "come around" once their anger subsided such that later the complaint will be retracted

thus wasting the barangays' meager resources if the barangay officials took all complaints of VAWC seriously.

The focus group discussions further exposed the nearly systematic practice of giving the perpetrator "another chance" by advising the victim to take time to "think things over" as it was simply *away mag-asawa*, or a "couple's quarrel" (WWTSVAW 2009: 32).

The intersection of Catholicism with law is also evident in specific provisions in the 1987 Constitution of the Republic of the Philippines. It is clear that the Philippine State has a hand in defining Filipinos' sexuality and in shaping their consciousness of what is acceptable and unacceptable and what is normal and what is deviant or perverse. Policies concretely link marriage, the family and the nation. For example, the constitution declares in Section 1, Article 15, "The State recognizes the Filipino family as the foundation of the nation. Accordingly, it shall strengthen its solidarity and actively promote its total development." In Section 12, Article 2, the constitution proclaims, "Being a basic autonomous social institution, the State considers, as a matter of policy, the protection of the family in all aspects, from marriage to motherhood, from birth to the end of life" (Section 12, Article 2). Subsequent laws, like Executive Order No. 209 of 1987, the "Family Code of the Philippines," reinforced this principle and further disregarded the rights of women, instead emphasizing the traditional view of a family as one with a mother, father and children.

Family relationships are therefore governed by law and in the case of disagreement or conflict over the fixing of the family domicile, Article 211 of Executive Order No. 209, "The Family Code," of 1987, affirms that "parental authority over the person and property of their children is given to the father/husband, whose decision shall prevail over the mother/wife, unless there is a judicial order to the contrary". In this legal concept of the family, same-sex relationships are excluded. Marriage between couples of the same sex is, therefore, not possible under Philippine law. In fact, "lesbianism or homosexuality" of one party in the marriage can be grounds for legal separation and the annulment of marriage. The homosexual spouse is considered the guilty party and loses his or her rights of inheritance from the other spouse as well as any claim to conjugal property and may lose custody of the children.

The heterosexual and patriarchal beliefs that prevail over family formation, personal relationships and cultural, spiritual and political practices in the Philippines demonstrate not only the limited extent of the legal system to capture the multiple identities and intersectionality of women's lives and voices (Crenshaw 1991), but also indexes the wide extent to which the "public" continues to be prioritized over the "private" (Edwards 2011: 87, see also Romany 1994, Sullivan 1995). In essentializing women to a common experience and identity and privileging male hegemony over public life, gender discrimination remains the unresolved issue in the close connection between gender-based violence and violations of human rights and fundamental freedoms (Edwards 2011: 179). In other words, the major forms of disenfranchisement, exclusion and oppression of women are bound up with the disadvantages they suffer in cultural, social, and economic realms (Charlesworth, Chinkin and Wright 1991: 635; Edwards 2011: 60). As Barrios (1990) poignantly writes in her poem, " . . . the cruelty of war / Lies not on heads that roll, / But tables always empty", a stark reminder that we must also "look at poverty's face". This section has sought to view violence against women in relation to these underlying causes while the next section explores women's strategies in escaping and dealing with domestic abuse. I argue that Filipino women are resilient, turning to opportunities outside of the home and nation for the physical safety, psychological comfort and even financial security that they cannot fully gain domestically through legal means.

Transnational sites of struggle and sacrifice

Hope Basias Abella, Chair of the Center for the Prevention and Treatment of Child Sexual Abuse, claims that abuse against women persist because they continue to be perceived as "the weaker sex" or to be regarded as second-class despite advances in the struggle for gender equality (Quismundo 2009). Abella stresses, "If she is regarded as the weaker sex, automatically, where is the voice of the woman [as compared to] those in authority?" (Quismundo 2009). I argue that a woman's voice is not necessarily found only in her speech but is also embodied in her actions. "To be a woman," as Neferti Tadiar (2008: 100) states in her reading of Barrios' poem, "is a way of life in a time of war; it is to make a living out of conditions of war," such that "women's being as a living . . . [is] an active undertaking". If we further read the "conditions of war" as being the colonial and Catholic ideologies and institutions that structure women's lives, then women's "being and becoming are cast as a form of work and survival as well as the practice of defiance under general, socialized terror" (Tadiar 2008: 100).

That is, as Barrios (1990) reveals: "No moment / Is without danger. / At home, / To speak, to defy, / Is to challenge violence itself. / On the street, / Walking at nightfall / Is to invite a stranger's attack. / In my country, / To fight against oppression / Is to lay down one's life for the struggle". The fear that comes from colonial and Catholic forces is, therefore, turned into a direct "challenge of violence itself," which requires a recognition that one's own body and life is the site of such a fight and that the transformative struggle must actively take place both at home and in society. As Barrios (1990) declares: "I seek to know this war. / To be a woman is a never ceasing struggle / To live and be free" despite the danger, terror and fear. "To speak, to defy," however, is clearly a risk-taking activity that Tadiar (2008: 100–101) suggests is "brought about precisely by the gambling gestures women make" to reclaim futures and achieve another destiny that are not defined by the men in their lives.

Laura[13] is a woman who dared to "make a living" out of abusive conditions by following in the footsteps of her mother. At the time of my fieldwork, Laura was thirty years old and had just returned after working in France for three years. She had left her four young boys at home with their father while she worked as a domestic helper abroad. She had married young and did not find out until she was married that her husband was physically and verbally abusive and also took drugs. Her best friend told me that Laura really loved her husband so she put up with him and even began to experiment with drugs to see what he was up to and eventually became addicted herself. Ultimately, Laura sought help for her addiction through her best friend, who was at the time a staff member of the local NGO, Atikha Overseas Workers and Communities Initiative, Inc. (Atikha), which provides families and children with counselling and social services, life skills trainings and orientations on migration, financial literacy, human rights issues, gender awareness and other issues. Realizing what her life had become, Laura decided to escape from her abusive husband by going abroad like her mother, who had left her at the age of seven. However, while she was overseas, her husband continued to threaten her, warning that he would harm the children if she had an affair. Yet, while Laura was away, it was well known in the barangay that he had numerous affairs himself and used the remittances she sent home to gamble.

When she returned to the Philippines, she was forced to separate from her husband (though it is unclear whether the separation was official) and is now waiting to return to Europe, to her mother and siblings who are there. Despite finding a solution to the domestic violence at home, Laura is tempted not only by the increased monthly income (around PHP100,000, or US$2,167) she would earn as an OFW, but also by the future opportunities and possibilities it affords. While the labour migration would mean leaving behind her children in the Philippines again, it is a sacrifice she has chosen to make, saying she has many dreams not for herself but, rather, for her family. "When I was a child," Laura recounts, "my dream was to have a good home. . . . I don't want my children to experience the hardships of life." She states, "OFWs work abroad for the sake of their family and loved ones. Because of the difficulties of life, we think we have to leave the family and migrate to other countries and work there".

Maria, 46 years old at the time of my fieldwork, is another woman who chose to escape. Her sister conveyed to me that she was always sad because of her older sister, Maria, who, like Laura, went to work in Saudi Arabia to escape the physical abuse her husband meted out. On a visit to the Philippines, she chose to go back to her husband. At first, everything seemed better so she decided she would just stay in the Philippines. She opened up a little *tindahan* (small grocery store) to help her three children, who remained in the Philippines; however, the abuse started again. Eventually Maria separated from her husband and went back to Saudi Arabia to work, but found herself again in a failed relationship there with her long-term partner cheating on her. Phone calls from Maria eventually were no longer filled with sadness as her sister reports that she was happier now, having found a stable and successful boyfriend who himself migrated to Riyadh for work.

For these two women, their bodies served as their voice. In a community with a long history of family migrations to France, Spain, Italy and Saudi Arabia (see Alipio 2009), going abroad is seen as a viable and convenient alternative to abusive relationships, especially with poor economic conditions and limited legal rights at home, where divorce is illegal in Catholic Philippines (Sobritchea 2007). Thus, the decision by Laura and Maria to become OFWs rather than abused wives at home proclaims that they are willing to escape abuse in search of a better life elsewhere. Many female migrant workers explain their decision to go abroad in terms of *pakikipagsapalaran,* or fate playing (Tadiar 2008: 99). This is an act of faith, where one risks and gambles on the chance of another future, of a different life hopefully free from abuse (Tadiar 2008: 98).

It may be due to the opportunities for self-transformation they find in their countries of destination that empowers them to return back to the Philippines and articulate their personal, social, cultural, or economic grievances (Edwards 2011: 61). The increased incomes and possibilities for a relationship free from violence, in addition to the mere act of leaving home or "running away," became a kind of "leveraging tool" through which women, like Laura and Maria, are able to negotiate the conditions of their domestic situations and to separate from their abusive husbands (Faier 2008: 636). In this empowered transformation, they undermine what Ratna Kapur (2002: 18) has criticized as the image production of a "truncated Third World woman who is sexually constrained, tradition-bound, incarcerated in the home, illiterate and poor". Instead, Laura and Maria represent a growing group of women from low-income families who are educated, mobile and participating in the global economy.

By contrast, Nicole Constable (1999: 212) has found that some women working overseas in Hong Kong were not eager to go back home to the Philippines due to "trouble at home". For example, she describes the case of Delores, who had first migrated out of a desire to help her family though now "had little choice" but to return to Hong Kong after learning that her husband was "going with" another woman (Constable 1999: 212). Delores turned a blind eye to her husband's infidelity, owning to her appreciation that he was looking after the children well, and subsequently became a "punching bag" with her face "blue and black all over" (Constable 1999: 213). A friend of Delores offered the following account of accusations made by the husband to Delores (Constable 1999: 213):

> . . . He would say I am so proud to have so much money. And I said, "No, I am not. If I had a lot of money I would not go back and clean other people's toilets. If I have lots of money I would not go back." "Now that you are rich, you act like this." I said, "No. I just want to make sure I still have my pride here; I still have my person, my being, here with all my spirit intact because of what you are doing to me. I thought I am doing something good for my family. Now you are doing this to me."

As we see from the cases of Delores, Laura and Maria, transnational labour migration does not wholly promise liberation or happiness. For Delores, family obligations and filial piety motivated her to work abroad but for having left and becoming economically independent, she faced the hostility of her husband. For Laura, the dream of giving a better life for her children is also what keeps her away from them as she works to add much needed resources to her family's low-income household. Her dream, however, was thwarted by her vice-filled husband, who recklessly partakes in "A-S-B," or "*Alak-Sugal-Babae*" (wine, gambling and women), with the remittances she sent home. For Maria, the move away from domestic violence at home did not end her struggle; she found herself again in an abusive relationship with a different partner.

The daily experience of domestic violence survivors, as Julie Goldscheid (2006: 356) argues, "reflects the ongoing legacy of sex discrimination, both in the persistent gender-based differences in who generally commits and is harmed by the abuse, and in the responses victims encounter". Seen in this way, VAW is "a symptom of a much wider social problem," requiring what Alice Edwards (2011: 189) insists must be "a systematic, political solution". In the absence of strong government policies and in the presence of widespread corruption in the Philippines, the solution must be recast to directly effect individuals and communities, a recognition that VAW is a "group-based harm, a practice of social inequality carried out on an individual level" (Goldfarb 2003: 254). Violence, then, is of public concern, a social justice issue of structural gender inequality, not just a crime committed in private against individuals as I detail below.

Conclusion

Filipino women have long gambled on the prospect of better lives, taking risks in spite of the fear of being "[u]ncertain of a future / Hinged / To the men of [their lives]" (Barrios 1990). Women, who choose to defy traditional gendered expectations and obligations in order to fight against oppressive abuse or poverty by migrating for work overseas, are more likely to come up against criticism than to encounter praise for their initiative. Discourses on the traditional, ideal family remain strong and calls for its stability echo throughout the nation, from the media to classrooms. Such media representations and national discourses vilify and shame migrating women, allowing the public an opportunity to further morally discipline women and resist changes in gender equality, family formation and household structure. As Arjun Appadurai (1999: 231) observes, globalization has commonly led to "ideas about gender and modernity that create large female work forces at the same time that cross-national ideologies of 'culture,' 'authenticity,' and national honor put increasing pressure on various communities to morally discipline working women". Filipino women, who migrate to challenge the very violence of unequal relations and conditions that Barrios (1990) suggests create their " . . . never ceasing struggle / To live and be free," are unable then to elude the traditional gender roles to which they are ascribed.

For instance, many could point to the cases of Delores, Laura and Maria and see the separation caused by overseas contract work as worse than the actual migration itself since it weakens the ties between family members (Medina 2001: 40). Although the prolonged absence of either a father or a mother leads to emotional costs and distance in the family, there is a tendency to denigrate more the transnational family of women working outside the Philippines. As an increasing number of women leave the Philippines for economic and personal reasons, they have no choice but to relegate maternal responsibilities to the father, kin relatives and even to older children. Despite this support, migrant women are judged and scorned on the basis of their performance as an absent mother, owning to the belief that women as nurturers are central to the emotional needs of the young. As was the case with the extensive use of European nurses during the eighteenth century by elite mothers (Donzelot 1997: 9), Filipina migrants are condemned for abandoning their children to outsiders and their potentially dangerous influences.

The disruption of the social relationship between mother and child has brought about national anxiety over the destruction of the "moral fabric" on which prevailing regimes of gender and kinship depend. In migrating to escape abusive relationships, Filipina mothers face guilt and criticism from others who control and normalize these regimes of power and knowledge. Transnational migration, consequently, is a contradictory process, exacting both freedom and costs in a "cosmic gamble of fate" (Tadiar 2008: 123). In confronting the contradictions between the ideals of a dominant Western feminism and the lives of women in non-Western societies, Lila Abu-Lughod (2002) asks: "What does freedom mean if we accept the fundamental premise that humans are social beings, always raised in certain social and historical contexts and belonging to particular communities that shape their desires and understandings of the world?" Tadiar (2008: 137) replies that "communities are not simply given but, indeed, shaped by and called into being by the very cultural practices of freedom and power that Filipinas exercise through their imaginative and bodily capacities". To lessen domestic violence in the barangay, community members must pay attention to the actions of women like Laura, Maria and Delores, who chose to leave rather than find solutions and support from within their communities. Members of the community must be aware of what is happening around them and to their neighbours in order to shape and transform their environments.

In a 2006 survey of 77 barangays, conducted by the WWTSVAW, 58 percent of the barangays indicated that their knowledge of RA 9262 came from NGO-conducted seminars, while the remaining said their knowledge came from government-sponsored seminars. This finding shows the significant role NGOs play in providing crisis intervention and support services. In San Pablo City, local NGO Atikha has taken on the task of spreading knowledge about women's rights and human rights. This is being done through the children of the city. In the particular barangay where I worked, children, both of OFWs and others, were particularly active in Atikha's children's programme, called Batang Atikha Savers Club. Primarily a savings programme to help children learn how to save and invest the remittances of their migrant parents (see Alipio 2009), the club also conducts activities like a "Gender Sensitivity" seminar, where one young girl stated: "I learned from Gender Sensitivity that a male and a female can have the same responsibilities and that whatever a man can do, a woman can also do the same. We should view them equally." To further cultivate children's knowledge and skills and boost their confidence, the club has puppetry and theatre arts workshops .

The children put on puppet shows at elementary schools and different public venues around town, throughout the province, and even in Manila. Their scripts deal with methods to cope with parental migration, save money from their OFW parents' remittances and prevent abuse of their rights, where children most importantly learn how to differentiate between "good touches" and "bad touches" (Atikha's description of sexual harassment). A regular and talented puppeteer is Laura's eldest son, John. John was a very shy and quiet sixth-grader at the time I knew him, something I attributed to the absence of his mother and the character of his father. However, when he was behind the curtains, lending his voice to the puppets he handled, he transformed. He was vocal, enthusiastic and very much a part of his community, teaching his peers and elders to value their rights, and how to play an active role in protecting them.

John's example gives us an alternative to Ruffa Gutierrez's much sensationalized story that began this chapter. It also offers an alternative to work around the legal limitations, economic constraints, social norms and cultural restrictions adults and children face everyday at home. The community-based interventions that Atikha advocates makes men, boys and children a part of the solution through their active participation in spreading knowledge on preventing domestic abuse and through their support in bringing attention to gender-based discrimination. As Atikha extends their programs to support those experiencing domestic violence, they may actually be preventing victim-survivors from seeking solutions from outside, like taking a chance on a better life by migrating.

For women who do leave violent relationships, it is indeed a gamble to migrate and leave their children behind with the abusive father, especially if social services, government offices and legal laws are unavailable or ineffective. Women, therefore, face the cruel decision of staying at home or leaving, one struggle of being a woman — as per Barrios' (1990) definition — "at a time of war". As women choose to migrate from home to work abroad, the risk does not seem to bring a clear benefit to women. Instead, as women struggle transnationally — still hinged — they move from one form of abuse to another with the patriarchal beliefs and spirituality that first structured the discrimination they are subject to in cultural, social, economic and legal realms, now ironically resurging as a coping measure, reaffirming their suffering and sacrifice as they free themselves from unbearable conditions of violence and poverty. "Religious faith," Laura poignantly expresses, "is important. You turn to 'Him' in times of trouble and when you are very down."

Acknowledgements

The research for this study was supported by the Fulbright IIE U.S. Student Fellowship under the sponsorship of the Philippine-American Education Foundation and the Visiting Research Associate program at the Institute of Philippine Culture at Ateneo de Manila University. The final writing of this research was supported by the Postdoctoral Fellowship at the Asia Research Institute of the National University of Singapore. I am grateful to Atikha Overseas Workers and Communities Initiative, Inc. for the support I received while in the Philippines.

Notes

1 The exchange rate for 21 May 2010 is 1 US dollar (US$) to 46.14 Philippine Pesos (PHP). For consistency, all subsequent exchange rates in the chapter are calculated for this date.

2 For more information on Avon's Speak Out Against Domestic Violence campaign and its partnership with Ruffa Gutierrez, see the press release, "Avon Strengthens Commitment to Empower Women to Speak Out", found on the website: http://www.avon.com.ph/PRSuite/speakout2010.page (accessed November 26, 2012).

3 Along with the 1987 Constitution of the Republic of the Philippines, the United Nations Universal Declaration of Human Rights (UDHR) and other

international human rights instruments to which the country is a state party, the Philippine government additionally cites the United Nations Convention on the Elimination of All Forms of Discrimination against Women (CEDAW) and the Convention on the Rights of the Child (UNCRC) as standards in addressing VAWC (WWTSVAW 2009: 6).

4 In Section 3(h) of RA 9262, children "refer to those below eighteen (18) years of age or older but are incapable of taking care of themselves. . . . it also includes the biological children of the victim and other children under her care."

5 It is the duty of law enforcers to investigate a complaint and when investigation shows a crime has been committed to file an official complaint with the public prosecutor. Under RA 9262, the public prosecutor then has to conduct either an inquest or a preliminary investigation to determine if there is probable cause. The investigating prosecutor subsequently files the appropriate information before the court, and a public attorney is assigned to the victim(s) while the prosecutor assists the victim(s) during the trial. If the courts prove that an individual is guilty of the crime, he may be imprisoned for a period ranging from one month and one day to life in jail (with the length depending on the gravity of the crime) and is additionally obliged to pay PHP100,000 (US$2,167) to PHP300,000 (US$6,502) in damages. The offender also has to undergo rehabilitative counselling from the DSWD and may have to submit to psychiatric treatment or confinement whenever deemed necessary by the court.

6 If the victim-survivor is a child, the DSWD is required to and responsible for providing protective custody, being guardian *ad litem*, referring the child to appropriate agencies for needed services and preparing social case studies if required by the court, among other things.

7 Besides the victim-survivor, any of the following may file a protection order on behalf of the victim-survivor(s): parent or guardian; grandparents; children and grandchildren; relatives (aunts, uncles, cousins and in-laws); local officials and DSWD social workers; police; lawyers; counsellors; therapists; health care providers (nurses, doctors and barangay health workers) and any two people who are from the city or municipality where the VAWC occurred and who have personal knowledge of the crime. A Temporary Protection Order is effective for 30 days and can be continuously extended or renewed until final judgment is issued on the application for a Permanent Protection Order, which is valid until the petitioner revokes it.

8 The lack of transportation or transportation fare posed a major problem at my field site since the barangay was located on the periphery of the city; thus, the mobility of those who lived there was often limited.

9 In Section 9(d) of RA 9710, "The Magna Carta of Women" of 2009, also requires LGUs to establish a Violence Against Women's Desk in every barangay "to ensure that violence against women cases are fully addressed in a gender-responsive manner".

10 In addition to these duties, under RA 9262, barangay officials must also support organizing efforts and development programmes for women in the community; prioritize livelihood projects for victim-survivors; involve women in planning and implementing all programmes and projects in the barangay; ensure that all barangay officials, health workers, nutrition scholars, and

other barangay workers and security officers undergo gender-sensitivity seminars to enable them to respond to victims of violence; develop a system to document and report cases of VAWC as well as an assistance programme for the victims and prescribe additional guidelines and standards that are consistent with the act, if necessary.

11 The English translation of Joi Barrios' poem can be found in the March-April 2009 issue of IBON International's *Education for Development Magazine* at the website: http://edm.iboninternational.org/2009/march-april-2009/244-to-be-a-woman-is-to-live-at-a-time-of-war (accessed November 26, 2012).

12 Recounting the history of divorce in the Philippines, Gina Mission (1999) reminds us that divorce is already legal for part of the society. The 1977 Presidential Decree No. 1083, "Code of Muslim Personal Laws," permits divorce in marriages where both spouses are Muslims or where only the male is Muslim but the marriage was solemnized in accordance with Muslim Law. Additionally, some indigenous cultures practice divorce. Divorce is, therefore, not a new concept in the Philippines.

In the pre-colonial period, absolute divorce was widely practiced among tribal communities. Under the Spanish, legal separation was allowed, while under the Americans, divorce was allowed only on the grounds of adultery on the wife's part and concubinage on the husband's. Under Japanese occupation, the grounds for divorce were expanded. However, by 1950, the Civil Code of the Philippines allowed only legal separation on grounds of violent abuse and in 1987, the Family Code of the Philippines further tightened the laws against divorce with nullification of marriage only allowed on grounds of psychological incapacity.

13 Throughout this chapter, I have changed the names of informants in order to protect their privacy.

References

Abu-Lughod, Lila. (2002). Do Muslim Women Need Saving? Anthropological Reflections in Cultural Relativism and Its Others. *American Anthropologist* 104(3): 783–790.

Alipio, Cheryll. (2009). Affective Economies: Child Debts, Devotions, and Desires in Philippine Migrant Families. Doctor of Philosophy dissertation, University of Washington, Seattle.

Amnesty International Philippines. (2010). Amnesty International says victims of domestic violence denied access to justice, despite RA 9262. Press release, March 8. Electronic document, http://www.amnesty.org.ph/news.php?item=news&id=137. Accessed November 26, 2012.

Appadurai, Arjun. (1999). Globalization and the Research Imagination. *International Social Science Journal* 160 (June): 229–238.

Avon. (2010). Avon Strengthens Commitment to Empower Women to Speak Out: Launches 2nd Year of Speak Out Against Domestic Violence Campaign. Press Release. Electronic document, http://www.avon.com.ph/PRSuite/speakout2010.page. Accessed November 26, 2012.

Barrios, Joi. (1990). *Ang Pagiging Babae ay Pamumuhay sa Panahon ng Digma (To Be a Woman Is to Live in a Time of War)*. Manila: Babaylan Women's Publishing Collective, Institute of Women's Studies, St. Scholastica's College.

Bunch, Charlotte. (1987). *Passionate Politics: Feminist Theory in Action*. New York: St. Martin's Press.

Chant, Sylvia and Cathy McIlwaine. (1995). *Women of a Lesser Cost: Female Labour, Foreign Exchange and Philippine Development*. Quezon City: Ateneo de Manila University Press.

Charlesworth, Hilary, Christine Chinkin, and Shelley Wright. (1991). Feminist Approaches to International Law. *American Journal of International Law* 85: 613–645.

Constable, Nicole. (1999). At Home but Not at Home: Filipina Narratives of Ambivalent Returns. *Cultural Anthropology* 14(2): 203–228.

Crenshaw, Kimberle. (1991). Mapping the Margins: Intersectionality, Identity Politics, and Violence Against Women of Color. *Stanford Law Review* 43(6) (July): 1231–1299.

Delfin, Claire. (2008). Victims of domestic violence: Attacked by husbands, trapped by society. *GMANews.TV*, July 11. Electronic document, http://www.gmanetwork.com/news/story/106465/news/specialreports/victims-of-domestic-violence-attacked-by-husbands-trapped-by-society. Accessed November 26, 2012.

Donzelot, Jacques. (1997 [1976]). *The Policing of Families*. Baltimore, MD: John Hopkins University Press.

Edwards, Alice. (2011). *Violence Against Women Under International Human Rights Law*. Cambridge: Cambridge University Press.

Faier, Lieba. (2008). Runaway Stories: The Underground Micromovements of Filipina *Oyomesan* in Rural Japan. *Cultural Anthropology* 23(4): 630–659.

Flores, Helen (2010). 30 Filipino Women Suffer Domestic Abuse Daily. *The Philippine Star*, May 21.

Foucault, Michel. (1990 [1978]). *The History of Sexuality Volume I: An Introduction*. New York: Vintage Books.

Glenn, Evelyn Nakano. (1992). From Servitude to Service Work: Historical Continuities in the Racial Division of Paid Reproductive Labor. *Signs: Journal of Women in Culture and Society* 18(1): 1–44.

Go, Stella P. (1993). *The Filipino Family in the Eighties*. Manila: De La Salle University.

Goldfarb, Sally F. (2003). Applying the Discrimination Model to Violence Against Women: Some Reflections on Theory and Practice. *American University Journal of Gender, Social Policy, and the Law* 11(2): 251–270.

Goldscheid, Julie. (2006). Domestic and Sexual Violence as Sex Discrimination: Comparing American and International Approaches. *Thomas Jefferson Law Review* 28(3): 335–397.

Israel-Sobritchea, Carolyn. (1990). The Ideology of Female Domesticity: Its Impact on the Status of Filipino Women. *Review of Women's Studies* 1(1): 26–41.

Kapur, Ratna. (2002). The Tragedy of Victimization Rhetoric: Resurrecting the "Native" Subject in International/Post-Colonial Feminist Legal Politics. *Harvard Human Rights Journal* 15(1): 1–38.

Mahmood, Saba. (2005). *Politics of Piety: The Islamic Revival and the Feminist Subject*. Princeton, NJ: Princeton University Press.

Medina, Belen T.G. (2001). *The Filipino Family*. 2nd edition. Quezon City: University of the Philippines Press.

Menjívar, Cecilia and Olivia Salcideo. (2002). Immigrant Women and Domestic Violence: Common Experiences in Different Countries. *Gender and Society* 16(6) (December): 898–920.

Mission, Gina. (1999). Breaking the ties that bind. *WIN Magazine* 27 (December). Electronic document, http://www.gina.ph/WIN/issues/issue27/win27c.htm. Accessed November 26, 2012.

Mohanty, Chandra Talpade. (1991). Under Western Eyes: Feminist Scholarship and Colonial Discourses. In Chandra Talpade Mohanty, Ann Russo and Lourdes Torres (eds.) *Third World Women and the Politics of Feminism*, pp. 51–80. Bloomington, IN: Indiana University Press.

National Statistical Coordination Board. (2006). Updates on Women and Men in the Philippines. *Fact Sheets*, March 1. Electronic document, http://www.nscb.gov.ph/factsheet/pdf06/fs2_06.asp. Accessed November 26, 2012.

National Statistical Coordination Board. (2007). Updates on Women and Men in the Philippines. *Fact Sheet*, March 8. Electronic document, http://www.nscb.gov.ph/factsheet/pdf07/FS-200703-SS1-01.pdf. Accessed November 26, 2012.

National Statistical Coordination Board. (2008). Updates on Women and Men in the Philippines. *Fact Sheet*, March 18. Electronic document, http://www.nscb.gov.ph/factsheet/pdf08/FS-200803-SS1-01.pdf. Accessed November 26, 2012.

National Statistical Coordination Board. (2009). Updates on Women and Men in the Philippines. *Fact Sheet*, March 19. Electronic document, http://www.nscb.gov.ph/factsheet/pdf09/FINAL%20factsheet%20on%20women%20and%20men%20march%202009.pdf. Accessed November 26, 2012.

National Statistical Coordination Board. (2010). Updates on Women and Men in the Philippines. *Fact Sheet*, March 1. Electronic document, http://www.nscb.gov.ph/factsheet/pdf10/Women_Men_March2010.pdf. Accessed November 26, 2012.

Otto, Dianne. (1999). A Post-Beijing Reflection on the Limitations and Potential of Human Rights Discourse for Women. In Kelly D. Askin and Dorean M. Koenig (eds.) *Women and International Human Rights Law: Volume 1*, pp. 115–135. Ardsley, NY: Transnational Publishers.

Parreñas, Rhacel Salazar. (2001). *Servants of Globalization: Women, Migration, and Domestic Work*. Stanford, CA: Stanford University Press.

Quismundo, Tara. (2009). Rise in domestic violence alarms police. *Philippine Daily Inquirer*, February 6. Electronic document, http://newsinfo.inquirer.net/breakingnews/nation/view/20090206-187867/Rise-in-domestic-violence-alarms-police. Accessed November 26, 2012.

Raj, Anita and Jay Silverman. (2002). Violence Against Immigrant Women: The Roles of Culture, Context, and Legal Immigrant Status on Intimate Partner Violence. *Violence Against Women* 8(3): 367–398.

Raposas, Tess. (2008). Marriage and Domestic Violence: A Fatal Combination in the Philippines, Where Divorce is Illegal. AlterNet, January 17. Electronic document, http://www.alternet.org/story/74044/. Accessed November 26, 2012.

Rodriguez, Luz Lopez. (1990). Patriarchy and Women's Subordination in the Philippines. *Review of Women's Studies* 1(1): 15–25.

Romany, Celina. (1994). State Responsibility Goes Private: A Feminist Critique of the Public/Private Distinction in International Human Rights Law. In Rebecca J. Cook (ed.) *Human Rights of Women: National and International perspectives*, pp. 85–115. Philadelphia, PA: University of Pennsylvania Press.

Rosal, Malou E. (2010). Speak to break free. *Manila Bulletin*, May 22. Electronic document, http://www.mb.com.ph/articles/258486/speak-break-free. Accessed November 26, 2012.

Sobritchea, Carolyn I. (1990). The Ideology of Female Domesticity: Its Impact on the Status of Filipino Women. *Review of Women's Studies* 1(1): 26–41.

Sobritchea, Carolyn I. (2007). Constructions of Mothering: The Experience of Female Filipino Overseas Workers. In Theresa Devasahayam and Brenda S.A. Yeoh (eds.) *Working and Mothering in Asia: Images, Ideologies and Identities*, pp. 173–194. Singapore: NUS Press.

Sokoloff, Natalie J. and Ida Dupont. (2005). Domestic Violence at the Intersections of Race, Class, and Gender: Challenges and Contributions to Understanding Violence Against Marginalized Women in Diverse Communities. *Violence Against Women* 11(1): 38–64.

Sullivan, Donna. (1995). The Public/Private Distinction in International Human Rights Law. In Julie Peters and Andrea Wolper (eds.) *Women's Rights, Human Rights: International Feminist Perspectives*, pp. 126–134. New York: Routledge.

Tadiar, Neferti Xina M. (2008). *Things Fall Away: Philippine Historical Experience and the Makings of Globalization*. Durham, NC: Duke University Press.

Tran, Carolee GiaoUyen and Kunya Des Jardins. (2000). Domestic Violence in Vietnamese Refugee and Korean Immigrant Communities. In Jean Lau Chin (ed.) *Relationships Among Asian Women*, pp. 71–96. Washington, DC: American Psychological Association.

Women Working Together to Stop Violence Against Women (WWTSVAW). (2009). Breaking the Silence, Seeking Justice in Intimate Partner Violence in the Philippines: A Review on the Implementation of Republic Act 9262 or the Anti-Violence Against Women and their Children Act of 2004. Electronic document, http://www.amnesty.org.ph/publications.php. Accessed November 26, 2012.

Philippine Laws

Executive Order No. 209, also known as the "Family Code of the Philippines", 1987.

Presidential Decree No. 1083, also known as the "Code of Muslim Personal Laws", 1977.

Republic Act 7610 or an act providing for stronger deterrence and special protection against child abuse, exploitation and discrimination, and for other purposes, also known as the "Special Protection of Children Against Abuse, Exploitation and Discrimination Act", 1992.

Republic Act 7877 or an act declaring sexual harassment unlawful in the employment, education or training environment and for other purposes, also known as the "Anti-Sexual Harassment Act", 1995.

Republic Act 8353 or an act expanding the definition of rape, reclassifying the same as a crime against persons, amending for the purpose Act No. 3815, as amended, otherwise known as the "Revised Penal Code", and for other purposes, also known as the "Anti-Rape Law", 1997.

Republic Act 8505 or an act providing assistance and protection for rape victims, establishing for the purpose a rape crisis centre in every province and city, authorizing the appropriation of funds therefore and for other purposes, also known as the "Rape Victim Assistance and Protection Act", 1998.

Republic Act 9262 or an act defining violence against women and their children, providing measures for victims, prescribing penalties therefore and for other purposes, also known as the "Anti-Violence Against Women and Their Children Act", 2004.

Republic Act 9710, also known as the "The Magna Carta of Women", 2009.

CHAPTER

6

Investigating Intimate Violence

A Problem of Law

NARAYANAN GANAPATHY

In 1995, domestic violence surfaced as a problem in Singapore. The awareness of the issue came in the form of the Family Violence Bill introduced to the Singapore Parliament that year. Fundamentally, the bill gave the police greater power to arrest an abuser without a warrant or court order, making it a *seizable offence* provided for by the Singapore Penal and Criminal Procedure Code. The police would have the authority to investigate all complaints of domestic abuse including "simple hurt", and the discretion to decide between prosecution and mandatory counselling. The bill also outlined police responsibilities towards the victim, such as finding alternative accommodation or refuge shelters, getting medical help and assisting the victim in collecting her belongings from the matrimonial home. Although the goal of the bill was to protect vulnerable family members, including the young and the elderly, it was rejected by Parliament. The state's response to the bill was clear — it feared that the bill would introduce litigation at an early stage, leading to the disintegration of the family. (The state's perspective on the limits of police intervention is discussed later in the chapter.)

Despite this failure to have the bill passed as law, the Singapore Police Force's (SPF) willingness to improve the policing of domestic violence can be traced to the implementation of the Domestic Violence Project at a police division later the same year. This project, organized around an elaborate network comprising the police and social service agencies, was essentially an administrative set-up designed to assist victims of domestic violence in making a formal complaint (CP 75/4 53 dated 5 May 1997, Public Affairs Department, SPF). The project, jointly administered by the SPF and then Ministry of Community Development (MCD) marked the first formal response by the state in recognizing and addressing the problem of domestic violence in Singapore.

An interesting feature of this "facilitated complaint and referral system", as the police phrased it, was the incorporation of the "Family Violence Monitoring Scheme". Under the scheme, the police referred the victim to a Family Service Centre (FSC) in non-seizable (non-arrestable) cases for counselling. The counsellor at the FSC then worked closely with the Neighbourhood Police Officer (NPPO) on one of the two options available: to prosecute the offender (a criminal perspective) or to monitor the victim's progress (a social work perspective). A significant development in the implementation of the Domestic Violence Project was the extension of the socio-legal control mechanisms that dealt with the problem of marital violence and the empowerment of FSCs to act as "official gatekeepers" of domestic cases of assault that entered the criminal justice system.

A notable legislative development arising from this police initiative was the Amendments to the Women's Charter (Chapter 353) that came into effect in May 1997. The amendments included a new section (Part IV "Protection of Family") in the charter to provide protection for family members. The application of a protection order was extended to other family members including former spouse, father, mother, father-in-law, mother-in-law, siblings, relatives and incapacitated persons besides the "traditional" categories of spouse and children. The definition of "violence" was also broadened to include intimidation, continual harassment or restraining someone against his/her will. Significantly, a breach of the conditions of any of the Protection Orders — Personal Protection Order, Personal Protection Order with Exclusion Order and Expedited Order — was made a seizable (arrestable) offence (except for failure to attend compulsory counselling sessions which remains non-seizable).

To rank-and-file police officers, however, it was business as usual. These changes implied marginal *operational* differences to the way most police officers responded to and investigated domestic violence. The disjunction between "street-level" policing and "managerial" policing raised some serious questions about the effectiveness of police or legislative reforms. Not only did it question the policies of various land divisions, the quality of training, and the effectiveness of police supervision and accountability systems, but it also cast doubt on the entire reform process as it related to making the police more responsive to marital violence.

The failure of the reform can be attributed to the fact that reform efforts have been primarily directed at changing the cultural assumptions of front-line officers and investigators with regard to marital violence without a corresponding and conscious change in the structural-legal framework that guides investigation in such cases. In the now voluminous literature on police subculture, many researchers and police reformers have documented police subculture as an impediment to police responsiveness to wider community concerns (see Chan 1997; Holdaway 1983). Brogden and Shearing (1993: 96), for example, observed that when existing rules were incongruent with practice, rank-and-file officers often found ways to "ingeniously" circumvent them. Therefore, to change police practice, as Brogden and Shearing suggested, "an attack on the police occupational culture [was] necessary" where the rule-making approach to police reform would be complemented by strategies to change police culture from within (1993: 97). Similarly, Reiner observed that before initializing police reform, "key changes must be made in the informal culture of the police, their practical working rules" (1992: 232), by redefining the police mandate and instituting new forms of accountability to curtail the imperatives of police culture.

Collectively, changing rank-and-file culture to reform police response to marital violence meant changing the predisposition of front-line officers towards marital violence. The cultural change approach thus focused on restructuring and delimiting the (deviant) practices of rank-and-file officers, thought to stem from police subculture, to make them more congruent with the organization's official policies.

What it failed to take into account, however, was that *a* police subculture emerged as a response to the structural conditions of policing and the structural contingencies police officers faced "as a way of coping with, and making sense of, a given environment" (Manning & Van Maanen 1978: 267) in the face of recurrent problems and common experiences. Thus, while the Amendments to the Women's Charter (Chapter 353) was designed to eliminate the discretionary powers of rank-and-file officers by directing them to arrest abusers whenever there is a violation of a PO, the structural-legal premise on which this legislation rests is problematic. First, the reclassification of the violation of a Protection Order as a seizable offence is not an attempt at criminalizing domestic violence *per se*. Instead, it is a response to an act that in the view of the police and judiciary amounts to a "Breach of Court Orders". Second, the legal source of criminalizing, and hence, the exercise of arrest powers in domestic violence is still to be found in the generic category of "Hurt" (Chapter 224), provided for by Section 323 (Voluntarily Causing Hurt) and Section 325 (Voluntarily Causing Grievous Hurt) of the Penal Code. This chapter argues that the "exclusionary" classification of Section 325 as it relates to arrest decisions in cases of domestic violence contributes to an under-reporting and under-recording of such cases in the police system. It also seeks to document the impact this classification has on victims's decision to involve the police in such cases and show how police response to this "crime" is circumscribed by a state discourse that discourages the criminalization of domestic violence in Singapore.

An overview of police response to domestic violence

The literature on policing domestic violence identifies two major perspectives that have informed criminologists in their formulation and conceptualization of the problem of policing "domestics". The first perspective, assumed by situational and non-feminist legal theorists, draws its inspiration from Black's (1971) research, which was among the few empirical studies that examined police arrest decisions based on exogenous factors. A significant contribution of Black's study, though it did not directly address the issue of police intervention in domestic violence, lies in its theoretical credence to developing a model of police decision-making rife with situationally determined contingencies. It precipitated a great deal of interest in the nature of police-citizen arrest encounters and the controversies over what constituted appropriate and effective (and, therefore, differential) police intervention. The model emphasizes that police assessment of the situation, and later justifications for their actions, depended in part on the ways in which the police actors themselves set the stage for police management in handling of situations (Bittner 1967). Using this model, researchers investigating police response to domestic violence attempted to determine and delineate aspects of police arrest decisions based on a variety of exogenous variables (Dutton 1995; Choi 1995; Loving and Farmer 1980; Dolon and Meagher 1986; Waaland and Keeley 1985; Ford 1987; Buzawa 1988; Berk and Loseke 1980; Bell 1984; Choi 1989; Brown 1984; Berk et al. 1984; Smith and Klein 1984; Worden and Pollitz 1984). Factors commonly cited as affecting arrest include the victim signing a citizen's arrest form, the victim requesting officers to charge the offender, the presence of weapons, the suspect's hostility towards the police, the relational social distance between offender and victim and the race of the disputants. The main limitation of this perspective is that it obscures an understanding of police *decisions of avoidance of arrests* as studies using this perspective have generated findings based on specific and discrete observations of police-citizen encounters, where arrest was inevitable. As Smith and Klein acknowledged: "while our quantitative results identify factors which significantly affect arrest decisions, they do not directly address the underlying processes: how do police chose to arrest in some disputes and not in others" (1984: 47).

To better conceptualize the issue of rank-and-file *decisions to avoid arrest*, feminist criminologists, in particular, have developed a perspective where they specifically seek to examine and delineate aspects of rank-and-file police culture that seem to determine handling of domestic situations (Field and Field 1973; Parnas 1967, 1971; Edwards 1989; Walter 1981; Hatty 1989; Zoomer 1989; Smith & Gray 1983; Hanmer 1989; Ferraro 1989a; Buzawa and Buzawa 1990). Studies using this perspective essentially presuppose that a negative police response, conceptualized as one equivalent to perfunctory or "non-arrest" intervention, is reflective of the normative values achieved during the process of social and organizational socialization of the police. A notable feature of this rank-and-file police culture, which most studies have highlighted, is the perception that attending to domestic situations is not an "appropriate" police duty. Although I subscribe to the basic premise of the cultural perspective that "no-arrest" outcomes are reflections of normative values developed and sustained by rank-and-file police culture, I argue that this approach to understanding the policing of marital violence inherits a similar theoretical weakness as the first perspective — an all-powerful and deterministic conception of police subculture *alone* fails to adequately explain and account for rank-and-file officers' *decisions of arrest.*

Using Pierre Bourdieu's (1977; 1990) relational concepts of "habitus" and "field", I argue for a need to take into account *both* the cultural dispositions of police subculture and structural conditions of policing to understand police response to domestic violence (Narayanan 2008). By structural conditions of policing, I am referring to the social, political and legal contexts in which the policing of domestic violence takes place in Singapore. For the purposes of the current objective, analysis of the "structures" will be confined to the legal framework that guides police intervention in domestic violence. The utility of this proposed framework is that it does not locate the problem of what is commonly perceived as perfunctory interventions on the part of the police solely within the domain of police subculture but shows how police investigation into domestic violence is constrained by existing statutory requirements with determined outcomes.

Conceptualizing police response to domestic violence

Theoretically, although my observations of police decisions of *arrest* and *non-arrest* were largely congruent with the findings of situational theorists (for example, see Berk and Loseke 1980; Bell, 1984; Smith and Klein, 1984; Worden and Pollitz, 1984) that combinations of variables — legal and extra-legal — act to influence a particular course of police action, data gathered through qualitative methodologies of observation and case-study was instrumental in developing a perspective that focused on the *meanings* patrolmen attached to these variables. As much as these meanings were constructed and sustained by the police occupational culture, they were equally acquiescent to "triggering" factors encountered within the political, social and legal context in which they exist, thus explaining the (seemingly) equivocal police response to domestic violence situations.

Examining the context in which police intervention occurred in domestic violence situations — and in a way that generated so few arrests — required an analysis as well as an explanation from the level of *inter-*

actions (everyday policing encounters) to that of *structures* (context in which everyday policing was to be situated). Although police officers exhibited reservations at having to deal with domestic violence cases and offered resistance to incorporating it into the ranks of "real crimes", the low arrest rate arising from domestic violence cases could not *solely* be attributed to the organized (cultural) resistance and circumvention strategies displayed by officers on the ground. That the majority of domestic violence cases did not result in arrest was a direct consequence of officers *merely* satisfying the statutory requirements of the law — most cases did indeed *legally* fall into the non-seizable category where the police cannot initiate arrest without a warrant. We shall see why this is so.

The central (legal) categories for the operational policing of family violence are drawn from provisions available in the generic category of "hurt" under Chapter 224 of the Singapore Penal Code. Typically, the definition of a "domestic violence incident" is based upon the classification of the incident as "voluntarily causing hurt" (VCH) under Section 323 (where the police cannot arrest without a warrant) or "voluntarily causing grievous hurt" (VCGH) under Section 325 (where the police can arrest without a warrant). My data reveals that the bulk of all family violence cases did not result in arrest because they could not justify the very "exclusionary" definition of "voluntarily causing grievous hurt". For a case of violence to be defined as "grievous hurt", the victim has to satisfy one of the following conditions: (a) emasculation; (b) permanent privation of the sight of either eye; (c) permanent privation of the hearing of either ear; (d) privation of any member or joint; (e) destruction or permanent impairing of the powers of any member or joint; (f) permanent disfiguration of the head or face; (g) fracture or dislocation of a bone; (h) any hurt which endangers life, or which causes the sufferer to be, during the space of 20 days, in severe bodily pain, or unable to follow his ordinary pursuits (Singapore Penal Code 1985: 102).

A consequence of this very "exclusionary" classification, lop-sided if you like, is that most cases of domestic violence are diverted from the criminalization process. This probably would explain why the "referral" and "advice" roles of the police have to be incorporated, institutionalized and legitimated within the operational framework, a point discussed later in the chapter. When an officer was asked how he would distinguish Section 323 (VCH) from 325 (VCGH), he stated:

> it's rather simple and straightforward. In most cases, as you know already, the women tend to scream and scream at the top of their voice especially when we are there, maybe to get our attention. If I see this, straightaway I know that this must be 323 because if you see how the law sees grievous hurt, the woman cannot or shouldn't be doing these kind of things . . . she must be deaf or blind . . . only then we can go in. . . . Sometimes, I think the law is a bit funny also. (explanation added)

In terms of the operational policing of domestic violence, the fulfilment of this legal requirement and thus classification of the case as "non-seizable" would explain why police intervention in most cases takes a *routinized* form. Typically, this involves advising the victim to make a police report at the nearest police post or division on her own in order to file a magistrate complaint against the perpetrator and then leaving the scene for the next job. As one officer remarked:

> we know from our experience that most cases of family violence are indeed non-seizable and therefore it makes no difference. Whether you go to the scene in three or thirty minutes you cannot do much. You are still there to perform a very *routine* response, give her the NP 301 (police report), NP 306 (medical report), ask her to report to the police station, which they will never do, and then we leave. . . . (emphasis added)

In such instances, domestic violence cases are typically categorized as either "No Offence Disclosed" (NOD) or "Police Assistance Required" (PAR), a legitimate classification that would expel such cases from the police system. Although the use of NOD and PAR is a way of *procedurally* and *legitimately* justifying the exit of such cases from the police system, their use, in effect, could mean one of five things: first, the victim refusing to substantiate the allegation; second, no physical evidence or bodily injuries to substantiate the allegation; third, not enough evidence to substantiate the claim or an exaggerated version of the episode led officers to discount the victim's account; fourth, no sign of the suspect or victim at the reported address or inability of the police to contact either of the disputants and fifth, "false alarm," where the victim called the police to frighten her husband with no intention of pressing charges against him. As there were no records pertaining to the classification of incidents as NOD/PAR maintained by any unit at the police division including the operations room, ascertaining the number of cases that had entered *and* exited at that single point is difficult. Police definitions and interpretations of a NOD/PAR situation are rarely questioned and it is not unreasonable to conclude that this could be the largest but the most undocumented single exit point from the police system.

If a particular domestic incident is "in progress" and restoration of peace is difficult, an arrest, theoretically, could be staged. However, when arrest was exercised as an option, officers were less inclined to invoke the legal categories of "hurt", resorting instead to provisions of Breach of Peace (BOP), Public Nuisance, and Disorderly Behaviour under Miscellaneous Offences, a fundamental legal precept to deal with public crime/disorder (as opposed to "private crime" in the case of family violence). Still, there is some ambiguity in the way officers understood the meaning of these categories, particularly Breach of Peace. Some officers flatly denied that such a charge could be used in a "domestic" situation.

Others claimed that they would use the powers of arrest invested in this provision, which basically relied on the subjective interpretation of the officer at the scene, even if the "breach of the peace" happens in the "suspect's own living room" (field notes). There were instances where officers lured the perpetrator outside the front door into the common corridor before effecting arrest under the BOP charge. One station inspector stated that from his experience this particular tactic was an effective way of dealing with cases where control of the situation was difficult, when victims failed to substantiate allegations of violence, or "when you feel like teaching him a lesson" (field notes). However, the use of these categories was mainly reserved for the recalcitrant and those who openly challenged police authority.

Victims' experiences of domestic violence policing

It must be emphasized that the processing of a "domestic violence incident" as accomplished by institutionalized policing hinges on whether the victim wishes to substantiate the allegation of assault by making a formal police report. A negative answer would result in the exit of the case at any stage even if the victim had earlier made a verbal complaint with the police. As an officer plainly stated:

> Policemen are like God, we help those who help themselves. You see, in domestic violence, there is nothing much we could do legally to help the victim. The most we could do is to offer advice and maybe offer some support to the victims to take up a PPO from the Family Court . . . our hands are tied in cases of domestic violence.

This would explain the predominance of the victim-choice model (Hoyle and Sanders 2000) in conceptualizing the majority of victims' relationships with the police where the victim must display an initiative throughout the criminal justice process to prosecute the abuser in court. The institutionalization of a victim-choice approach by the Singapore police, however, could be challenged on several different grounds. First, it allowed individual victims to decide what may be best for them without considering the impact of non-prosecution on perpetrators and victims of marital violence in general. Second, the idea that the police should act on women's choices also presupposed that women could achieve the "right" decision without accurate information, support and advice. It assumes that the social and structural context that victims of violence inhabit is conducive to making "free choice" and that they are able to express their wishes uncoerced — both structurally and interpersonally. Third, the victim-choice approach also exposes women to the manipulation of others — perpetrators, police officers and family members — who might have an interest in the criminal justice process not being invoked (Buzawa and Buzawa 1990). As Edwards (1989) noted in her research, the police, in particular, had used a victim-choice approach as a cloak to cover up their own disinclination to treat domestic violence the way they treat other crimes. My own perspective on this is that this effect comes about because of the way officers, especially patrolmen, marshal the institutionalized categories at their disposal. Of particular importance here, are the categories set up as polarities: "victim" and "suspect"; "innocent" and "guilty"; "no-crime" and "crime". These terms are, perhaps, familiar to most people, but they perform a special function in the semantic network of police work. Within the confines of operational response and subsequent processing of a domestic violence incident, there must be both a "suspect" and "victim". However, if the person with injuries in a domestic incident does not wish to step into the labelled box of a "victim", it is difficult for the police to process the incident as a "criminal" one. To the officers on the ground, such cases amounted to "victim failing to substantiate an allegation", an analytical as well as an operational category that functions as a hinge between the polarities of "victim" and "suspect", "guilty" and "innocent", "no-crime" and "crime", before the case is admitted into or evicted from the police system. Thus, the policing of domestic violence becomes essentially a problematic category because the protracted and complex situation in which the violence takes place between known individuals makes it difficult to readily identify an offender and victim from the perspective of the police and as warranted by formal procedures. This issue is also one of the more significant factors adversely affecting the initial success of the mandatory and presumptive arrest policies where dual-arrest outcomes seem to be the more prevalent and preferred mode of intervention by responding officers, which, to an extent, is motivated by a desire to circumvent established procedures (Balos and Trotzy 1988; Buzawa and Buzawa 1990; Ferraro 1989b; Stanko 1989).

Contrasting the victim-choice model is the pro-arrest policy, which occupies a position at the other extreme of the continuum of police response. A major irony in the case of domestic violence as far as the Singaporean experience is concerned is that a victim tends to lose her choice the moment she exercises it (by seeking a Protection Order for instance) as the "system" assumes control of the criminal justice process henceforth with little regard for victim's needs. Nevertheless, the shift from discretionary to pro-arrest policies is perceived, among others, to have four key advantages. First, pro-arrest laws would provide more clarity in terms of the police role in *criminalizing* domestic violence (Stanko 1992) as much as it signifies the moral unacceptability of male violence against women (Edwards 1989; Stark 1993). Second, the responsibility of initiating arrest decisions is transferred from the victims to the police officers on the scene (Beul 1988). Third, it would lead to a more equitable law enforcement system by eliminating discriminatory and exogenous factors (such as race and social class) in determining police intervention. Finally, criminalization would enable the state to "intervene, usually by prosecuting, in order to exact retribution, produce specific deterrence and perhaps, treat the offender, thereby reducing further offending in a more constructive manner" (Dobash and Dobash et al. 1996).

In Singapore, elements of a pro-arrest policy are embodied in the Amendments to the Women's Charter (Chapter 353). As noted earlier, the amendments included a new section to provide protection for family members, with a breach of the conditions of any of the Protection Orders resulting in a *seizable* offence for which the responding policemen could arrest the perpetrator without an arrest warrant even if the incident did not meet the stringent criteria of VCGH. The function of the amendment, as far as this aspect is concerned, is (a) to delimit the discretionary powers of the police by directing them to make mandatory arrests whenever there is a violation of a PO by the person against whom the PO had been issued, and (b) transfer the responsibility of initiating criminal proceedings against the offender from the victim to the police regardless of victim-choice.

This is not simply a pro-arrest policy but a *pro-charge* policy as well since charges against the suspect are filed immediately upon arrest. An officer remarked:

> I think the amendments are effective as the policy clearly states that the police must arrest the offender whatever the situation is. It not only offers a solution to the problem of police officers evading arrest when they should but puts a stop to women's fickleness about wanting their husbands arrested and the next minute withdrawing their complaints which can leave a very lousy feeling at the end. With this policy, no one can withdraw or is allowed to withdraw once the charges are filed.

This policy reflects the assumption of the Singapore police that arrest and prosecution are desirable outcomes for victims and, therefore, the goal of police intervention. The "Guidelines for Patrol Officers", issued to all front-line officers following the Amendments to the Women's Charter, stated:

> Police must arrest the perpetrator when it is established that physical violence was inflicted on the victim even though the victim may request that Police do not arrest the perpetrator. . . . Police, not the victim, should decide whether to effect the arrest or not.

Whilst the police aim — to reduce further violence — is appropriate, the method advocated to achieve that aim is not necessarily so. It is based on the problematic assumption of the deterrent effect of arrest in cases of marital violence and that the (temporary) removal of the offender from the scene would ensure the victim's long-term safety and security. Further, the pro-arrest approach assumes that victims of domestic violence have little agency and that the police and policy-makers know what is best for them. Based on their British experience, Hoyle and Sanders (2000) suggested that it seemed presumptuous that policy-makers or even feminist advocates who have been successful in having pro-arrest policies instituted could easily determine what is best for, or in the interests of, a diverse group of battered women. It is as much a conceit as the theory of deterrence in this area, which assumes that both violent men and victims of violence are a homogenous group with identical and identifiable needs.

As I have stated elsewhere (Narayanan 2006), victims' experiences of policing in domestic violence in Singapore can be contextualized in terms of two extreme but interrelated sets of responses. At one end of the continuum, criminal justice sanctions are strictly contingent upon victim willingness to initiate criminal proceedings against the perpetrator, and at the other, victims's rights, needs and preferences seem to be usurped by the justice system regardless of their choice. Neither of these positions takes victims' interest into account. Nor do they stem from an understanding of the socio-cultural, economic and structural circumstances in which victims experience violence and continue to experience it, long after a police intervention. As such, criminalization as an ideological and legally practical tool is not only rendered ineffective but irrelevant to the experiences of women in the Singaporean context. Two factors may account for this phenomenon. First, the absence of support structures to achieve criminalization and address victims' needs in the aftermath of criminalization, and second, the paternalistic and patriarchal state impedes processes aimed at the empowerment of women victims by prescribing the limits of police intervention in domestic violence. It is the latter point that the next section deals with.

State discourse on the limits of police intervention

The discourse surrounding police intervention in cases of domestic violence in Singapore occurs within a specific political regime and within the boundaries defined by the authoritarian and "hetero-patriarchal" state (Chan 1996). In Singapore, the People's Action Party (PAP) is practically synonymous with the state (Rodan 1993). The Singapore State is also a patriarchal and paternalistic one. Paternalism refers to a relationship of exchange: an exchange of submission for protection (Lerner 1986: 239), involving a relationship of mutual obligations and rights. In a paternalistic discourse, protection takes precedence over empowerment or equal treatment. An analysis of the Family Violence Bill provides an excellent opportunity to appreciate the state's perspective on police intervention in domestic violence. As mentioned earlier in the chapter, the bill was rejected after 30 days on the grounds that it would introduce litigation at an early stage, which could be detrimental to the family. Singapore has a definitive and unproblematic view of what constitutes the family and its role in society:

> We believe that the state of our families, the building blocks of any society, determine not only the moral tone of the society but its economic health as well. As our families prosper, so does the nation. (Abdullah Tarmugi, 1995: 89–90)

Given the Singapore government's desire to promote the family as the "building block of society" and its constant warnings against "decadent western values" — thought to pose a threat to the well being of the family — a Family Violence Bill that did not accept the state's defined role for the family was deemed problematic. This was particularly evident in light of the state's intent to ensure the preservation of the family unit whose role is clearly prescribed in the White Paper (1991: 3): "the family is seen as the 'fundamental building block' out of which larger social structures can be stably constructed".

Despite attempts by the supporters of the bill to tailor its contents and method to fit into the political discourse of the "family", the bill was described by various political actors as being "harsh, high-handed and detached" (*The Straits Times*, 3 November 1995) as well as confrontational and punitive.

> Mandatory intervention made many MPs as well as concerned Singaporeans outside parliament, men and women, uncomfortable, not least because they just do not think the problem warrants such a drastic solution. (*The Straits Times*, 4 November 1995)

This subsequently led to a reworking of the definition of "family violence", in which Abdullah Tarmugi, the then Acting Minister for Community Development, Minister for the Environment, and Minister-in-charge of Muslim Affairs, states:

> a problem but not endemic . . . without belittling the suffering of these victims . . . the reality in most cases is not as gruesome and the victims not as helpless as put. There is a wide of range of abuse with various shades of gravity. (*The Straits Times*, 3 November 1995)

Objections to the bill were, therefore, not confined to the measures against domestic violence. There were objections to the idea of having a bill that would focus exclusively on family violence and overly emphasize and amplify the seriousness of the problem.

> We do not want to frighten our young citizens into thinking that marriage is a declaration of war, the home a battle zone, and the bedroom the scene of war crimes! Neither do we want the Bill to be viewed as a piece of legislation that will result in constant conflict between the two genders, that is, men and women. (*The Straits Times*, 2 November 1995)

The above is particularly revealing, given the government's concern that its young citizens are marrying later, having fewer children, and in some cases, eschewing marriage altogether. A telling argument against the bill was that it would send the message that marriage, and, therefore, the "family" (for the Singapore State does not separate the two) is a dangerous affair, which was contrary to the discourse on Shared Values. Recognizing this, supporters of the bill attempted to re-work the Family Violence Bill to prevent the state from rejecting the bill altogether, by arguing that the family unit would be kept safe; that mandatory counselling would contribute to keeping the "family" intact; that the bill did not intend to pit women against men, creating an atmosphere of mistrust, but rather that it meant to include other vulnerable family members like the elderly and the physically challenged. The one constant refrain throughout the debate was that of preserving the family unit.

Thus, the strategy adopted by proponents of the bill was to avoid making it solely a women's issue but rather one in which whoever takes to violence should be stopped ("Abuse issue is not a male-female battle, *The Straits Times*, 28 September 1995). The emphasis on women's rights and needs, as Purushotam (1992) argues, makes Singapore state uncomfortable because it does not deny either being a patriarchal state or supporting the patriarchal family. For women's needs to be addressed, they have to be made politically relevant by locating those needs within the context of the family. For example, in addressing the recommendation for the setting up of a Women's Affairs Bureau "to identify the problems confronting women today, and then, to design policies and solutions", the then Prime Minister Goh Chok Tong (1993: 22) said

> I do not think, however, that the proposed Women's Affairs Bureau should confine itself to *problems confronting women*. . . . The rationale for its setting up should be whether it can address *family and societal problems* more effectively. (Emphasis added)

Reinforcing the state's conception of the family and women's position in the family, the then Minister without Portfolio, Lim Boon Heng, stated:

> The majority of women continue to accept the traditional marriage

contract where the man is the natural head of the household by virtue of his role as the breadwinner, while the woman plays the supportive role in home-making and nurturing the young and old dependents, even though she also works and contributes financially. (1994: 70)

Similarly, Seet Ai Mee, the Minister of State then, argues:

In today's age, women can complete their housework more quickly and have more time on their hands. They are therefore in a better position to pursue careers and contribute to the economy. (1989: 94)

Feminists in Singapore, and proponents of the bill in particular, were compelled in a sense to accept and participate within the dominant political discourse that maps out the state's locations for "women" and women's role in the "family". They were also confined by the state's definition of legitimate actors who may introduce such an issue and legitimate strategies that emphasize negotiation and consensus-finding. The latter, however, was deemed problematic by the state as the bill was perceived to have contravened the Shared Values (1991: 4) on how differences are to be resolved:

Resolving issues through consensus instead of contention complements the idea of putting society before self. It means accommodating different views of the way the society should develop, and working hard to develop a consensus on particular courses of action which have the majority but not unanimous support, in order to bring as many people aboard as possible.

The criticism of the bill, therefore, stems from the point that

Dr Soin [a nominated member of parliament representing women's issues] came across as advocating just the kind of approach which some feminist groups and liberals elsewhere favour — roping in the state to fix everything that they think is not right. (*The Straits Times*, 4 November 1995)

Her strategy of using the law as a tool to legislate protection for victims of violence was interpreted as a more Western and confrontational way of solving issues instead of "a more Asian and less legalistic way of sorting out family problems" (*The Straits Times*, 4 November 1995). There is again a creation of categories: one Western and litigious and detrimental to the family and the other Asian and consensus-seeking, displaying a concern for the preservation of the family.

Clearly, the state has not ignored the issue of domestic violence since it certainly has a vested interest in ensuring stable families and preservation of the family unit. However, given that the discourse on family violence in Singapore takes place within the context of a paternalistic and patriarchal state, the defining element of that discourse must necessarily be protection over empowerment, and consequently left to the state to decide and implement.

Institutionalizing "alternative" categories: Authoritative intervention, referral and advice roles of the police

It is against such a social and political context of policing domestic violence — the *structural* conditions of policing — that the *operational* rank-and-file response to domestic violence is to be located. The operational policing of domestic violence in Singapore has an extended meaning and dimension, in that it has incorporated and institutionalized "alternative" categories of "referral" and "advice" (Sheptycki 1993) as legitimate operational categories. When anything less than arrest and diversion from the criminalization process has been interpreted by observers as "perfunctory" intervention by the police (Buzawa and Buzawa 1993), the Singapore experience suggests otherwise. There are a number of factors accounting for the establishment of the extended operational framework to deal with family violence. First, full criminalization of domestic violence incidents is indeed difficult and rare because of the problematic nature of the application of the seizable and non-seizable clause. As shown in this chapter, most cases do not *satisfy* the legal requisites of a seizable offence where the police can arrest the perpetrator without a warrant. The referral and advice roles of the police are thus developed to absorb cases diverted from the criminalization process.

Second, even if a case is criminalized, followed by the arrest of the perpetrator, investigators are unwilling to retain it within the police system for the purpose of prosecution because of the widespread perception that victims will eventually withdraw their charges. This led to officers discharging "problematic" cases — sometimes throwing the baby with the bath water — from the police system (by this I mean the criminalization process) at the first available opportunity, by referring them to FSCs and social work agencies without even acknowledging the case as an "incident" in the police system. The Amendments to the Women's Charter addressed the uncertainty issue by compelling officers to arrest and prosecute offenders whenever there was a violation of PPO but as shown earlier, it has its own setbacks. Third, the peace-keeping role of the police is preferred to criminalization in domestic violence because of the futility of appropriating "guilt" and assigning the label of "offender" to a family member who is *known* to the victim. Many officers remarked that criminalization is neither an appropriate nor an effective method to deal with wife abusers. In fact, a majority of them were of the view that social service agencies instead of the police should attend to cases of domestic violence where the former should aim for reconciliation and reintegration of the family. This view was reinforced by the results drawn from a National Survey of Singapore that revealed that a good majority of respondents (45 percent) "wanted the police to ask the couples to solve the problem themselves" (Choi and Edleson 1995: 243–258). Fourth, the officers' perspective on the potential threat criminalization poses to the family institution is a reflection of the Singapore State's discourse on the moral limits of police intervention in family violence cases. Outlining the police role in safeguarding the family as a "cornerstone of Singapore society", the then Home Affairs Minister argued:

> We should not hastily or mindlessly apply the *full intrusive and coercive force of the law* when this may not be the best course of action in the *interest of the family*. (Parliamentary Debates, Vol, 65: 116) (emphasis added)

Echoing the Home Minister was the then Senior Minister of State for Health and Education, Aline Wong:

> Where the law intervenes or is resorted to readily, people will be much less inclined to solve family problems through reconciliation or take moral responsibility for their own behaviour. In the long run, we may all be the losers. (*The Straits Times*, 3 November 1995)

The next section documents the operational aspects of the use of the "alternative" categories for cases classified as "non-seizable"; the procedural part of these has already been charted earlier.

Referral and advice roles of the police

These two roles of the police are frequently conflated into one idea. The use of these categories became increasingly formalized after the implementation of the Family Violence Referral System in 1996, where the police established a network with Voluntary Welfare Organizations (VWOs) around the island to refer victims of family violence — a majority of whom are women — to any of the MCD (now MCYS)-funded FSCs. However, this should not be seen as anything other than an addendum to the formal processing of calls. "Referral" meant informing the victim of a non-seizable crime of the services available to her, such as those offered by the FSC and shelter homes. Advice is often given to the victim at the same time as she is being referred to the FSCs; it is most often associated with informing her to make a police report at the nearest police station or Neighbourhood Police Centre (NPC). She is also given a copy of the medical examination form (NP 306) to seek medical assistance and is advised on the existence and use of protection orders (PO). The latter is available through either filing for a civil suit at the Magistrate Court if the victim intends to seek legal redress against her perpetrator, or the Family Court for non-legal pursuits.

Authoritative intervention

This is yet another police use of an "alternative" category that I have termed as "authoritative intervention". By this I mean police officers intervene in a situation to put an immediate halt to the violence and to exit the call almost immediately afterwards. This is an important aspect of the police role in these situations, and its role as the custodian of the state's monopoly of legitimate coercion (Waddington 1999: 31) means that the police was, and still *is*, the only organized response that has the potential to stage an authoritative intervention. It could be argued that this is central to the police response and, as such, it might be artificial and arbitrary to separate it from the operational processing of domestic violence cases I have outlined earlier. While it is no doubt true that this is a formal part of "within-the-job" (Chatterton 1978: 49) duties and that the "order-maintenance" role of the police is a long established one in police history and research (Reiner 1985), it does make sense to maintain the distinction. By doing so, "authoritative intervention" is seen as a precursor to, and in most cases is used instead of, a more involved and organized response by the criminal justice system to criminalization.

Documentation of the use of this "alternative category", though not officially sanctioned by the police organization nor officially accounted for in police records of any form, is an everyday practice amongst patrolmen. The difficulty in tracing the frequency of the use of this alternative category is exacerbated by police classification of such instances as "NOD/PAR" — an official category facilitating the exit of such cases from the police system. "Authoritative intervention", apart from putting a stop to the violence and restoring order, carried with itself advice, counselling and warning.

The victims themselves seemed to prefer this type of intervention to put an immediate halt to the violence but without compromising the position of their husbands in the family. In the words of a policeman, "the victims want the cake and eat it too". Certainly, this form of intervention is quite far removed from the operational processing that would gain "results", or be organizationally relevant, in a manner recognized by superiors. This might explain why many officers have categorized domestic violence cases as a "lose-lose" situation, something not worth responding to.

Regardless, it is obvious that these authoritative interventions, while built on legitimate use of coercive force by the police, are not interventions calculated to produce "results"; rather, they operate to facilitate an exit from the police system. The use of the "alternative" categories — referral, advice and authoritative intervention — in situations of domestic violence creates a "paradox" in the processing of these kinds of cases. I call it a "paradox" because very often such a response seems to "relocate" the victim to the same position she was in when she made her initial call to the police. This "paradox" is a portion of the police response to domestic violence that is quite systematic and institutionalized as officers simply tend to advise victims to seek medical assistance and court orders while routinely classifying such cases as NOD or PAR.

Conclusion

Given the desire of the Singapore State to promote the family as a "building block of society" (Tarmugi 1994, 1995), it should, therefore, come as no surprise that "radical" reforms such as mandatory and presumptive arrest policies do not even enter the debate on local reforms. This also means that reformers who wish to place family violence on the political agenda have to ensure that the issues discussed and measures suggested do not contradict the state's view on the role of the family in Singapore society. It is not uncommon for reformers and organizations with an interest in issues relating to violence against women to be reminded by the state not to "dwell on inequalities" (Tarmugi 1994: 69) for such inequalities should be expected in a patriarchal and paternalistic society. As Prime Minister Goh Chok Tong (1993: 29) points out:

> In a largely patriarchal society, minor areas where women are not accorded the same treatment should be expected as long as the welfare of women and of the family is protected.

Consequently, this leads reformers to abandon their philosophical views on *empowering* women as a strategy against male violence and choose *protection* from the state instead.

Choosing protection, however, subjects women to further abuse. Leaving protection to the state — both as motivator and dispenser of that protection — is equally problematic since it may, through the organization of the police, set boundaries to what constitutes violence. In responding to women who report violence, the police are involved in a (social) process of defining which attacks are to be criminalized and made arrestable and which are to be condoned and "no-crimed". The categorization of violence into seizable and non-seizable offences, for example, which informs patrolmen to make an immediate arrest or not, is a classic illustration of how the police make a distinction between violence they deem justifiable and violence they deem as requiring police attention.

A consequence of this process of defining and categorizing violence is the separation of victims into those "deserving" and "undeserving" of police attention. Thus, the police do not offer unconditional protection to *all* victims against *all* forms of violence, but rather any protection they offer is conditional upon victims meeting police notions of "deservedness"' and the circumstances of the attack meeting their definition of "crime" (Hanmer, Radford and Stanko 1989: 6). These categories of "deserving" and "undeserving" victims are often reinforced by the policemen's understanding of class, race and sexuality (Reiner 1985, Marenin 1983). It is through policing violence to achieve a degree of *general order* that the social divisions of class, race, gender and sexuality — *stratified order* — are reproduced in Singapore society.

References

Abdullah, Tarmugi. (1994) 'The Family: The Foundation of Society,' *Speeches*, 18(1): 68–72.

Abdullah, Tarmugi. (1995) 'Singapore's Approach to Social Development,' *Speeches* 19(2): 88–92.

Balos, B. and Trotzky, J. (1988) 'Enforcement of the Domestic Abuse Act in Minnesota: A Preliminary Study,' *Law and Inequality*, 6(1): 83–125.

Bell, D. J. (1984) 'The Police Response to Domestic Violence: A Replication Study,' *Police Studies*, 7: 136–43.

Berk, S. F. and Loseke, D. R. (1980) '"Handling" Family Violence: Situational Determinants of Police Arrest in Domestic Disturbance,' *Law and Society Review,* 15(2): 317–46.

Berk, R. A., Berk, S. F., Newton, P.J., and Loseke, D.R. (1984) 'Cops on Call: Summoning the Police to the Scene of Spousal Violence,' *Law and Society Review*, 18(3): 479–98.

Beul, S. M. (1988) 'Recent Development: Mandatory Arrest for Domestic Violence,' *Howard Women's Law Journal*, 11: 213–226.

Bittner, E. (1967) 'The Police on Skid Row: A Study of Peacekeeping,' *American Sociological Review,* 32(5): 699–715.

Black, D. (1971) 'The Social Organization of Arrest,' *Stanford Law Review*, 23:1087–1111.

Bourdieu, P. (1977) *Outline of a Theory of Practice*, Cambridge: Cambridge University Press.

Bourdieu, P. (1990*) In Other Words: Essay Towards a Reflexive Sociology*, Cambridge: Polity Press.

Brogden, M. and Shearing, C. (1993) *Policing for a New South Africa*, London: Routledge.

Brown, S. E. (1984) 'Police Response to Wife Beating: Neglect of a Crime of Violence,' *Journal of Criminal Justice*, 12(3): 277–88.

Buzawa, E. (1988) 'Explaining Variations in Police Responses to Domestic Violence: A Case Study in Detroit and New Zealand,' in H. Hotaling, D. Kinkelhor, J.T. Kirkpatrick and M.A. Straus (eds) *Coping with Family Violence: Research and Policy Perspectives*, pp. 169–182. Newbury Park, CA: Sage.

Buzawa, E. S. and Buzawa, C. G. (1990) *Domestic Violence: The Criminal Justice Response*, London: Sage.

Buzawa, E. S. and Buzawa, C. G. (1993) 'Opening the Door — The Changing Police Response to Domestic Violence,' in R. G. Dunham and G. P. Alpert (eds) *Critical Issues in Policing: Contemporary Readings*, pp. 551–567. Prospect Heights: Illinois Waveland.

Chan, J. B. L. (1997) *Changing Police Culture: Policing in a Multicultural Society*, Cambridge: Cambridge University Press.

Chan, J. (1996) *Legislating Feminism in a Paternalistic State*, Paper Presented at the Joint International Conference of the Law and Society Association and Research Committee on Sociology of Law (ISA), July 10–13, 1996 in Glasgow, Scotland.

Chatterton, M. R. (1978) 'The Supervision of Patrol Work under the Fixed Points System,' in S. Holdaway (ed.) *The British Police*, pp. 83–101, London: Edward Arnold.

Choi, A. (1989) *Policing Domestic Disturbances: Police Responses and Risks*, PhD Dissertation, York University, Canada.

Choi, A. (1995) *Policing Domestic Disturbances: A Research Review of Police Response*, Working Paper Series, Department of Sociology, National University of Singapore.

Choi, A. and Edleson, J. L. (1995) 'Advocating Legal Intervention in Wife Assaults,' *Journal of Interpersonal Violence*, 10(3): 243–258.

Dobash, R., Dobash, R., Cavanagh, K., and Lewis, R. (1996) *Research Evaluation of Programmes for Violent Men*, Edinburgh: The Scottish Office Central Research Unit.

Dolon, R. & Meagher, M. S. (1986) 'Police Practices and Attitudes Toward Domestic Violence,' *Journal of Police Science and Administration*, 14(3), 187–192.

Dutton, G. D. (1995) *The Domestic Assault of Women: Psychological and Criminal Justice Perspectives*, Vancouver: UBC Press.

Edwards, S. (1989) *Policing 'Domestic' Violence: Women, the Law and the State*, London, Sage.

Ferraro, J. K. (1989a) 'The Legal Response to Woman Battering in the United States,' in J. Hanmer, J. Radford, and E. A. Stanko (eds) *Women, Policing, and Male Violence: International Perspectives*, pp. 155–184, London: Routledge.

Ferraro, J. K. (1989b) 'Policing Woman Battering,' *Social Problems*, 36(1) 61–74.

Field, M. and Field, H. (1973) 'Marital Violence and the Criminal Process: Neither Justice Nor Peace,' *Social Service Review*, 47(2): 221–40.

Ford, D. A. (1987) *The Impact of Police Officers' Attitudes Towards Victims on the Disinclination to Arrest Wife Batters*. Paper Presented at the Third Conference for Family Violence Researchers, Durham, NH.

Goh Chok Tong (1993) 'Guarding the Sacred Institutions of Marriage and Family,' *Speeches* 17(3): 28–33.

Hanmer, J. (1989) 'Women and Policing in Britain,' in J. Hanmer, J. Radford, and E. A. Stanko, (eds) *Women, Policing, and Male Violence: International Perspectives*, pp. 90–124, London: Routledge.

Hanmer, J., J. Radford, and E. A. Stanko, (eds) (1989) *Women, Policing, and Male Violence: International Perspectives*, London: Routledge.

Hatty, S. E. (1989) 'Policing and Male Violence in Australia,' in J. Hanmer, J. Radford, and E. A. Stanko, (eds) *Women, Policing, and Male Violence: International Perspectives*, pp. 70–89, London: Routledge.

Holdaway, S. (1983) *Inside the British Police*, Oxford: Basil Blackwell.

Hoyle and Sanders (2000) Police response to domestic violence: from victim choice to victim empowerment, *British Journal of Criminology*, 40(1), 14–36.

Lerner, G. (1986) *The Creation of Patriarchy*, New York: Oxford University Press.

Lim Boon Heng (1994) 'Family Values,' *Speeches*, 18(6): 67–74.

Loving, N. and Farmer, M. (1980) *Police Handling of Spouse Abuse and Wife Beating Calls: A Guide for Police Managers*, Washington DC: Police Executive Research Forum.

Manning, P. and Van Maanen (1978) *Policing: A View from the Street*, Santa Monica, CA: Goodyear Publishing.

Marenin, O. (1983) Parking Tickets and Class repression: The Concept of Policing in Critical Theories of Criminal Justice, *Contemporary Crises*, 6, 241–66.

Narayanan, G. (2006) 'Between the Devil and the Deep-Blue Sea: Conceptualising Victims' Experiences of Policing in Domestic Violence in Singapore,' *The Australian and New Zealand Journal of Criminology*, 39(1): 90–108.

Narayanan, G. (2008) *Policing Marital Violence in Singapore*, Leiden: Brill.

Parnas, R. I. (1967) 'The Police Response to Domestic Disturbance,' *Wisconsin Law Review*, 2(4):914–60.

Parnas, R. I. (1971) 'Police Discretion and Diversion of Incidents of Intra-Family,' *Law and Contemporary Problems*, 36(4), 539–565.

Purushotam, N. (1992) 'Women and Knowledge/Power: Notes on the Singaporean Dilemma,' in K. C. Ban, A. Pakir, and C. K. Tong (eds) *Imagining Singapore*, pp. 320–361, Singapore: Times Academic Press.

Reiner, R. (1985) *The Politics of the Police*, London: Harvester Wheatsheaf.

Reiner, R. (1992) *The Politics of the Police*, 2nd Edition, London: Harvester Wheatsheaf.

Rodan, G. (1993) 'Preserving the One-party State in Contemporary Singapore,' in H. Robinson and G. Rodan (eds) *Southeast Asia in the 1990s: Authoritarianism, Democracy and Capitalism*, pp. 75–108, Australia: Allen and Unwin.

Seet Ai Mee (1989) 'Women: Maximise Your Potential,' *Speeches*, 18(3): 92–96.

Sheptycki, J. W .E. (1993) *Innovations in Policing Domestic Violence*, Aldershot: Avebury.

Smith, D. and Klein, J. (1984) 'Police Control of Interpersonal Disputes,' *Social Problem*, 31(4): 468–81.

Smith, D. J. and Gray, J. (1983) *Police and People in London*, London: Policy Studies Institute.

Stanko, E. A. (1989) 'Missing the Mark? Policing Battering,' in J. Hanmer, J. Radford, and E. A. Stanko, (eds) *Women, Policing, and Male Violence: International Perspectives*, pp. 46–69, London: Routledge.

Stark, E. (1993) 'Mandatory Arrest of Batterers: A Reply to Critics,' *American Behavioral Scientist*, 36(5): 651–80.

The Straits Times, 28 Sep 1995, 2 Nov 1995, 3 Nov 1995, 4 Nov 1995, 3 May 1997, Sep 9 1998, Nov 17 1998.

Waaland, P. and Keeley, S. (1985) 'Police Decision-making in Wife Abuse: The Impact of Legal and Extra-legal Factors,' *Law and Human Behavior*, 9(4), 355–366.

Waddington, P. A. J. (1999) *Policing Citizens: Authority and Rights*, London: UCL Press.

Walter, J. D. (1981) 'Police in the Middle: A Study of Small City Police Interaction in Domestic Disputes,' *Journal of Police Science and Administration*, 9(3): 243–261.

Worden, R. E. and Pollitz, A. A. (1984) 'Police Arrests in Domestic Disturbances: A Further Look,' *Law and Society Review*, 18(1): 105–119.

Zoomer, J. O. (1989) 'Policing Woman Beating in the Netherlands,' in J. Hanmer, J. Radford, and E. A. Stanko, (eds) *Women, Policing, and Male Violence: International Perspectives*, pp. 125–154, London: Routledge.

Government documents

Singapore Penal Code (1985) Government of Singapore, Singapore

White Paper on Shared Values (1991) Government of Singapore, Singapore

CHAPTER

7

Malaysia's Domestic Violence Law

An Epic Passage and the Clash of Gender, Cultural and Religious Rights

MAZNAH MOHAMAD

The twenty-six years during which a plethora of interest groups lobbied for the Domestic Violence Act (DVA) of Malaysia became an outstanding example of drafting a law from the basics. Epic in nature, the outcome of the struggles led by feminist organizations resulted in a piece of legislation that reflected numerous and varying degrees of compromises and accommodations. Although it was hailed as a landmark law, the relevance of the DVA's concepts and provisions and the effectiveness of its implementation continue to be tested and challenged. Why is this so?

One of the ironies of the DVA's weaknesses can be traced to the process of its passage, which was democratic and inclusive. It was also a contest that saw women battling at least four forces — the executive and the legislature (politicians), Syariah Islamists, police and the judiciary. In this context, women range from women's civil society groups to ordinary women victims and plaintiffs in the court. Such an extensive and intensive engagement over the issue of gender-based violence resulted in the DVA as it stands today. Malaysia's DVA is a success story in so far as it reflects the interests of a variety of stakeholders involved in the statute's passage. However, the law is not wholly satisfactory as a tool for protecting vulnerable women or punishing offenders. The literal *body*, replete with its rights and autonomy and the crux of the legislation's motive, was meant to be freed, but remains trapped within family and the state.

This chapter documents and analyzes the history of the DVA's passage in Malaysia. By doing so, I hope to show that the ambiguity of family and of control over one's body remains the most contentious issue in the modern state. The historical development of the DVA follows three periods — the early years, the campaign years and the stocktaking years. As these periods are uncovered, I show how law-making is a highly involved movement, although what is being negotiated and contested ultimately reflects a compromise rather than the completion of an agenda. Domestic violence is to a family what war is to a nation. The underlying logic of both is territory and power — both family and the nation-state guard the former and use the latter in the event of a transgression (see Das 2008). However, the struggle to enact a domestic violence law is also about building rights consciousness, something which neither the family nor the state will be able to suppress, once the project takes off.

The chapter is organized as follows: I first trace the consciousness around gender-based violence in its early years and the language and meaning attached to it by the legal system. I question how violence in the home is conceived by the judiciary. Judgements in the Syariah and civil courts are compared to differentiate the experiences of Muslim and non-Muslim women when they seek justice in an untenable marriage. Before the late 1980s it was a time when the "subjectivities of suffering" had yet to be legally recognized (see Sen 2010: 378), with gender-based violence ambiguously, if not improperly, conceived by legal constructions.

The second part of the chapter is an account of the campaign years, the most intensive period of contestation and negotiation between feminists, government, media, police and various other civil society groups over how a law to curb violence against women (VAW) would be shaped. It describes the collaboration and conflict between autonomous women's groups and others and the contentious debates waged between secular feminists and Syariah Islamists. I hope to demonstrate that the discourse on domestic violence was not merely about law-making but also about struggles to constitute new political and linguistic consensus and cultural and legal norms.

In the final part of the chapter, I assess the aftermath of the DVA and its limitations in resolving gender-based violence, calling this the stocktaking years. While the DVA may be less effective than expected, it has also been most successful in sustaining women's agenda in public life. The notions of control, discipline and punishment of the family, or rather the *body* of its wayward members, underscore the dynamics of contestation behind the DVA's passage and implementation.

The early years

Violence is only real, pending divorce

Before the mid-1990s, domestic violence was interpreted differently in various courts in Malaysia. The civil or secular court had access to the Penal Code, under which acts of battery and assault would be considered criminal offences, causing hurt and liable to be punished under the law. Nevertheless, wife-battery was never charged under this law. Women could only use battery as grounds to apply for restraining orders against their husbands; however, only in the case of a pending divorce application could the Penal Code be applied to restrain abusers. Judges were also able to cite case British judgements as precedents, as long as the applicable English common law was passed before 1956. Such legal moves favoured women's application for protection, as in the cases of *Jayakumari a/p Arul Pragasam v. Suriya Narayanan a/l v. Ramanathan* (1996) and *Chan Ah Moi v. Phang Wai Ann* (1995).

Jayakumari, for example, was successful in getting a court order to evict her violent husband from their matrimonial home. This was in 1996, before the DVA came into effect. Jayakumari first left her matrimonial home after being assaulted by her husband. However, in March 1996, she filed a petition for judicial separation and sought an order to restrain her husband from further assaulting her and to get him to vacate the matrimonial home. Although the DVA was not in force yet, the judge applied a precedent used in an English court. He cited a 1953 case, in which the English judge noted that it is the right of the wife to stay in the matrimonial home while keeping the husband away from it as "otherwise the wife will be bullied out of her remedy or deterred by pressure from seeking the help of the court" (*Jayakumari a/p Arul Pragasam v. Suriya Narayanan a/l v. Ramanathan* 1996).

A similar judgement, using the English common law as precedent, was that in the case of *Chan Ah Moi v. Phang Wai Ann* (1995), in which Chan had applied for a non-molestation order pending the release of her convicted husband from jail. He had earlier been convicted of causing her serious injuries and had been imprisoned for two years. The order was to exclude him (after his release from prison) from any part of the matrimonial home and its vicinity. English cases were cited to grant Chan the exclusion order to prohibit her husband from entering her home.[1]

This was how judgements were handed down to women who sought justice from their intimate but violent partners. Domestic violence was wholly attached to a matrimonial condition, and it was only if women decided to end the marriage that spousal abuse could be used as a justification. The above cases dealt with women plaintiffs who were ready and able to do so. If they chose to stay in a violent marriage, no amount of complaints over wife-battery could lead to conviction, since the law did not recognize it as an offence.

However, there were some highly inconsistent court rulings in cases of violence against Muslim women. In all cases, a complaint of violence could only be made to the Syariah court upon application for divorce under either *taklik* or *fasakh*. *Taklik* divorce is automatically and judicially granted to a woman (without spousal consent) if the court is satisfied that a husband has breached some stipulations inserted in the marital contract, wife-beating being one of them. If wife-beating is not stipulated in the marriage contract for divorce, then a woman can apply for divorce under the terms of *fasakh*. One of the conditions for a *fasakh* divorce is cruelty and wife-beating.

Nevertheless, in earlier legislations, in order to be valid as grounds for divorce wife-abuse had to be interpreted as a form of cruelty traversing the bounds of "Islamic law and adat". In *Hasnah v. Saad* (1983), Hasnah complained of being beaten on the face, right ear, chest and back. A doctor's report was also submitted as evidence. On the marriage certificate, signed by her husband, was the following condition for *taklik*:

> I cannot assault, beat or torture or hurt my wife Hasnah bt. Hashim by any means that exceeds the bounds of Islamic law and adat. Whenever I commit any of these, and that she files a complaint with the kadi and upon verification of her allegations, the kadi shall witness the divorce of one *talaq* on my wife Hasnah bt. Hashim. (ibid)

Hasnah's divorce application was granted based on the *kadi*'s (the judge of an Islamic court) assessment that the assault had "exceeded the bounds of Islamic law and *adat*" (*melebehi hukum syarak dan adat).* Clearly, this stipulation seemed to indicate that some form of violence may be considered acceptable and within the bounds of Islam.

If the judge was not convinced that the violence was "habitual", the application would be rejected as in the case of an application for *fasakh* divorce in *Hairun v. Omar* (1993). The evidence of assault was supported by reports from two separate doctors. The *kadi* accepted the veracity of Hairun's allegations, but did not grant the divorce as he was not satisfied that the offence committed could be classified as being "habitually hurting" (*lazim menyakiti*).[2] Since the beating was inflicted twice (as admitted by the husband), the *kadi* interpreted that this did not indicate habitual assaults.

Islamic stipulations, such as the rejection of female witnesses and the acceptance of sworn oaths as claims to truth in courts, were also applied to deny women their right to be free from their violent husbands. In the case of *Adibah v. Abdul Rani* (1986), Adibah was denied *fasakh* despite providing a witness to the assault and submitting a medical report as evidence of her injury. The *kadi* ruled that the testimony of Adibah's witness, her female domestic helper, could not be accepted. According to the *kadi*, under Islamic law (*hukum Syarak*), only the testimonies of two male witnesses or one male witness together with two female witnesses can be accepted in court. To add insult to injury (literally), the *kadi* then asked if Abdul Rani would swear upon the Quran (*sumpah Syarie*) to deny his wrongdoing. He did, and read out the following oath: "Wallahi, Wabillahi, Watallahi, I, . . . hereby named swear that I did not assault or beat or torture or hurt my wife . . . as alleged by her in this case". Based on this declaration, Adibah's application to leave her abusive husband was rejected.

It was only in the mid-1980s, when Islamic Family Law statutes (such as the Administration of Islamic Family Law Enactment 1985 of Selangor) were passed in almost all states, that Muslim women were able to securely use domestic violence as grounds for divorce. Under the Islamic Family Law statutes, the definition of wife-abuse was expanded to include non-physical hurt and the notion "habitual assault" was no longer applied to verify or deny women's claims of spousal violence against them.

In *Hairun v. Omar* (1993), Hairun's divorce application was rejected (before her appeal) by the *kadi* court on the grounds that she was not "habitually assaulted" by her husband. She appealed against this decision to the Selangor Syariah Appeals Committee (*Jawatankuasa Ulang Bicara Syar'iah*)[3] and her appeal to obtain divorce under *fasakh* was granted. The Appeals Committee ruled that the term "habitually assaults", as contained in the legislation, was wrongly interpreted by the *kadi*, and that the beatings suffered by Hairun were indeed sufficient to fulfil the *fasakh* clause. This judgement expanded the definition of cruelty towards wives to include non-physical hurt:

> the principle of marriage dissolution or *fasakh* due to abuse or *dharar* is not merely admissible only if the hurt and cruelty is afflicted upon the physical body, but includes a wider range of actions. This includes refusal to speak with one's wife, ignoring her or turning away one's face away from hers in bed, preferring to be hospitable to other women other than the wife, any form of beating which brings hurt and it does not mean that the beating has to be done repeatedly or habitually. (*Hairun v. Omar* 1993)

By 1995, the judicial system appeared more accepting of wife abuse as grounds for divorce. At the Syariah High Court of Terengganu, a woman's application for divorce in *Hasnah v. Zaaba* (1995) was granted without reference to the habitual nature of the abuse or if the beating was within Islamic limits. The judge even acknowledged that the husband, "had not only beaten and disparaged his wife, but also forced violent sexual intercourse on her". The judgement seemed to be drawing upon the precedence of *Hairun v. Omar* (1993). The definition of cruelty towards wives as extending beyond physical assault was restated in this case.

No protection against violence for Muslim women

To protect themselves against violence by spouses, while a divorce is pending, women could apply for a restraining order through civil courts. For the most part, only non-Muslim women could make use of this right, as in *Jayakumari a/p Arul Pragasam v. Suriya Narayanan a/l v.*

Ramanathan (1996) and *Chan Ah Moi v. Phang Wai Ann* (1995). Muslim women were not able to do so, as the case *Faridah bte Dato Talib v. Mohamed Habibullah bin Mahmood* (1990) illustrates. Faridah had sought divorce by *fasakh* at the Syariah court on the grounds of assault and battery by her husband Mohamed Habibullah. However, she had to apply to the civil court for an injunction to restrain her husband from further abusing her. The High Court judge considered assault and battery as a civil and criminal wrong and ruled that although it involved a Muslim marriage, such an offence did not fall within the jurisdiction of the Syariah enactment and court. As the acts of battery and assault had caused hurt, they were considered criminal offences under the Penal Code.

However, on 28 April 1989, Faridah's husband Habibullah challenged the High Court order by appealing to the Supreme Court. The question posed in *Mohamed Habibullah bin Mahmood v. Faridah bte Dato Talib* (1992) was whether the High Court had the jurisdiction to hear the case as it involved a Muslim marriage and should have, therefore, been heard in a Syariah court. The judges referred to the new amendment to the Constitution, Article 121 (1A), that came into effect on 10 June 1988. Under this new provision, in cases involving Muslim personal laws, the jurisdiction of the civil court was separated from the Syariah court. In trying to decide if the case fell under the jurisdiction of civil or Syariah courts, the judges referred to the Islamic Family Law (Federal Territory) Act 1984, which gave the Syariah court power to "order any person to refrain from forcing his or her society on his or her spouse or former spouse and from other acts of molestation". Thus, Faridah's allegation of assault and battery was interpreted to fall within the jurisdiction of the Syariah court. Hence, the interim injunction granted to Faridah by the High Court was dissolved. According to the judges, the complaint related to the husband's conduct during the course of a Muslim marriage; thus, it was considered neither a civil nor a criminal matter as suggested by the High Court judge. To the Supreme Court judges, the alleged assault and battery merely constituted a *matrimonial offence or misconduct* to be dealt with by the Syariah court. Faridah was also not entitled to sue her husband for damages since the Married Women Ordinance 1957 considered a husband and wife as one entity and taking up a suit would be like suing oneself. [4] To quote the judgement:

> the root of her complaint relates to the conduct of Habibullah as a husband during the course of a Muslim marriage. It is not really a civil or criminal matter simpliciter as suggested by the trial judge. *In fact and in law, the alleged assault and battery constitute matrimonial offence or misconduct by Habibullah* which may entitle Faridah to a dissolution of her marriage under Muslim law . . . *Since the complaint relates to marriage, the matter should, if at all, be dealt with by the court in its matrimonial and not in its general civil jurisdiction* . . . the application

> under O 18 r 19 *ought to have been allowed forthwith on the ground of prejudice and unfairness to Habibullah* in the proceedings pending against him in the Syariah Court. (emphasis added) (*Mohamed Habibullah bin Mahmood v. Faridah bte Dato Talib* 1992)

Faridah's husband, Habibullah, had the law on his side based on the following legal concept of being married and Muslim:

- Muslim couples come under the jurisdiction of the Syariah as there are clauses under Islamic statutes to protect women from assault by husbands.
- Civil courts cannot adjudicate on matters under the Syariah court because of the amendment to Article 121 (a) of the Constitution.
- Spouses cannot sue each other under tort (for claims arising from injury to person or reputation) under Section 9(2) of the Married Women Ordinance 1957.

The legal system, Syariah or civil, treated violence against married women as mere matrimonial misconduct rather than an offence punishable by law. The Married Women Ordinance 1957 considered a man and a woman in marriage to be one person and, therefore, not entitled to damage claims against one another when an injury is inflicted upon their persons (or body). This law allowed the couple to sue one another if there was damage to their *property*, but not to their *bodies* or *reputation*! Yet another legislation that worked against Muslim women at that time was the separation of civil and Syariah jurisdictions on matrimonial matters. This proved to be a great obstacle in Faridah's attempts to obtain justice, compelling her to renounce her status as a Muslim during the course of her legal action. It was stated in the court statement that Faridah believed that "Islam could not provide enough protection for battered wife (*sic*)", and thus took steps to revoke her faith by means of a statutory declaration before a Commissioner of Oath. It was ascertained later that she retracted this renunciation.[5] Nevertheless, it suggested that at that time, the Syariah court was less reliable in guaranteeing women safety from their abusive spouses.

The campaign years

Rising awareness about the battery of women in their own homes, the unequal treatment that abused women experienced under different jurisdictions and the accumulated experiences of women's shelters in dealing with domestic abuse cases were some of the many reasons for public support for a domestic violence law in Malaysia. One of the first few conceptual issues that arose was whether this law, covering family matters, would be drafted as a criminal or a civil legislation and whether it would cover Muslims as well. In Malaysia, it was the legal aspect of family that was being debated rather than its cultural significance. This was because Malaysia did not have an explicit "family code" or any written constitutional provision extolling family as the moral fibre of the nation (as in the Indian, Philippine and Indonesian cases); instead, the family's supposed sanctity was guarded by civil or Islamic law. In the 1970s, a Royal Commission was set up to study and propose reforms to marriage and divorce laws affecting non-Muslims. This resulted in the Law Reform (Marriage and Divorce) Act 1976, which, among other stipulations, abolished polygamy and set eighteen as the minimum age of marriage for non-Muslims. Although the commission's brief did not cover Muslims, Islamic marriages were also scrutinized around the same concerns. This resulted in the first Islamic Family Law Acts, with three state enactments passed in Kelantan, Malacca and Negri Sembilan in 1983, and one covering the Federal Territory in 1984 (Siraj 1994: 563–565). Hence, the delineation of jurisdictional turfs between the "Islamic family" and the "Other family" was established. Much of the DVA campaign was thus taken up by advocacy, debates and resistance around the question of who had authority over the Islamic family. There followed a long, combative and arduous process of organizing and negotiating. There were several watershed moments during the course of this campaign, covering the years below:

- 1985–1994: VAW campaign started, DVA drafted
- 1994: DVA adopted by Parliament
- 1996: DVA re-questioned, debated, defended and gazetted
- 1997: DVA implementation issues/police versus women

1985–1994: VAW campaign started, DVA drafted

A two-day workshop/exhibition/festival on VAW organized by five women's groups in 1985 now serves as the most iconic marker of the campaign's beginnings.[6] Eventually dubbed the Joint-Action-Group (JAG) event, and later as the JAG-VAW group, this was one of the more memorable events that ushered in a new era of the autonomous women's movement in the country (see Ng, Mohamad and tan 2006).

As one of the participants of this event, held in a worker's community hall in Petaling Jaya, I recall the festive atmosphere of the occasion. The two-storey hall was filled with some 2,000 women, men and children. Some men were recruited to take charge of childcare at the event. The organizational effort put into this event was considerable; it was driven by spirited women, most of them young professionals. People were drawn to "women's events", partly because women's issues were new then and not given much public airing. The occasion was meant to be inclusive with the target group being the multicultural community. The print and television media covered the event well and helped to launch the cause in a visible way. Ivy Josiah, a long-serving executive director of the Women's Aid Organization (WAO) recounted the "atmosphere and momentum" of the event as "incredible":

> We had so many people involved. We had artistes like Marion D'Cruz and dancers as well as stage performers participating. My role at that particular time was to dance in the item 'Arise'. It was great.[7]

Following this momentous JAG event and VAW campaign, the Rape Law was successfully amended (Siraj 1994: 570–571). A (woman) deputy minister in the Prime Minister's Department, Siti Zaharah Sulaiman then announced that the department's Women's Affairs Secretariat would be inviting views and opinions of women's organizations, relevant ministries such as the Home Ministry and the Attorney-General's chambers to participate in the drafting of the DVA (Zahara 1989). A National Committee to draft the DVA was chaired by Mehrun Siraj, the then president of the Association for Women Lawyers (AWL). At this point, the government seemed serious in committing to women's rights and even devoted an exclusive chapter to women's development in its Sixth Malaysia Plan for 1991–1995 (Siraj 1994: 572).

AWL together with the All-Women's Action Movement (AWAM) and WAO embarked on a nationwide campaign against domestic violence. A Mother's Day workshop titled "Confronting Domestic Violence" was coordinated by AWAM in 1989. A postcard signature campaign by WAO collected some 14,000 signatures in the same year. In Penang, for example, even a lesser-known organization such as the Federated Kar Har Tong Youth Division worked with the Women's Crisis Centre (WCC) to rally local support by collecting signatures for a national petition to demand the bill (Zahara 1989).

The WCC also published a series of informative pieces in the June 1990 issue of its newsletter *Herizons*. There were articles such as "Why the Need for the DVA", "Present Legal Framework for Victims of Domestic Violence" and "Common Questions/Issues Raised on DVA and Suggested Answers".[8] Later, when DVA was beginning to attract the attention of Muslims, the magazine carried a piece on "The Islamic Perspective of Domestic Violence" (Salbiah 1991).

Four years after it was first announced by the government, the proposed bill had still not been tabled in Parliament. By then, there was a new minister in charge of women's affairs. Napsiah Omar became the new Minister for National Unity and Social Development, replacing Siti Zaharah and her portfolio. In 1992, at a public ceremony, the minister officially received the draft bill prepared by the National Committee. However, more lobbying and pressure were needed to push the bill through the parliament. In 1993, a public forum organized by AWAM assessed the progress of the bill. According to Cecilia Ng, one of the early movers of the project:

> The DV Act is more complicated because of the Muslim-non-Muslim implications in it — probably that was why feet were dragging. AWAM came out with a booklet on how to lobby members of Parliament, so the campaign activities shifted more towards community-based lobbying of policy makers.[9]

Religion seemed to have come between the bill and its passage. There was a lot of resistance, not just from the Muslim/Syariah faction (or the Syariah Islamists), which considered anything pertaining to Muslim marriage within their jurisdiction, but also from those reluctant to accept domestic violence as a criminal offence. Mehrun Siraj, who chaired the National Committee for the draft bill, reflected on the process:

> The police kept telling us why they do not like to record the reports because when it was time to investigate and take action, the women would draw back, saying that the perpetrator is the father of their children and so forth. That's why they tell us that women do not really want to take criminal action against their husbands, they should be given the alternative of instituting civil action.[10]

There was still uncertainty over whether the original DVA was meant to be civil or criminal because some sections believed that family offences did not deserve criminal treatment. More immediately, the committee had to find a way to avoid the conflict of jurisdiction between Muslims and non-Muslims. Ostensibly the way out, to include all Muslims and non-Muslims under a common law, was to have the DVA drafted as a criminal legislation (Afida Mastura 2000: 79; Ng, Maznah and tan 2006: 52–57). However, the bill also needed to accommodate the views of Islamic scholars who had expressed dissatisfaction with marital rape being included in the definition of domestic violence, claiming that this was not acceptable under Islamic law (Mohd Shahrizad 1994). Neither a civil nor a criminal domestic violence legislation seemed likely to please all factions all the time.

1994: DVA adopted by Parliament

By 1994, the campaign had seen two different women ministers. Finally, when it was tabled in the parliament, the bill's passage was dubbed the "Cinderella Act" because of its "turbulent midnight passage" through the House of Representatives (Padman 1995a). On the very last day of the parliamentary session, amidst opposition from other legislators, Minister

Napsiah Omar was determined to push the bill through before midnight since failure to do so would mean presenting it at another sitting, to be held two months later; such a wait, although not long, could spell uncertainty for the future of the bill.

Although the DVA was finally approved by the parliament, the struggle to have it gazetted and implemented continued. It was two more years later, in 1996, that the "Cinderella Act" or the DVA 1994 could be enforced. English dailies, such as the *New Straits Times* (*NST*) steadfastly supported women's interests in getting the DVA enforced. Women journalists at these publications carefully strategized the publication of public debates to suit the agenda of the law's final adoption. In 1995, the paper started running a fortnightly column under its Woman's Desk section called "Women Behind Closed Doors". The column carried news and features on domestic violence as a means of exerting pressure to have the act enforced (Padman 1995b). Notable journalists responsible for keeping the issue alive through their writings included Padmaja Padman, Muharyani Othman, Pang Yin Fong and Esther Tan.

Momentum was sustained through reportage of women's activities such as the campaign carnival on 26 March 1995. Jointly organized by AWAM, WAO, WCC, Persatuan Sahabat Wanita Selangor (PSWS) and Women's Development Collective (WDC), the occasion was timed to celebrate International Women's Day. The event, attended by more than 2,000 people, replicated the festive atmosphere of the historic 1985 JAG event:

> There were people in wheelchairs, parents pushing their children in prams, students, housewives, office and factory workers, domestic workers, professionals and businessfolks. Orange and purple-coloured balloons and banners with anti-violence messages, as a school band and a kompang group further boosted the enthusiasm of the participants. (Pang 1995)

By mid-1996, the DVA was still not in force. Islamic religious authorities, who were represented at meetings to draft the act, were purported to be changing their minds. Another lady, Zaleha Ismail, was appointed Minister of National Unity and Social Development, replacing Napsiah Omar. She was quoted as being hesitant about the implementation of the DVA, passing the buck to the Islamic faction that was "not in favour of the Act applying to Muslim women as they feel all matters pertaining to Muslims should come under the jurisdiction of the syariah court, the power of which they fear could be undermined if the Act applies to all" (Muharyani 1996a). This news was met with furious reactions from women's groups. The JAG–VAW swiftly shot off a memorandum to the minister stating:

> the Act is a criminal law as it operates within the Penal Code, a Federal

> Law which applies to all persons in Malaysia. This means that the courts that have jurisdiction over the DVA will be the general civil courts and not the syariah courts . . . A conflict of jurisdiction does not arise . . . In the same manner that the Child Protection Act was passed by Parliament and implemented to apply to Muslims and non-Muslims, so should the DVA. (*NST* 1996a)

On 8 March 1996, in conjunction with International Women's Day, women's groups confronted the minister at the opening of a national seminar on women. At the hotel where the seminar was held, she was handed a memorandum from JAG-VAW. Outside the hotel, about 50 women held an "International Women's Day" banner and chanted, "DVA. Act now, right now". The news report the next day published the minister's defensive response to the demonstration:

> There are sensitive issues involved and they have to be handled delicately — as the Malays say — *seperti menarik rambut dalam tepung — rambut jangan putus, tepung jangan berselerak* (Roughly translated, it means 'in settling a dispute, one must not antagonize any party but work towards an amicable solution'). (Muharyani 1996b)

1996: DVA re-questioned, debated, defended and gazetted

Following the minister's response, the *NST* wasted no time in reporting that the Secretary-General of the opposition Democratic Action Party (DAP), Lim Kit Siang, would be tabling a question in the parliament to enquire why the act had yet to be enforced (Muharyani 1996b). The very next day, Cabinet Minister In-Charge of Islamic Affairs, Abdul Hamid Othman, defended the delay by claiming that a study on the effect of the DVA's implementation on Muslims had yet to be completed, noting that "a few things under *syarak* are not considered violent but under the Act, they are considered violent" (Azeman 1996).[11]

As the issue of Muslim versus non-Muslim jurisprudence began to rear its insistent head, the campaign for the DVA turned into a multi-pronged contest which saw feminists battling the Syariah Islamists or those who did not want Muslims to be covered under the DVA. Even after parliamentary endorsement of the DVA in 1995, the government and politicians representing the ruling party were anxious about how the law would resonate with their "sensitive" constituencies, namely the Islamic lobby which was then aggressively pushing for exclusive judicial control over Muslims.

To put this issue in context, the *NST* ran an interview with one of the early drafters of the law whose identity was, however, not revealed. The drafter explained the split in what seemed to be two camps around the DVA. On the one hand, there were people who "wanted to classify domestic violence as a crime in itself rather than simply an attachment to the Penal Code because they felt that a crime against a family member was in some ways more serious than that against a stranger". On the other hand, there were those who considered this "too drastic" and were worried that, "the Act creates the crime of marital rape, and allows a wife to bring this charge against her husband". This "worried" camp wanted the DVA to be merely pegged with the Penal Code, thus only emphasizing the protective rather than the punitive aspect of the law (*NST* 1996b).

The charting of divided opinions opened the floodgate of vigorous debates around the act. The newspaper compiled a story detailing the divided opinions on the Act. A team of their reporters researched the cause for this and found that Islamic authorities believed the Act:

- Contained certain provisions contrary to Islamic laws.
- Caused an overlap of jurisdiction between civil and Syariah law since cases of ill-treatment of wives were covered under the latter, which meant Muslims did not need protection under the DVA.
- Treated marital rape as domestic violence, which Islam did not consider valid.
- Was applicable only to non-Muslims.

Arguments by women's groups in opposition to the above were:

- The DVA was a criminal law and not a civil law (hence it covered Muslims and non-Muslims).
- The act did not just protect wives but all family members, unlike Islamic law which only applied to married couples.
- For a domestic violence law to be passed for Muslims, each state would have to enact a separate legislation, meaning that the country would need 14 laws in all provided that each state legislature was able to pass such a law. The content of each state's law could also vary.

The report ended by opining that, "it obviously looks strange and unfair for one ethnic group to be left out from enjoying the benefits of the DVA when the incidence of domestic violence which transcends race and religious belief, appears to be on the increase" (Muharyani, Pang, Juneita and Alina 1996).

A week after the publication of this feature, the government relented and announced that the DVA would be enforced for all — Muslims and non-Muslims. A high-ranking bureaucrat, in-charge of Muslim affairs under the Prime Minister's Department, conceded that Pusat Islam (the Islamic Centre) had given its "full blessings for the law to be implemented", with written consent delivered to the National Unity and Social Development Ministry (*NST* 1996c).

Oddly enough, even this did not convince Minister Zaleha Ismail that the DVA could finally be used. There seemed to be pressure exerted on her to continue stalling the implementation of the DVA from other quarters. She said that a committee comprising police and ministry officials would submit a report to the cabinet before deciding if the act could be enforced (Choong 1996). Simultaneously, Muslim professionals began entering the fray by stating their position on the DVA in letters to the press. News about the minister's dithering was followed by a letter from Zaitoon Othman, the President of the Muslim Lawyers Association of Malaysia. She objected to the DVA and insisted on the Muslim and non-Muslim jurisdictional separation in family matters:

> In respect of the provisions in the Domestic Violence Act, which are clearly against Islamic doctrines, Article 11 (1) of the Federal Constitution applies... Central to this proposal is the recognition of the constitutional and historical reality — that laws affecting Muslim family matters, be they criminal or civil — have always been within the jurisdiction of the State Legislature. (1996)

The next day, Padmaja Padman, a senior journalist who initiated the "Behind the Doors" column in the women's page shot a rebuttal:

> the way the DVA was hijacked by quarters with no direct jurisdiction over its implementation is without precedent. How most of us stood by quietly and allowed this to happen must be beyond comprehension to survivors of abuse. Official explanations have been less than satisfactory or convincing, given that this is a law that has been passed by Parliament, assented to by the Yang di-Pertuan Agong and gazetted according to procedure. (1996c)

An editorial on this was equally scathing, especially of the minister's role:

> Following the withdrawal of Islam-related objection that delayed enforcement of the Act, Minister Datin Paduka Zaleha Ismail now sees it fit to prolong the agony of domestic violence survivors with inept touches of her own . . . what makes this thoroughly unacceptable situation is that the minister had, on March 8, asserted she would implement the DVA "today" if it were left to her. It has, but she has not even set a date. (*NST* 1996d)

Even a statement from the opposition was published in the *NST*, which was unusual given the paper's pro-government bent. Lim Kit Siang, the DAP secretary-general, urged the minister "to immediately put her signature" to the regulations (*NST* 1996e). Karpal Singh, another opposition politician, proposed a motion of disappointment in the parliament to chide the minister for her failure to enforce the Act. Although the motion was rejected, this did not stop the *NST* from publishing his admonishment of the minister, "who should be leading the cause", but "has now turned out to be the stumbling block" (1996f).

Within 10 days of what appeared to be a continuous repartee communicated through the press, the minister finally relented by announcing in Parliament that the Act would be enforced in early June (Choong, Ramlan and Mohd Yusof 1996). To back up this new commitment, a letter by Noor Farida Ariffin, representing the AWL, was published on the same day. This was in reply to the letter sent by Zaitoon Othman. Noor Farida expressed her astonishment at Zaitoon's statement claiming that the DVA's provisions were "clearly against Islamic doctrines":

> Zaitoon has also advocated that the Act be enforced with immediate effect, but to exclude Muslims. This is a position which is strongly opposed by the Association of Women Lawyers, Sisters in Islam and other women's groups. We cannot see any valid reason why Muslim women should be excluded from protection against violence within the family afforded by the Act. (1996)

The debates persisted for a month after the minister's agreement. Rahmah Hashim, head of the Women's Affairs Bureau of the Muslim Youth Movement of Malaysia (ABIM), wrote to the press insisting on the primacy of the Islamic position on this issue, condoning some form of violence and "stealthily" using the disciplining of children as an example:

> Islam has its own perspective on the roles of parents and children, and education within the context of the family circle. For example, a parent is allowed to a limited extent to physically discipline a child who is 10 years old and above who refuses to carry out the obligation of the five daily prayers . . . The extent to which this duty can be carried out by the parent and his defences will be relevant only in a Syariah Court. In this respect, Islam does not take an apologetic stance in the face of the move in some Western countries to totally abolish physical disciplining by parents towards their children even to educate them. (1996)

Zainah Anwar, of Sisters in Islam, retorted by asking if the "murder and rape of family members" was also considered to "fall within the jurisdiction of the Islamic Family Law of each State"?:

> The DVA and Muslim women should not be turned into victims, yet again, in the battle over turf. We do not believe that the civil courts, in their dispensation of justice, are any less Islamic. Placing the DVA under the civil courts does not reduce the importance of the syariah system. (1996)

By mid-1996, it seemed that the government's waffling and Muslim scholars's diatribes over jurisdiction had finally ended. What followed were daily newspaper reports of how the law was finally being used in society. After the DVA was enforced, *NST* headlines noted the government's role in making good the legislation: "Four centres to house domestic violence victims in Malacca" (8 June 1996); "Rising domestic violence in Penang" (2 July 1996); "23 Domestic violence cases since June 1" (7 August 1996); "Court gives two women protection from husbands" (13 August 1996) and "Domestic violence: more cases reported" (30 December 1996).

1997: DVA implementation issues/police versus women

Amidst the seemingly positive atmosphere surrounding the acceptance of the DVA, a new controversy erupted in 1997. The police, perhaps playing its role as the *de facto* vanguard of the patriarchal state, seemed to resist the law's implementation. Oddly enough, Minister Zaleha Ismail, who had been hesitant about the DVA's enforcement, found herself at the receiving end of police and male "power". It started with women politicians from the ruling party, the National Front (the Barisan Nasional), expressing concerns about the police not taking women's complaints of abuse seriously (*NST* 1997a). The stance of the women leaders displeased the Inspector-General of Police, Rahim Nor, who audaciously set up a police team to interview the said women, all high-ranking officials within their parties — Ng Yen Yen, secretary-general of Wanita MCA (Malaysian Chinese Association); Sarasa Pasamanickam, head of Wanita MIC (Malaysian Indian Congress) and Zaleha Ismail, the minister (*NST* 1997b).

The chief of police insisted that his men had acted professionally in dealing with these cases. He claimed that the women politicians had not provided evidence to prove their allegations (Raja 1997). The minister responded by identifying three police stations, in Klang, Petaling Jaya and Gombak, as being responsible for the actions that spawned the allegations (Singh and Nelson 1997). A supporting news report by Shareem Amry verified these allegations, noting that: "Those who have been witnesses in the frontlines of spousal abuse argue that Zaleha has a strong case" (1997).

The police continued to defend themselves, issuing press statements with the following headlines in the *NST*: "Police: All cases raised by Zaleha were dealt with" (4 July 1996); "Domestic Violence: IGP Defends Police Role" (5 July 1997); "Use proper channel to voice disapproval" (5 July 1997) and "Police probed 12 domestic violence cases in Klang" (5 July 1997). A male leader from the MCA, Michael Choong, defended the police and disagreed with his own party's Ng Yen Yen, asserting that the victims "just want the abuse to stop and do not usually want the police to intervene. Instead, they want someone to help them talk to their spouses" (*NST* 1997c).

Ultimately, the exchange of accusations took a disconcerting turn. Shareem Amry, the journalist who wrote the story in support of the minister, was called in for questioning. A police report had reportedly been lodged against her for "malicious publication of false news", making her liable to be charged under Section 8(A) of the Printing Presses and Publications Act. After she was interviewed on 3 July 1997, others who were cited in her article, were also called in for questioning by the police. Zaitun Kassim and Manohari Subramaniam of AWAM and Irene Xavier of Persatuan Sahabat Wanita, who had first-hand experience in dealing with victims of domestic violence, were quoted as being critical of the police's role in the DVA's implementation (*NST* 1997d). In reaction to this show of police high-handedness, 21 organizations issued a statement expressing their concern over police treatment of this matter (*NST* 1997e). The "women versus police" conflict had become so heated that Lim Kit Siang, the opposition leader, brought up this issue for debate in the parliament. Although the motion was turned down by the speaker, this sparked even greater public interest over the issue (*NST* 1997f).

The dispute was finally settled when then Acting Prime Minister, Anwar Ibrahim, intervened, noting that the police should have conducted their investigations into reports of domestic violence "in a manner acceptable to all" (Ashraf and Ainon 1997). Police officers were subsequently asked to attend courses on public relations, so that they could be "more courteous" and "hopefully, help improve the public image of the police" (Deutsche Presse-Agentur 1997). All these measures appeared to have worked, according to a subsequent report about the police becoming more cooperative in accepting reports lodged by women (Murhayani 1997).

The stocktaking years

With the termination of the conflict between police and women activists, the system seemed to be on women's side. However, the DVA was still not a satisfactory piece of legislation. It was a version that accommodated the interests of many parties. It was not the law envisaged by its early initiators, who wanted to introduce a bill that explicitly recognized domestic violence as an offence, "as a statement from society that domestic violence won't be tolerated":

> Unfortunately, the bill that has been passed doesn't do that but simply refers to the Penal Code again. The committee sat for two years and made sure that the definition of domestic violence and various other provisions were included in the bill. Unfortunately, those have been thrown out and a small bill has come out which is not very satisfactory.[12]

This unease was justified. For example, soon after the DVA was enforced in June 1996, a case came up before the High Court in Kuala Lumpur. In September of that year, the court quashed an interim order sought by a Muslim woman to restrain her husband from assaulting her. The judge found no mention of any pending investigation in the notes of the proceedings in the magistrate's court, where she was granted the Protection Order (*NST* 1996g). In another case, the judge confirmed that any investigation into domestic violence must involve criminal proceedings. In *Ngieng Shiat Yen v. Ten Jit Hing* (2001), Ngeing did not succeed in obtaining a Protection Order against her husband, Ten, despite her harrowing experience:

> Approximately a year after the marriage, the respondent started beating her up and on one occasion following an argument between them, the respondent locked her and their three children outside their shared residence. Things got out of hand when an attempt made by the appellant to resolve their differences turned into a fight where she was kicked and beaten up by the respondent for which she sustained minor injuries which required medical treatment. (*Ngieng Shiat Yen v. Ten Jit Hing* 2001)

It was not that the account recorded in her case file was not acceptable to the judge, but since there were no investigations by the police she was denied the Protection Order. It is not wholly convincing that the court is unable to award a Protection Order in the absence of a pending investigation. In the case of *Jennifer Patricia A/P Thomas v. Calvin Martin A/L Victor David* (2005), a judge was able to use Section 5 of the 1994 DVA to grant a Protection Order even without a criminal investigation into the offence. Accordingly, "the only requirement for a protection order to be given is that there must be proceedings involving a complaint of domestic violence", and since Jennifer had lodged police reports in connection with her abuse, the judge was satisfied that this was sufficient basis for the Protection Order. However, it did seem that "who is awarded a protection order is mainly a function of law's literal nature and of violent men's generosity" (Lazarus-Black 2001: 391).

A Protection Order and the arrest of a perpetrator are guaranteed only when grave and obvious physical hurt has been inflicted. Yet, a bigger conundrum facing advocates of the law is that many survivors of domestic violence do not persist in convicting their offenders (see Hare 2010; Noraida 2011a). In Malaysia, from June to December 1997, of 1,611 cases there were only 27 prosecutions, while 113 reports were withdrawn (*NST* 1997g). Those who lodge reports with the police differ from those who actively use the services of women's organizations and shelters. Those seeking help from the latter do so with the serious intention of taking practical action. Women's shelters report that of the 64 battered women they dealt with in one year, 24, or less than half, decided to return to the abusive situation (Chin 2007). That the number of cases handled by women's centres was lower than the reports lodged with the police was said to be an indicator of how many more women prefer to use the "police" channel to serve as a "warning" to husbands rather than take action against their abusers (Siti Hawa 2010).

The availability of Protection Orders under the DVA is perhaps the most significant, and also the most elusive, of the benefits arising from the Act. Women's groups and service counsellors complain about how difficult it is to get a Protection Order for women, often due to the ignorance of police personnel about Protection Orders or their perception of the offence itself. Hence, investigations are abandoned once the abused person retracts the report, something that would not happen with other crimes. Ivy Josiah, the executive director of WAO, expresses indignation over domestic violence not being equated to other crimes:

> Now, if I make a police report that 'A has stolen my car', and later A comes forward and says how sorry he is, well, the police will still have to prosecute, right? But it's not the case when it comes to wives retracting their reports! (Chin 2007)

The difficulty and inadequacy of the DVA as a tool for dealing with the prosecution process is aggravated by the method of justice itself. The mode of enquiry, examination, interrogation, cross-examination and inquisition in the courtrooms would be enough to separate the extremely determined plaintiff from the faint-hearted and under-resourced victim. In Malaysia, the adversarial system of procedure is used in courts, through a method of examination and cross-examination for the extraction of evidence. Much significance is given to individual autonomy and dignity in the presentation of arguments and evidence. Judges are also expected to remain impartial. Such a system actually works against victims of domestic violence who would be exposing themselves to greater danger and stigmatization if forced to testify against their partners and family members. This is in contrast to the inquisitorial system, where systems and procedures are said to be less rigidly applied and more conducive to resolving family-related cases (Tan 2009: 406–407).

A second round of reforms

Issues such as those listed above resulted in a call to review the DVA as early as 1999. The drive was initiated by the WCC of Penang, which submitted a 20-point memorandum to the government. Loh Cheng Kooi, the executive director of WCC, highlighted that some of the recommendations were for a broader definition of domestic violence, to encompass mental, psychological and emotional harm (*NST* 1999).

The call seemed to have been heeded by the then prime minister, Abdullah Badawi, who accepted the recommendation for review, remarking that he was proud that Malaysia was the first Asian and Islamic country to introduce the DVA. The seriousness of the problem was backed up by police statistics that showed an increase in reported domestic violence cases, from 1,409 in 1995 to 5,799 cases in 1997 (Senyyah 2000). Azalina Aziz, who had just been made head of Puteri UMNO (the newest UMNO wing for young women), touted the DVA as a government achievement. In her first keynote address as Puteri UMNO chief at the movement's maiden assembly, she cited the DVA as an example of government-formulated laws that were not discriminatory to women and rebuked the opposition PAS (Islamic Party of Malaysia) for their inability to do the same (*NST* 2003). The DVA was indeed useful as a political platform for upcoming politicians to gain legitimacy among an important constituency, women. Abdullah Badawi had just taken over as prime minister after Mahathir Mohamad suddenly stepped down in 2002 and was seeking a mandate on his leadership through the 2004 general election. So too was Azalina, as she prepared for her first contest in a general election.

In 2005, in response to the high-level endorsement of the DVA reform, the Parliamentary Select Committee on the Penal Code and Criminal Procedure Code proposed that the DVA get its own separate section in the Penal Code to enable criminalizing of not just physical assault, but also sexual, emotional, mental and financial abuse. The committee considered amending both the DVA and the Penal Code to take into account varying forms of domestic violence (*NST* 2005).

Another six years passed before the amendments to the 1994 DVA were effected. In June 2011, a bill cited as the Domestic Violence (Amendment) Act 2011, was tabled for debate in Parliament by the Deputy Minister for Women, Family and Community Development Heng Seai Kie. The amendments were not in accordance with the proposal of the Parliamentary Select Committee in 1995, but included the following new provisions (Ganesh and Mazlinda 2011):

- Recognizing psychological abuse, including emotional injury, as a form of abuse. This includes threats of harm or abandonment, intimidation, humiliation, verbal abuse and controlling another person's behaviour.
- Recognizing as domestic violence the illegal use of intoxicating substances to cause victims, including children, to suffer delusions.
- Prohibiting the person against whom the order is made from inciting others to commit domestic violence against his victim by specifying the mode by which an interim Protection Order may be sought.
- Extending the Protection Order to include a safe place and shelter

in the list that the perpetrator is prohibited or restricted from entering.

- Prohibiting or restricting the perpetrator from communicating, by whatever means, with the protected person, not just using "written or telephone communication" but also other means of communication technology.
- Making it compulsory for the court to attach a warrant of arrest together with the Protection Order or interim Protection Order if the court is satisfied that the perpetrator is likely to cause actual physical injury to the protected person.

The bill was passed without much objection, debate or fanfare in October 2011. The amendment fell short of what was previously recommended by JAG-VAW as well as by the Parliamentary Select Committee. In spite of having come a long way, the DVA reforms have yet to succeed in criminalizing domestic violence. The amended law still prioritized protection of victims rather than punishment of offenders. The definition of domestic violence, although stretched to include non-physical forms of abuse, was only useful to protect victims subjected to varying degrees of cruelty. In the end, the punishment of offenders still depended on how his/her acts were read by the Penal Code. More importantly, the procedures for getting protection remained as circuitous and discouraging as before.

The law is still a problem

Although the definition of what constitutes domestic violence has now been expanded to cover acts such as emotional and psychological hurt, a distinction is still made between a "seizable" and "non-seizable" offence. A "seizable" offence would be one where the victim's hurt is of a physical nature, with injuries such as cuts, wounds, lacerations or broken bones. Malaysia's DVA has to be read together with the Penal Code for the act of battery itself to be charged as a criminal offence (Amirthalingam 2006: 685–690). The Penal Code only empowers the police to investigate "seizable" offences, which means that violent spouses inflicting other forms of assault may still not warrant an arrest under the law. Automatic arrests of perpetrators can only be made when there is a "seizable" offence, although most women can be battered regularly without any visible evidence of grave physical injury. Given that the post-reporting period can be even more traumatic for the victim, since a Protection Order is not immediately granted, there is a high dependence on shelter facilities to provide pre-protection or protection before the Protection Orders (Noraida Endut 2011b: 56–161).

A controversial exclusion of a form of gendered violence from the definition of domestic violence is marital rape. The DVA does not recognize forced sexual intercourse between married persons as an act of violence. Hence, Section 2 (c) of the Act implies that a victim does not have the right to be protected against the imposition of certain conduct (namely, sexual intercourse) even if inflicted by force or threat upon the victim. This is because domestic violence is still treated as falling within the ambit of matrimonial law (Noraida 2011b: 56).

As the DVA needs to be read with the Penal Code, the law is quasi-criminal, combining civil and criminal procedures (Ng, Maznah and tan 2006: 53). It is also referred to as "a strange hybrid of criminal law with provisions pertaining to civil law remedies", such as the non-legal remedy of counselling (Afida Mastura 2000: 79). The ambiguity of the law, being both civil and criminal, is not the actual obstruction to the solution. Even if gendered violence is defined within the ambit of the Penal Code it will not be sufficiently addressed by it, given the complex nature of "hurt" and "harm" inflicted by intimate partners on each other.

How should domestic violence be criminalized?

There is a dilemma in this. If domestic violence is to be considered a crime (like burglary of murder), then the victim does not have the right to decide whether or not the alleged offender should be prosecuted. This stance takes away the autonomy of wives and mothers whose lives could worsen if their only source of support is incarcerated. If victims do not have autonomy in determining whether the system should intervene in their lives, the results (such as mandatory imprisonment for their partners) could be rather painful for the entire family. Hence, while punishment of offenders is the preferred option among feminist advocates of the law, given its deterrence value, this could mean taking away victim "autonomy". Concerns such as this probably explain why very few cases actually go from reporting to seeking actual intervention to prosecution. Much to the dissatisfaction of DVA advocates, domestic violence has remained a "quasi-crime". If domestic violence is to be fully-criminalized, then the victim cannot assume autonomy in the matter:

> mandatory policies have had staying power not because they have actually protected women in the ways that their proponents originally hoped, but because they are written in a language that makes sense in a retributivist and prosecutorially-focused criminal justice system. If batterers are going to be considered criminals, then they need to be arrested and prosecuted. There is no room for victim ambivalence or hesitancy . . . (Bailey 2010: 1271)

Home and marriage is often still the only source for women's sustenance, social network and status. A criminal justice system that includes mandatory punishments will only work well if we can assume that victim autonomy does not create further misery for the victim. To arrive at that conclusion the *body* as sovereign needs to be freed from the fetters of family, community and state. However, it is not in a position to do so, as the subjectivities of self and its material sustenance are still entrenched within the very sites that it seeks freedom from — family and the state.

Law in practice

To conclude this section, Malaysia's DVA is a success story insofar as it mirrored the compromises and accommodations that contributed to the statute's passage. However, the law does not satisfy all parties nor does it have sufficient provisions to fully criminalize the offence of domestic violence. The literal *body* was meant to have taken on a sovereign identity after the subjectivities of its sufferings had been "named, blamed and claimed" (Felstiner, Abel and Sarat, cited in Kuo 2012: 592). However, in reality it is still trapped within family and the state, with the law assigning the crime only a quasi-criminal or hybrid quality and continuing to protect the boundary of "conjugal patriarchy" (see Kuo 2012: 551).

Having analyzed all of the above, the significance of the DVA — the result of an expansive collaboration in spite of multiple debates — lies in the possibilities it offers. In law-making and in use of the law lies the ability to shape and re-articulate cultural meanings and the concept of rights (Merry 2003: 973, Douglas 2012). We may have to contend that laws, no matter how limited, can still instil an empowering ideology within familial bounds and relationships (Lazarus-Black 2001: 391). Douglas, citing Carol Smart, sees the efficacy of law in its *practice* as it is only by seeing the operation of the law that the possibility of decentring it from its over-centralized sense of power to be the be-all and end-all of the solution can be explored (2012: 122).

Conclusion: Losing the battle but winning the war?

I have traced the history of the passage of the DVA by illustrating how marital violence was conceived and defined by the courts in the early years before the DVA campaign took root. Legal judgements in the Syariah and civil systems revealed the dissimilar experiences of Muslim and non-Muslim women when they sought justice against their abusers in court. The basis for much gender angst and unity was provided by this moment of inconsistent and inappropriate justice. By the mid-1990s, domestic violence began to be slowly recognized and named as a grave offence; the right to guard the body against harm was recognized. This period saw an intense contestation involving the government, media, police and civil society interests. In this spirited discursive terrain, and largely through the organizational weight of autonomous women's groups, the DVA was shaped, contested and claimed, in a pattern similar to that observed in the East and the West (see Htun and Weldon 2012 and Spehar 2012). It was an unmistakable moment for gender consolidation. Although epic in nature, the outcome of the struggles led by feminist organizations resulted in a piece of legislation that reflected numerous and varying degrees of compromises and accommodations. Although it was a historic law, the relevance of DVA's provisions and the effectiveness of its implementation are continually being assessed and critiqued. In the final part of the chapter, I discuss the stocktaking years by evaluating some of the difficulties of the DVA in resolving family matters, ranging from the seemingly simple procedure of obtaining a Protection Order to intimidating court procedures unsuitable for family deliberations, as well as the dilemmas around intervention and the autonomy of victims to decide if and how violence upon them should be criminalized.

In this historical account, the double-sidedness of the domestic violence discourse and practice is presented. On the one hand, it has been a potent force in raising rights consciousness and providing legal clout to the erstwhile unnamed subjectivities of intimate agony. On the other hand, it is also a manifestation of the limited capacity of law and the state in affecting social transformation. However, like most statutes introduced in the modern nation state, the Malaysian DVA took on a life of its own; its most meaningful impact in Malaysia being the sustainability of a secularizing women's movement in competition with forces tending towards ethnic and religious separatism and exclusiveness. The campaign for the DVA allowed for much rethinking around the question of one's own subjectivity (and empowerment) in relation to gender, family, ethnicity, religion and nation. However, the implications of the law also drove home the realization that domestic violence has yet to be deeply understood as a form of gendered violence and explicitly criminalized under the Malaysian legal system. Yet, criminalizing this offence alone does not resolve the multifaceted nature of the problem, rooted in the ambiguity of family. Home is the site of many "domesticities", the violent one being one of these, and filled with complex emotions where, for some, only a thin line separates passion from aggression (see Das 2008). This ambiguity is the root of the ineffectiveness of the law, although the effectiveness of women's agenda in public life has been enhanced by the possibility of further reforms around this issue.

Notes

1 The judge held that "there is no provision in the Act for an exclusion order. However, where there is a lacuna in Malaysian law, English common law principles can be invoked as provided under Section 3 of the Civil Law Act 1956".

2 In the legislation, a *fasakh* divorce shall be affected under the following conditions: "when a husband abuses his wife, among others through i) habitually

hurting or causing her life to suffer due to his abusive behavior)" (Section 52(1)(h)(i) of the Selangor, Islamic Family Law Enactment, 1984).

3 This committee was chaired by Tan Sri Mohamed Azmi. The other members were Dr Mahfodz bin Mohamed and Professor Dr Mahmud Saedon bin Awang Othman.

4 The Married Women Ordinance 1957 provides remedies for protection and security of property for married women. However, this law only provides protection or security of the individual's property and does not safeguard against injury to person or reputation. For the latter, no husband or wife shall be entitled to sue the other for a tort under this law. This rule is derived from the common law of England, where it was held that marital status made the husband and wife one person in the eyes of the law and, therefore, a suit by one against the other was like suing oneself. The Married Women Ordinance 1957 was subsequently amended, allowing a husband and wife to "sue each other in tort or damages in respect of injuries to his or her person, as the case may be in the like manner as any other two separate individuals" (Section 4A in the Married Women Act 1957).

5 A document was provided to the court in the form of a letter from the kadi of Petaling Jaya, Selangor, notifying that on 16 May 1989, Faridah had retracted her renunciation of Islam and renewed her faith in the religion, at his office.

6 The five were the Association of Women Lawyers (AWL), the women's section of the Malayan Trade Union Congress (MTUC), the women and media sections of the Selangor and Federal Territory Consumers Association, University Women's Association and Women's Aid Organization (WAO).

7 Personal interview with Ivy Josiah as part of the WCC's project to commemorate its tenth anniversary. January 1999.

8 Academics such as Goh Beng Lan (from University of Science Malaysia), Cecilia Ng (from the Agricultural University of Malaysia) and Salbiah Ahmad (from the International Islamic University) contributed the articles in this special issue.

9 Personal interview with Cecilia Ng held in January 1999 as part of the WCC's project to commemorate its tenth anniversary.

10 Personal interview with Mehrun Siraj in January 1999 as part of the WCC's project to commemorate its tenth anniversary.

11 "Syarak" is the local term for Islamic law.

12 Interview with Mehrun Siraj, January 1999.

References

Afida Mastura, Binti Muhammad Arif (2000) "A Study on Remedies for Domestic Violence in Malaysia", a dissertation submitted in partial fulfilment of the Requirement for the degree of Master of Comparative Laws of Master of Comparative Laws, International Islamic University Malaysia (Kulliyah of Laws), April.

Amirthalingam, Kumaralingam (2005) "Women's Rights, International Norms, and Domestic Violence: Asian Perspectives", *Human Rights Quarterly*, Vol. 27, No. 2 (May, 2005), pp. 683–708.

Amry, Shareem (1997) "Making sure women are protected under Domestic Violence Act", *New Straits Times*, 2 July, p. 2.

Ashraf, Abdullah and Ainon Mohamad (1997), "Exercise care in abuse cases, Anwar tells police", *New Straits Times*. 18 July, p. 2

Azeman, Said (1996) "Reason for not enforcing Act yet", *New Straits Times*, 10 March, p. 2.

Chin Mui Yoon (2007) "Home is Where the Hurt is", *The Star*, 25 November, online: www.thestar.com.my/lifestyle/story.asp?file=/2007/11/25/lifefocus 19548266&sec=lifefocus, last accessed 15 October 2012.

Choong, Alex (1996) "Act won't be enforced just yet", *New Straits Times,* 27 March, p. 1.

Choong, Alex, Ramlan Said, Mohd Yusof Talib (1996) "Domestic Violence Act enforced in June", *New Straits Times,* 10 April, p. 4.

Das, Veena (2008) "Violence, Gender, and Subjectivity", *Annual Review of Anthropology*. Vol. 37: pp. 283–99.

Deutsche Presse-Agentur (1997) "Malaysian cops to undergo ethics course to polish image", *Deutsche Presse-Agentur,* 27 August, online source: http://www.lexisnexis.com.libproxy1.nus.edu.sg/ap/academic/ , last accessed 15 October 2012.

Douglas, H (2012) "Battered Women's Experiences of the Criminal Justice System: Decentring the Law", *Feminist Legal Studies*, 20: 121–134.

Ganesh, V. Shankar and Mazlinda Mahmood (2011) "Protection from emotional abuse", *New Straits Times*, 30 June, p. 10.

Hare, Sara C (2010) "Intimate Partner Violence: Victims' Opinions About Going to Trial", *Journal of Family Violence,* published online, September.

Htun, Mala and Weldon (2012) "The Civic Origins of Progressive Policy Change: Combating Violence Against Women in Global Perspective; 1975–2005", *American Political Science Review,* vol. 106, no. 3, pp. 548–569.

Kimberly D. Bailey 92010) "Lost in translation: Domestic violence, "the personal is political," and the criminal justice system", *Journal of Criminal Law and Criminology*, vol. 100, no. 4, pp. 1255–1300.

Kuo, Margaret (2012) "Spousal Abuse: Divorce Litigation and the Emergence of Rights Consciousness in Republican China", *Modern China*, vol. 38, no. 5, pp. 523–558.

Lazarus-Black, Mindy (2001) "Law and Pragmatics of Inclusion: Governing Domestic Violence in Trinidad and Tobago", *American Ethnologist*, 28 (2): 388–416.

Merry, Sally Engle (2003) "Constructing a Global Law-Violence against Women and the Human Rights System", *Law & Social Inquiry*, Vol. 28, No. 4, pp. 941–977.

Mohd. Shahrizad, Mohd. Diah (1994), "The Legal and Social Issues of Wife Battering and Marital Rape in Malaysia: A Comparative View with Islamic Law", Masters of Comparative Law, Kulliyah of Laws, International Islamic University, Malaysia, May 1994.

Muharyani, Othman (1996a) "Still waiting for the Act", *New Straits Times,* 1 February, p. 8.

Muharyani Othman, Pang Yin Fong, Juneita Johari, Alina Rastam (1996) "Objections put the Act in Limbo", *New Straits Times*, 14 March, p. 6.

Muharyani, Othman (1996b) "Women's groups call for speedy action on Domestic Violence Act", *New Straits Times,* 9 March, p. 1

Muharyani, Othman (1997) "Controversy has positive effects", *New Straits Times*, 24 November, p. 7.

Ng, Cecilia, Maznah Mohamad and tan beng hui (2006) *Feminism and the Women's Movement in Malaysia: An Unsung (R)evolution,* London: Routledge.

Noor Farida, Ariffin (1996) "Astonishing to say that law is against Islamic doctrines", letters, *New Straits Times*, 11 April, 13.

Noraida, Endut (2011a) "The Nature and Impact of Domestic Violence: A Study of Survivors of Wife Abuse in Malaysia", in Cecilia Ng, Rashidah Shuib and Noraida Endut (eds.) *Our Lived Realities: ReadingGender in Malaysia,* Penang: Penerbit Universiti Sains Malaysia; pp. 43–64.

Noraida, Endut (2011b) "Women, Law and Justice: The Case of Domestic Violence in Malaysia", in Cecilia Ng, Rashidah Shuib and Noraida Endut (eds.) *Our Lived Realities: Reading Gender in Malaysia*, Penang: Penerbit Universiti Sains Malaysia; pp. 150–163.

New Straits Times (1996a) "DVA should apply to all races", 9 March, p. 4.

New Straits Times (1996b) "Act an important stand against violence", 14 March, p. 6.

New Straits Times (1996c) "Domestic Violence Act to be enforced this year", 26 March, p. 1.

New Straits Times (1996d) "Move it, minister", 30 March, p. 12.

New Straits Times (1996e) "Delay a Disservice to women's cause, says DAP", 30 March, p. 8.

New Straits Times (1996f) "House rejects Opposition bid to amend motion of thanks", 2 April, p. 6.

New Straits Times (1996g) "Order restraining man from harassing wife quashed", 14 September, p. 6.

New Straits Times (1997a) "Police: we are serious in dealing with abuse reports", 26 June, p. 6.

New Straits Times (1997b) "Police hope to meet Zaleha over statement", 27 June, p. 19.

New Straits Times (1997c) "Records show most domestic violence cases go unreported", 28 June, p. 14.

New Straits Times (1997d) "Police interview NGO representative over report", 12 July 12, p. 6.

New Straits Times (1997e) "21 organizations express concern over police response", 11 July, p. 3.

New Straits Times (1997f) "Kit Siang's debate bid fails", 15 July, p. 9.

New Straits Times (1997g) "Police on why domestic cases left hanging", 14 June, p. 4.

New Straits Times (1999) "Plan for drive to review Domestic Violence Act", 22 February, p. 15.

New Straits Times (2003) "Get feedback from women says Azalina", 19 June, p. 7.

New Straits Times (2005) "Penal code section on Domestic Violence", 3 August, p. 22.

Padman, Padmaja (1995a) "Legal Protection for the Battered", *New Straits Times,* 16 February, p. 39.

Padman, Padmaja (1995b) " Interim Protection Order help for abuse victims", *New Straits Times*, 2 March, 31.

Padman, Padmaja (1996c) "Vital to keep momentum going", *New Straits Times*, 28 March, p. 6.

Pang, Yin Fong (1995) "Embracing the carnival's cause", *New Straits Times*, 30 March, p. 31.

Rahmah, Hashim (1996) "Consider complexities before implementation Act, say group", *New Straits Times*, 11 May 11, p. 15.

Raja, Gerald (1997) "IGP: Zaleha could not prove allegations", *New Straits Times*, 29 June, p. 1.

Salbiah Ahmad (1991) "Islamic perspective on domestic violence", *Herizons*, February, p. 7.

Sen, Rukmini (2010) "Women's Subjectivities of Suffering and Legal Rhetoric on Domestic Violence: Fissures in the Two Discourses", *Indian Journal of Gender Studies*, vol. 17 (3), pp. 375–401.

Senyyah, Patrick (2000) "Domestic violence laws for review", *New Straits Times*, 5 April 5, p. 2.

Singh, Satwant and Nelson, Charlotte (1997) "Zaleha identifies three stations that refused to accept reports", *New Straits Times*, 30 June, p. 1.

Siti Hawa, Ali (2010) "Preserving Family Values: Experience of WCC in Challenging Violence Against Women", paper presented at Workshop on 'Domestic Violence in Asia: The Ambiguity of Family as Private–Public Domain, held at the Asia research Institute, National University of Singapore, Singapore, 7–9 October.

Siraj, Mehrun (1994) "Women and the Law: Significant Developments in Malaysia", *Law and Society Review*, vol. 28, no. 3 (Law and Society in Southeast Asia); pp. 561–572.

Spehar, Andrea (2012) "Women's Movements as Agents of Change: The Politics of Policymaking and the Reform of Domestic Violence Laws in Croatia and Slovenia, 1991–2004", *Journal of Women, Politics and Policy*, vol. 33, no. 3, pp. 205–238.

Tan Seng Teck (2009) "Battered Women, Provocation and the Criminal Justice System: An Inherent Mismatch", *The Law Review*, pp. 403 – 413.

Zahara, Shariman (1989), "Increase in Domestic Violence: Law to Protect Battered Women", *New Straits Times*, 22 May, p. 3.

Zainah, Anwar (1996) "Polemics on jurisdiction obscuring issue of justice", *New Straits Times*, 20 May, p. 13.

Zaitoon, Datuk Othman (1996) "Domestic Violence Act needs further study", Letters, *New Straits Times*, 27 March, p. 17.

Legal cases cited*

Adibah v. Abdul Rani (1986): Adibah Yasmi lwn Abdul Rani (1986) 3 *JH* 44.

Chan Ah Moi v. Phang Wai Ann (1995) 3 *MLJ* 130.

Faridah bte Dato Talib v. Mohamed Habibullah bin Mahmood (1990) 1 *MLJ* 174.

Hairun v. Omar (1993): Hairun bt Mohd Shariff lwn Omar bin Mohd Noor (1993) 8 *JH* 289.

Hasnah v. Saad (1983): Hasnah Bt Hashim lwn Saad B. Arof (1983) 3 *JH* 84.

Hasnah v. Zaaba (1995): Hasnah Bt. Omar lwn Zaaba bin Mohamad Amin (1996) 10 *JH* 59.

Jayakumari a/p Arul Pragasam v. Suriya Narayanan a/l v. Ramanathan (1996) 4 *MLJ* 421.
Jennifer Patricia A/P Thomas v. Calvin Martin A/L Victor David (2005) 6 *MLJ* 728.
Mohamed Habibullah bin Mahmood v. Faridah bte Dato Talib (1992) 2 *MLJ* 793
Ngieng Shiat Yen v. Ten Jit Hing (2001) 1 *MLJ* 289.

(* The mode of citation for all legal cases in this chapter is as follows: In the case of a publication, "(1996) 4 MLJ 421", 1996 denotes the year, 4 denotes the volume of the *Malayan Law Journal (MLJ)* and 421 denotes the first page number. The abbreviation JH stands for *Jurnal Hukum*, a journal for reporting Syariah cases.)

CHAPTER
8

The Indonesian Family as a Contested Site of Women's Rights

Implementation of the Domestic Violence Act

NURSYAHBANI KATJASUNGKANA

Background

In Indonesia, women's subordination and discrimination are based on patriarchal interpretations of culture and religion, particularly Islam. These are presented as "traditional" and may lead to violence against women (VAW). The Indonesian Ministry for Women's Empowerment estimated that 11.4 percent of the 217,000,000 citizens of Indonesia or around 24,000,000 women, especially in villages, admitted that they have experienced violence, particularly domestic violence.[1] The National Commission on VAW (2009) reported that the number of victims of domestic violence increased by 100 percent from 2004 to 2008 and by 263 percent in 2009. Yet, activists believe that most domestic violence cases are not reported.

Culturally, domestic violence is considered a private matter; the culture of silence surrounding the issue is a hindrance in implementing the Domestic Violence Act (DVA) adopted in 2004. Based on LBH APIK's[2] experiences and the study on the implementation of the DVA conducted by the Kartini Asia Network/APIK (2009) and a follow up desk study[3], it is clear that patriarchal religious teachings and culture are the most important obstacles in implementing the DVA. Patriarchal religious tenets and cultural norms are embedded in various family laws, such as the 1974 Marriage Law. The socio-political context that allows fundamentalism to grow and influences the law-making process further weakens women's position in the family and society. Fundamentalist groups managed to influence law makers at the local level to such an extent that by the end of 2011, 207 regional by-laws used "traditional" cultural values and religious teachings as their sources; 78 of these were discriminative towards women (Komnas Perempuan, 2011). Lack of capacity among legal authorities and failure of the institution (the Ministry of Women's Empowerment and Child Protection/MoWE & CP[4]) mandated by law to uphold the DVA also create impunity and limit female victims of domestic violence from exercising their rights and accessing justice.

The 2004 Domestic Violence Act: Some progressive provisions

Indonesia's DVA uses a holistic approach that goes beyond criminalization and includes preventive and protective support measures. It includes principles of non-discrimination, gender equality and justice, human rights and victim protection. These principles form the basis of a stipulation included in Article 15 of the DVA, which requires that everyone who hears, sees or knows about a domestic abuse incident reports it to the police or to the courts; it also allows victims to request a protection order. Based on this article, each person is to the best of his/her ability obliged to: (a) prevent a criminal act, (b) protect the victim, (c) provide emergency assistance and (d) facilitate the process of requesting a protection order; Article 15 of the DVA stresses that VAW is everybody's business. This also means there is a paradigm shift in viewing domestic violence: it is no longer a private matter but a public concern. Moreover these DVA stipulations are progressive regulations for the following reasons:

Firstly, an integrated approach is used, which is not only a deterrent, since it criminalizes the perpetrator, but also contains some preventive and rehabilitative provisions that emphasize support to victims.

Secondly, the definition of family and household has been broadened in relation to the definition used by the Criminal Code in which family members are limited to husband, wife and their children. The DVA definition has been extended beyond the nuclear family, since the extended family is more common in Indonesia. The DVA definition includes all members related by blood, marriage or employment (in the case of domestic helpers) and living under the same roof. Article 2 of the DVA provides protection to: (1) husband, wife and child/ren and (2) persons living in the same household as the individuals (as stated in 1) and who are related by blood and breastfeeding[5], guardianship or custody. Persons who work in the household are also considered family members for as long as they live under the same roof. According to Article 356 of the Criminal Code, assault of a family member (limited to wife, parents and children only) is considered a crime; the perpetrator can be sent to jail for a period that is up to one-third as long as other cases of assault.[6] Earlier, this crime was hardly punished because of the culture of silence surrounding domestic violence; the new DVA emphasizes that domestic violence must be penalized.

Thirdly, based on the victim protection principle, Paragraph 10 of Chapter IV of the DVA deals with the rights of victims, including (a) protection from family members, police, prosecutors, courts, lawyers, social institutions or other parties, whether on a temporary basis or based on court orders; (b) access to health services according to medical needs; (c) special treatment to maintain confidentiality of the victim; (d) welfare and legal assistance at all levels of the investigation, according to existing laws and (e) religious guidance/spiritual counselling. The social institutions referred to are the organizations concerned with the issue of domestic violence, for example, legal aid groups. Social workers refer to those who are formally trained or those who have practical experience in social work. This means that the issue of gender-based violence, materialized in the DVA as well as other conventions related to the elimination of gender-based violence, must be included in the curricula of legal aid, social work, health and legal education. Thus, law students, health providers as well as social work students should be introduced early to the DVA as well as to other laws related to human rights and gender equality. The state is also obliged to provide education to law enforcers, service providers and to the wider society and to provide support services, such as rehabilitation centres.[7]

Fourthly, the victim protection principle is further strengthened by a stipulation known as the protection order (Article 16 Paragraph 3), which rejects the perception that the DVA tends to cause family breakups and high rates of divorces. This protection order ensures that no repressive action is immediately taken against perpetrators of domestic violence, that is, they are not reported to the police immediately as is required for other crimes in the Criminal Code. A protection order can be requested on behalf of the victim; similarly, a restraining order can be requested against perpetrators. This is a significant breakthrough in the Indonesian legal system, because it obliges the state to provide protection to victims. Hence, it is important to disseminate information about this important stipulation to the public to avoid the common misconception that reporting domestic abuse contributes to divorces and breakups and brings dishonour to families. In fact, according to the Vice Chief of Justice of the Shariah Court, in 64.89 percent of the 221,520 divorce cases filed by women, domestic violence, including polygyny, was cited as the major reason for seeking a divorce; he made this statement at the National Seminar on the Integration of DVA in the Shariah Court, conducted by Rifka Annisa[8] and LBH APIK Jakarta (2009).[9]

Fifthly, Articles 5 and 6 of the DVA define violence to include physical, psychological and sexual violence. The inclusion of psychological and sexual violence, including marital rape, in the new law — which are not recognized in the Criminal Code — is a progressive development. However, implementation of the DVA may need to be adjusted, since there are no specific procedures to enable law enforcement officers to determine whether a domestic abuse case constitutes psychological violence.[10] Research has shown that domestic violence is closely related to the mental health of both the victim and the perpetrator. A study of 951 cases at the Sanglah Hospital in Bali discovered that the majority of victims suffered from post-traumatic stress disorder with symptoms of nightmares about violent events, hyper-arousal accompanied by mood swings, insomnia and suicidal tendencies. It was also found that patients who experienced domestic violence were inclined to be twice as violent as alcoholics and drug addicts. Inwardly directed aggression, in the form of depression, and outward aggression, by abusing others, was reported.[11]

Sixthly, the DVA also introduced another form of abuse, economic abuse or economic neglect. The conceptual and legal notions of economic abuse have long been included in Article 304 of the Criminal Code. Yet this article does not incorporate domestic violence. According to Article 304 of the Criminal Code, economic abandonment occurs when a man does not provide the basic necessities of life to his wife and children or to those persons whose care and maintenance are his legal responsibility. Economic abuse is more broadly interpreted to include the prohibition to work. Article 9 of the DVA states that "(1) it is forbidden to neglect persons living in the same household; as it is stipulated by laws, consensus or agreement that a person is obligated to provide a livelihood, care or maintenance to those persons living in the same household", (2) neglect as referred to in Paragraph 1 also applies to all persons who cause economic dependence by limiting and/or forbidding other persons within the household from working or earning a suitable income within or outside the household, such that they become victims under his control.

The struggle for the law: Transformative legal aid and the triangle of empowerment

APIK has used the concept "transformative legal aid" since 1995 (Katjasungkana 2004). A legal case is used as an entry point to look at women's experiences in dealing with the legal system and those experiences are used as research data and translated into policy advice. APIK developed its legislative advocacy, where public awareness campaigns, training for law enforcers and policy studies are used as the basis to create various bills and policy briefs. APIK also uses the concept of the triangle of empowerment (Wieringa and Vargas 1998: 3) in which civil society, parliament (feminist politicians) and government (femocrats) together play a critical role in drafting and advocacy. This triangle, when it works well, bridges civil society and the state, articulating women's demands, translating them into policy issues and fighting to get political support for their agenda.

During the first year of its formation in 1995, APIK handled 111 cases, 65 percent of which were domestic violence cases. The difficulty in handling them was mainly attributed to the lack of awareness — not only among victims but also among law enforcers, religious leaders, family members and the public in general — that domestic violence is a crime.[12] APIK demonstrated that the only legal regulation on sexual assault in the Criminal Code was very ineffective: the article does not respond to a woman's need to protect the autonomy and integrity of her body and mind from violence in her family/household. APIK argued that domestic violence is a crime that falls under public law although it occurs in the domestic sphere, because it threatens the whole integrity of a woman's body, soul and mind and her well-being. Article 352 of the Criminal Code, on minor abuse or violence, does not provide protection to women and is liable to biased implementation. An element of Article 352 of the Criminal Code states that minor abuse "does not result in physical pain or does not prevent the victim from working". "Work" in this article refers to formal employment (in the factory or in the office) and does not include women's work in the household. In addition, this article only protects family members (wife, parent and children) from physical violence. Although a minimum legal remedy is provided by the Criminal Code, because of corruption and lack of legal capacity as well as the failure of the MoWE&CP in upholding the law, access to justice for female victims of domestic violence became more limited and usually resulted in impunity for the perpetrators.

The most contentious aspect of advocating the DVA is the culture and belief system, especially in the Muslim community. An interpretation of the Quran commonly used to justify a husband battering his wife is Verse 34 of the Surah An-Nisa (the fourth chapter of the Quran), which contains the word "wadhribuhunna", almost always interpreted as "hit or beat her up". This particular verse is also often used to depict the unequal relationships between men and women by construing that men have absolute power over women. This gender-biased and misogynist interpretation exacerbates the impunity of domestic violence, making it a crime justified by religious teaching. There is, however, an alternative interpretation of the same verse, in which the word "wadhribuhunna" is translated as a "moral forewarning"; this provides an alternative to resolving marital problems with the help of a mediator.[13] Misogynist *hadith* (traditions relating to the deeds and sayings of the Prophet Muhammad) and interpretations of the Quran are considered official teaching materials in many Islamic boarding schools for women. The widely-used book of Imam Nawawi al Bantany entitled *Uqud-u al-Lujain* is characterized by its gender-biased explanations of *hadith* and of the Quran.[14] In the context of sexual relations, one can find verses that are always used to mute women; these verses depict the woman as a "field" that can be sowed by her husband anytime and anywhere he wishes (Quran, Al-Baqarah 223). Another well-known *hadith* is the belief that angels curse a woman who refuses to have sex with her husband. There are also many Quranic verses and *hadith* that describe the beauty of sexual relations between married partners as well as equality between men and women, but these are used less often.

Indonesia has some 300 ethnic groups with their own spiritual traditions and customs. Most of them share the notion of women's subordination which contributed to the impunity of domestic violence. Women's economic dependence on men is another factor that made it difficult to punish perpetrators of domestic violence.

Social institutions formed to maintain and protect "family harmony" — such as the Badan Penasihat Perselisihan Perkawinan (Board of Advisors on Marital Disputes), an official marriage counselling office — ignored domestic abuse problems by counselling victims to be patient and understanding towards their husbands who are the breadwinners. Similarly, the police frightened abused women by claiming that if they reported abuse, their husbands would lose their jobs and eventually their children would be abandoned. These institutions often blamed female victims for the abuse, thus creating double victimization. Consequently, many domestic violence cases were never reported by the victims. Many opted to go to religious courts to initiate divorce proceedings, but even there they were unlikely to get a positive response. There is a widespread belief among religious court judges that domestic violence problems do not fall within their jurisdiction and authority. In other words, religious courts did not have the ingenuity to create a breakthrough decision that would provide justice for abuse victims.

The dual system of courts — shariah and general court as well as criminal and civil procedures — inherited from the Dutch colonial legal system also contributed to the limited access to justice for women victims of domestic violence. It created a financial barrier for victims since they were required to go to the shariah court to file their divorce case and to the general court to report their domestic violence experience. As the legal authorities can exploit victims' ignorance, this became another cause for impunity or even corruption.

Misogynist norms such as those relating to *nusyus*, (violation of spousal obligations, mostly interpreted as women's disobedience) were often applied in divorce cases to avoid paying alimony or dividing assets to wives and children, particularly in cases where wives had been forced to leave their households. In fact, the 1974 Marriage Law as well as the 1991 Compilation of Islamic Laws clearly stipulated the unconditional obligations that husbands must fulfil with respect to former wives and children upon the termination of marriage. Government Regulation No 10/1983, which regulates procedures on marriages and divorces of civil servants (including the armed forces, the police and employees of state-owned companies), elucidated the equal division of income between former wives and children: each gets one-third of the husband's salary. In addition, as mentioned above, Article 304 of the Criminal Code penalizes a person who neglects their legal obligations.

In addressing the legal system's inadequate response to women's interests as explained above, in 1997, APIK organized a seminar on "The Social and Legal Responses toward Domestic Violence". In addition to abuse victims and legal experts, participants of the seminar included six leaders representing various religions. In essence, legal experts and practitioners as well as the religious leaders affirmed that the legal system and religious interpretations contributed significantly to the subjugation of women. The outcome of the seminar was a mandate to APIK to begin the process of formulating a draft of the DVA.[15] Some of APIK's activities to achieve this goal included the following:

1. APIK conducted media campaigns to promote monthly activities that enabled abused women to report grievances. In addition, APIK collaborated with other organizations such as Jaringan Kaulan Perempuan (Women's Pledge Network) and 17 radio stations throughout Indonesia and published campaign materials such as stickers, T-shirts, posters, fact sheets, case studies and booklets.
2. Policy studies were conducted to compare the Indonesian Criminal Justice Code with domestic violence acts in Malaysia, Turkey, Australia and the United States. Life stories of female victims of domestic violence and their experiences in dealing with the legal system were also collated.
3. APIK's Coalition was formed to coordinate activities to raise awareness and strengthen the formulation of the draft DVA and disseminate it to stakeholders. There were also numerous discussions, workshops and media campaigns conducted by various organizations concerned with the issue of domestic abuse. Some of these activities were organized under the auspices of the National Commission on VAW following its formation in 1998. The final outcome was a draft of the DVA as well as an academic paper produced by the drafting team in collaboration with the Centre for Gender and Law Studies of Brawijaya University in East Java. These were then disseminated and discussed in several cities in Indonesia.
4. In 2002, the engagement of law makers started. The draft of the DVA (the bill) was submitted to the Indonesian Parliament and the Indonesian Government by APIK's Coalition. Regretfully, there was no response by the government, represented by the MoWE, although parliament members were actively involved in reviewing the draft. However, the Legislative Council considered it seriously, especially with the active participation of its Chair, Professor J. E.

Sahetapy (the author's professor in criminology), and the Vice-Chair Tumbu Saraswati, a co-founder of APIK and a member of the drafting team. As the legislating process was going on, lobbying and campaigning activities continued. Weekly briefing sessions were held with members of parliament in collaboration with the Parliamentary Forum on Population. After many pressures including a "One Thousand Umbrellas" demonstration, the parliament finally enacted the DVA on 14 September 2004, and the law became effective on 22 September 2004, during the term of President Megawati Soekarnoputri.

Implementation of the DVA and access to justice

UNDP defines access to justice as "the ability of people to seek and obtain a remedy through formal or informal institutions of justice and in conformity with human rights standards" (2006: 5). Using this definition and the 2006 UNDP Conceptual Framework on Access to Justice,[16] the Kartini Asia Network and APIK conducted a desk study that concluded that most of the components in the framework have not been fulfilled by the state.

The first component of the 2006 UNDP conceptual framework is the normative one. It means that all laws and procedures must be in place and understood by duty and claim holders. This element requires that the DVA is understood by legal authorities, other institutions mandated by the law and claim holders. This element is problematic since the government has no national action plan to implement the DVA and there is no indicator to fulfil this requirement. The failure of the MoWE & CP, as coordinator, in upholding the DVA also contributes to the lack of understanding of legal authorities, service providers and claim holders.

The second component is legal awareness, which victims of domestic abuse need in order to pursue justice. Experience shows that individuals with limited knowledge and awareness of the law will also have an inadequate perception of the law; at the very least, their perception will differ from those who are knowledgeable about the law. Legal awareness enables abuse victims to have a better understanding of the legal aspects of their cases and also of the circumstances that triggered the abuse. It is correlated to an understanding of what action to take when one experiences mistreatment. In Indonesia, the public's familiarity with the law and legal processes is generally very low (Bappenas 2009). This also applies to awareness of the DVA. Since its enactment, several initiatives have been undertaken to improve the public's knowledge about the DVA. The office of the MoWE & CP was active in disseminating information about this law on television for a full month following its adoption. The Parliamentary Forum on Population, which actively participated in the parliamentary discussions of the DVA draft, printed and distributed thousands of booklets on DVA. Non-governmental organizations focusing on gender violence, such as LBH APIK and its affiliates all over Indonesia, are also active in raising legal awareness. However, these efforts are inadequate in view of Indonesia's population of more than 240 million, its large geographical area and the low level of legal awareness especially among women. An effective legal awareness and information strategy needs to be drafted to ensure not only that information becomes available to people, especially women, but also that women can avail of that legal information whenever they need it.

The third component is access to appropriate forums. An appropriate forum, either formal or informal, must be adequate to the needs of abused women both financially and geographically. It is clear that the availability of legal remedies and legal awareness alone is not sufficient for women to gain access to justice. Victims must have access to forums or other forms of mediation through mechanisms that are in their interest. Law enforcement agencies must also facilitate victims' access to justice and be open to accepting domestic abuse cases. The dual court system — shariah and general court — and the dichotomy between the civil and the criminal court systems, compounded by the issue of legal pluralism, are a major obstacle for abused women in their quest for justice. In fact, existing forums of resolution, such as the criminal courts that handle domestic violence cases, are still inaccessible to victims seeking justice. This is mainly because law enforcement officers are unresponsive to victims' needs. The criminal court system is oriented towards punishment, while family members are often influenced by cultural and religious interpretations as well as economic considerations (the possible absence of the breadwinner). Consequently, victims are often reluctant to take advantage of criminal courts. The legal structure and court administration are also imbalanced with respect to membership.[17] Gender bias in the court system is reflected in the organizational structure and administration. Women's groups identified this phenomenon long ago; they stress that larger participation and representation of women in decision-making institutions will influence legislation and produce a more gender-sensitive implementation of laws. Secondly, although the definition of "family" in Article 2 of the DVA is quite broad, people with non-normative gender identities or sexual orientations as well as couples who have not registered their marriage and children considered illegitimate face various obstacles in accessing legal remedies provided by the DVA. The long and complicated criminal procedure is also a barrier for abused women. It may take months or even years for the court to give its verdict. This makes the procedure very costly because of court and lawyers' fees; free legal aid for women is limited and mostly located in big cities.

The fourth component in the 2006 UNDP framework is access to effective handling of grievances and provisions of remedies. It implies that duty bearers or legal enforcers and service providers must take necessary action to provide remedies for a grievance. Our study shows that it is difficult for victims to access such services. The DVA gives victims the right to health, social, spiritual, psychological and legal services. However, we found that these services were not available in many locations. Even where they were available, law enforcers might not provide relevant information or might withhold these services from the victims. The management of a case is considered effective when law enforcement agents and service providers take the appropriate action to resolve abuse cases. The results of monitoring activities by Rifka Annisa (2009) and LBH APIK Jakarta (2009) indicate that law enforcers and service providers were not adequately carrying out their duties and taking appropriate action to help victims, including the most basic action such as issuing a protection order.

The fifth component is satisfactory remedies obtained. A legal settlement is considered satisfactory, from the point of view of abuse victims, when all procedures are carried out in accordance with the DVA and human rights standards are fulfilled. An investigation by the Centre for Human Rights Studies at Padang University[18] concluded that legal resolutions on domestic abuse cases are still not satisfactory. Thus, the requirements stipulated in the 2006 UNDP Conceptual Framework on Access to Justice are generally not fulfilled in Indonesia. However, there is one important point to be noted, namely that the Judicial Commission has included rulings on domestic violence cases to evaluate the capabilities of judges when considering their promotions.

Conflicting laws and regulations

Apart from the problems noted above, the DVA conflicts with other laws, especially the 1974 Marriage Law. There are also contradictions between the DVA and the many regional by-laws promulgated following the adoption of a policy of regional autonomy since 2001. Given the limitations of space, I cannot discuss the influential 1991 Compilation of Islamic Laws or the Labour Law.

Contradictions between the DVA and the 1974 Marriage Law

Several articles in the 1974 Marriage Law are contradictory to the principles of the DVA. These are discussed below:

1. **Discriminatory rules on domestic relationships:** Domestic abuse occurs within the home, which indicates not only the scene of the offense or *locus delicti*, but also the relationship between the perpetrator and the victim. The 1974 Marriage Law limits a domestic relationship to that between husband and wife and between parent and child. The DVA,

however, expands the scope of the household to include other individuals related by blood, marriage, breastfeeding, foster care and guardianship to the husband, wife or child, and who reside in the same household; even individuals who work and live in the same household are included. However, legal authorities may ignore the wider definition of the DVA, which may disadvantage couples whose marriage is unregistered or children who are born out of wedlock. Since same-sex relations are not recognized in the marriage law cases of VAW may not be dealt with by legal authorities either.

2. Gender stereotyping: The 1974 Marriage Law stipulates an unequal relationship between men and women through a rigid division of labour by which a husband is the head of the family and main wage earner and a wife is the household caretaker (Article 31 in conjunction with Article 34). These provisions legalize gender stereotyping that according to the Convention to Eliminate all forms of Discrimination against Women (the Women's Convention/CEDAW Article 5)[19] is a form of discrimination. The provision clearly assigns power to the man, who as head of the household is expected to make all family decisions and as wage earner will have control over economic decisions. This Marriage Law regulation can inspire men to prohibit women from working outside the house, which is considered an economic abuse in the DVA. This gender stereotyping contradicts social reality. Historically, Indonesian women have always worked outside the house; they work in the rice fields or earn income in the informal and formal sector. If household work were to be monetized, the contribution women would make to the national income would be significant. In the context of religious teaching, women are considered accessories to their husbands; for instance, a wife must be obedient to her husband, she must ask his permission if she wants to go out of the house, she must fulfil her husband's sexual needs and accept time-sharing with her husband if she is in a polygamous marriage. There is a long list of a wife's responsibilities to her husband that are being widely publicized by the print media as well as through proselytizing activities (see, for instance, Talib 1996). Hence, the potential for domestic abuse is high because of the tension between the norms (religious, legal or general) that regulate husband-wife relationships and the social reality. A study on the impact of gender stereotyping roles on low-income women in Jakarta indicates that such standardization of gender roles potentially provides venues for abuse of women (Wilujeng et al. 2005).

3. Polygamy as domestic abuse: The law that gives husbands the right to adopt and practice polygamy[20] as stipulated in the 1974 Marriage Law in Article 3 (2) is not only discriminatory but also male-biased as it places the woman as a household caretaker who must serve her husband's sexual needs, a producer of children who is not allowed to be sick [Article 4 (2)]. If a wife does not fulfil any of these criteria, the husband has an excuse to practice polygamy. To marry more than one woman, a man needs permission from the court and if he is a civil servant or a member of the police or the military, he needs similar permission from his superior. Other requirements include agreement from his wife, ability to support another wife economically and his guarantee that he will give equal and fair treatment to his wives. The court will waive approval if a wife does not respond to her husband's request or if it is considered impossible to obtain one. However, in practice, most polygamous marriages do not meet the above requirements, as the general view is that polygamy is the husband's right as legitimized by religion, and that the state has no right to enforce the law. Furthermore, many polygamous marriages are not legal because of failure to obtain court approval. The significant number of women who cite their husband's polygamy as the reason for divorce indicates that women see polygamy as a source of injustice, psychological pain and abuse.[21] Polygamy also causes distress among children. The restriction on polygamy as stipulated in the 1974 Marriage Law implies a reinterpretation of Paragraph 3 of Surat An-Nisa (a chapter in the Quran on women) that is often used to justify polygamy. The reinterpretation states that an Islamic marriage is basically monogamous. The only official reference that stipulates that the 1974 Marriage Law is based on the principle of monogamy is Judgement No 12/PUU-V/ 200728 by the Constitutional Court.[22] However, even this judgement is unable to prevent supporters from conducting campaigns in defence of polygamy. One manifestation is the formation of Polygamy Clubs in several cities. These clubs were established and are led by female "victims" of polygamy. Ikhwan Chodijah binti Am, founder and head of a Polygamy Club, claims that polygamy is an effective medicine to acquire God's love, because with polygamy one will always experience suffering in one's life. This statement is an admission that polygamy causes domestic abuse. This is in agreement with the assertion of well-known feminist Muslim scholar Musdah Mulia that "polygamy is fundamentally a humiliation of women" (Mulia 1999: 50).[23] In 1998, the CEDAW Committee praised Indonesia as a nation with the largest Muslim population that has provided protection to its women by restricting the practice of polygamy. The committee expressed the hope that Indonesia would eventually be free of polygamy and encouraged the government to take immediate steps to eradicate polygamous practices in Indonesia and amend discriminatory laws.[24] However, the number of polygamous marriages actually increased from 2002. This trend started when the then Vice President Hamzah Haz revealed publicly that he officially had four wives, followed by the presentation of the so-called Polygamy Award to practitioners of polygamy by a restaurant owner — a polygamist himself — by the name of PuspoWardoyo.[25]

4. Polygamy as a form of marital crime: The Criminal Code (Articles 278 and 279) considers marriage while in another marital relationship a criminal act or a marital crime. However, polygamous marriages are seldom exposed by law enforcers. The 1991 Compilation of Islamic Laws determines that a marriage can be substantiated if the following requirements are fulfilled: (a) bridegroom, (b) bride, (c) a male relative or guardian of bride, (d) two witnesses and e.) marriage solemnization. The groom must also pay a dowry or *mahr*. If all these marriage requirements are satisfied, the marriage is considered legitimate according to Islam. Thus, many marriages are conducted "under the table" or unofficially, which means that a marriage is considered valid if the marriage requirements and principles according to shariah are fulfilled. Without civil registration, however, the marriage is not legal according to the Marriage Law. In an "unofficial" marriage, the woman and children will have no legal recourse in terms of claiming income, assets and the "husband's" inheritance.

5. Status of children born out of wedlock: The birth of children outside a legitimate marriage is mainly the result of "unofficial" marriages or marriages that are not legally registered. These also include children born because of rape or out of a relationship in which the father has abandoned the mother. Article 43 in the 1974 Marriage Act and Article 100 of the 1991 KHI state that children born out of wedlock have civil ties only with their mothers and the mothers' immediate families. Although the 1974 Marriage Law pledged that a government regulation would be issued to regulate the status of illegitimate children, 37 years later, no government regulation has been issued. The lack of policies to protect the status of illegitimate children makes the children and their mothers vulnerable to domestic abuse. Fortunately, a Supreme Court Jurisprudence stipulates that the biological father is responsible for the costs of the education and health of his biological children (Supreme Court Jurisprudence in the case of Desrina and Nugraha Besus, 1997). In February 2012, the Constitutional Court annulled Article 43 of the 1974 Marriage Act and stated that "children born out of wedlock have a civil relationship with the mother and the mother's family as well as with the father including a civil relationship with the father's family as long as it can be proved by science and technology, and / or other evidence under the law that there is a blood relationship"[26]. This ruling was applauded by the women's movement but also "led to outrage with critics saying that the court condoned adultery".[27] However, as the Chief Judge of the Shariah Appelate Court of Semarang, Central Java, observed, this verdict gives a good legal foundation for the Civil Registry Office to provide birth certificates to the children; the ruling is also not against the shariah.[28]

6. A husband's right to deny paternity of his child: A husband can deny the legitimacy of a child born to his wife, if he has evidence that his wife committed adultery and the child is the result of the adulterous relationship (Article 44, 1974 Marriage Law). This regulation provides a relatively easy opportunity for a husband to deny the paternity of a child. It was produced at a time when patriarchal religious values played a prominent role in the formulation of laws and regulations. This does not conform to the principles of gender equality and can lead to various forms of domestic violence. Fortunately, the advancement of technology can facilitate verification of the blood relationship.

7. Parental permission for children below the age of twenty-one: Basically, a marriage is carried out with the approval of the bride and bridegroom (Article 6 Paragraph 1, 1974 Marriage Law). This conforms to the freedom to choose a partner, as guaranteed by the State Constitution, Paragraph 16(2), by CEDAW and several other international conventions. However, the freedom to choose is not unconditional, particularly for those below the age of twenty-one, who require permission from parents to get married (Article 6 Paragraph 2). This can potentially lead to domestic violence or forced marriage.

8. Age of marriage: The minimum age for marriage is sixteen years for a girl and nineteen years for a boy. The legal basis for these limits is unclear. However, it reflects the influence of patriarchy in that the minimum age is higher for men. The perception is that the man must be respected as one traditionally respects an older person. The difference in age is aimed at preserving the patriarchal values that conflict directly with the principle that forms the basis of the DVA — that of equality between men and women.

Contradictions between the DVA and regional by-laws

Since 2000, some 78 regional regulations have been promulgated that perpetuate and institutionalize gender discrimination (Komnas Perempuan 2011). These include forbidding a woman from going out at night without a male relative, regulating a specific dress code for women and criminalization of prostitution and homosexuality. These regulations clearly violate freedom of expression, the right to bodily integrity and sexual rights. Religion-based values are publicized within the community by disseminating interpretations of the Quran or verses that stipulate the presumed obligations of wives to their husbands. Religion-based values become more powerful because of state support and these by-laws. These discriminative regional laws ultimately create a misogynist culture that could lead to domestic violence.

Conceptual contestations

In Indonesia, the family is seen as the fundamental unit of the society. However, four decades ago, feminist scholars challenged this notion in the West and pointed out that the locus of inequality between men and women lies within the family (see for instance Oakley 1974, 1976). They also argued that paternal dominance is at the root of the problem. The husband and father is the patriarch, literally the father and ruler of the tribe. In the Indonesian context, this concept still exists and is even legalized in the 1974 Marriage Law. Compounded by Islamic teachings and patriarchal customs this leads to a culture of silence where different kinds of discrimination and violence experienced by women go unvoiced. Sis (name changed), a victim of domestic violence from Jogjakarta illustrates this point:

> I never told anyone that I was being abused. My relatives learnt about it when my husband and I were in the process of getting a divorce, which he requested, as he was no longer happy with me. My family couldn't accept the fact that I was being battered. I never reported it to the police because I didn't want our child to have a father who had a problem with the law. My family supported my efforts to save our family for the sake of our child. I also didn't report it to the police because I don't want to quarrel and don't want to make matters worse than they already are. Although I have been abused I want to maintain my family and hope I can save my marriage because I believe that a marriage is like a service to God. So, I believe that all the problems that I experienced are just trials and tribulations of a household and I have to protect my child so that he can have a complete family.

It is clear that Sis will do everything to save her marriage and her family even if her safety is threatened. The fear of family and children being stigmatized if an abusive father is reported to the police as well as the religious belief that a marriage is sacred and a woman is obliged to maintain the unity of the family, are obstacles that prevent abuse victims from reporting the abuse to the police or other law enforcement agencies or even to their own family.

"Do not meddle in the family matters of others (*jangan ikut campur urusan keluarga dan rumah tangga orang lain*)" is a well-known saying among Indonesian people. It illustrates the culture of silence that shrouds domestic violence. APIK's Coalition, as the proponent of the domestic violence bill, is fully aware of the importance of the family in Indonesian society. For that reason, even while using the principles of gender equality, human rights and non-discrimination, the "save our family" discourse was consciously incorporated as a core value in promoting and advocating the domestic violence bill. In 1994, when women's groups and then APIK's Coalition started promoting the need for a new law on domestic violence, the United Nations launched the International Year of the Family and the Indonesian Government embraced it by launching a Family Day that is celebrated every year on 29 June. Taking traditional values into account, APIK's Coalition demanded a new law on domestic violence. They succeeded in managing their differences with religious and community leaders as well as members of Islamic political parties in parliament, who opposed the bill. Gender-neutral wording such as "anyone" or "victim" were used to convince the opponents of the bill that it would protect all family members, including men. APIK's Coalition also took into consideration the situation of domestic workers who may be abused by their female employers who treat them as family property. This is why APIK's Coalition used the term "domestic violence" rather than "family violence". Domestic means domicile, a place where two people or a group of people, for one reason or another, having a relationship such as by marriage, blood, employment or other, live.

Another reason, as suggested by Kurz (1989), is that when the term domestic violence is used, the abused women tend to be the unit of analysis (of abuse) while the term family violence indicates that the family is the basic unit of analysis. APIK's Coalition was able to convince society, government and the opponents of the bill that the law on domestic violence was not meant to send a husband to jail or to make a criminal case, but that it was built on values of equality, peace and unity within the family, also known in Islam as maintaining a "harmonious family" (*keluarga sakinah*, a safe and peaceful family).

The success of APIK's Coalition in advocating the DVA means that the rigid separation of the domestic and the public arena was broken down. The DVA did away with the concept of family as a private domain although in most cases the blurring of the division makes legal authorities shy away from intervening. Moreover, the sphere of the family and household is now wide open to plans for better legal protection for the people within it, bound by relationships of marriage, blood, work and other social and intimate reasons. That this trend continues is borne out by the recent study of Iriyanto and Cahyadi (2008). They concluded that the separation of the criminal and civil courts in cases of domestic violence is broken down.

Conclusion

The notion that domestic violence is an internal family problem or a private matter reinforces the tendency to resolve such abuse within the family or by customary law. This type of resolution is also favoured by law enforcement officers, for instance, by recommending reconciliation between the perpetrator and the victim. Consequently, the legal mechanism does not function as it should. Only extraordinary cases exposed by the media capture the serious attention of law enforcement officers, especially if the cases involve celebrities. When domestic helpers experience abuse, particularly in cases involving minor physical injury, the police often reverse the circumstances in favour of their employers by accusing the domestic workers of stealing, etcetera.[29]

The silence around domestic violence and the inability of victims to report the abuse they experience are linked to the weak structural position of women vis-à-vis their husbands, their families and the public at large, due to the prevalence of gender stereotyping in Indonesian society. Various policies and laws further formalize gender stereotyping. The public's perception that it is an honour for a woman to be a wife and a mother, and that a mother's primary role is manager of the household (as defined in the Marriage Law) tends to influence victims of abuse to remain dependent — economically, socially and emotionally — on the perpetrators of abuse. These norms have been legalized into various laws and policies. The legalization of discrimination and violence has made it impossible for women and children to exercise their rights, because these rights are not protected once women find themselves within the institution of the family. Also, the condoning of domestic violence in religious and customary law prevents efforts to address gender-based discrimination and violence, especially domestic violence.

The legal system, policies and regional regulations that discriminate against women not only tolerate domestic violence and other forms of gender-based violence, but also prevent women from obtaining access to and control over economic, political and other developmental resources. Although there have been some changes in laws protecting women's rights, gender disparity is still very wide in the fields of education, health (maternal mortality in Indonesia is the highest in the ASEAN region), employment (most women are employed in blue-collar and low-level jobs) and decision-making (although the number of women in decision-making positions has significantly increased, gender-sensitivity is still low).[30] So far, both governmental and non-governmental organizations have focused on the implementation of legislations with hardly any consideration for the rehabilitation of victims, in particular the economic empowerment of victims. The recent introduction of national policies and regulations, such as the Anti-Pornography Law and regional regulations that discriminate against women and members of non-normative groups based on gender identity and sexual orientation, reflects acts of violence by the state and encourages violence by hardliner groups.[31]

Various data, based on records of the National Commission on VAW, the National Planning Agency (Bappenas) and other relevant institutions, indicate that reporting of domestic violence increases annually. These figures, however, represent only the tip of the iceberg. Accurate and reliable data that reflect the magnitude of the problem are unavailable, making it difficult to investigate many aspects of domestic violence scientifically. Accordingly, the government should include domestic violence as a variable in the population census. Characteristics such as reticence, the culture of silence and the feeling of shame prevalent among victims of abuse pose unanswered questions related to reporting, punishment and different forms of violence, including non-physical and sexual abuse. Another obstacle is that the prevalence of domestic violence is widespread. In general, the public and victims do not report incidences of domestic violence, because of the strong belief in the superiority of men that has been transmitted by male-biased teachings and interpretations of religion and because of patriarchal social attitudes and cultural traditions. In the Indonesian context, with more than 300 ethnic groups and languages, the challenge in implementing the DVA is great. It should also be noted that domestic violence occurs not only among legally married couples but also in marriages conducted by religious authorities and not legally registered. These unregistered marriages are not recognized by civil and religious courts, and hence not protected by the law. Other marginal groups face a similar dilemma; these groups include household helpers, children and parents of the mentally disturbed and the disabled, as well as LGBTI couples. There are legal remedies in place for children; however, legal protection is still needed for the remaining marginal groups because of the specific characteristics of their circumstances. Laws to protect these groups should be based on the main tenet of the UN Declaration on Human Rights (Article 1): "all human beings are born free and equal in dignity and rights". This principle has also been adopted by Indonesia's State Constitution.

The dichotomy between the private and public domains, with domestic violence placed in the private domain (under the jurisdiction of civil courts), should be abolished because it no longer conforms to the concept introduced by CEDAW, which has merged the two domains as an inseparable unit of women's rights. The relegation of domestic violence into the private domain and of legal interventions for domestic abuse cases to the public legal system (criminal justice system) has made it difficult for victims to seek justice. In other words, the criminal legal system remains unresponsive to the legal requirements of abuse victims. In addition to the dichotomy between civil and criminal laws, the legal system is also pluralistic in that Islamic religious law, customary laws and state law are applicable. At the community level, legal cases are often resolved through mediation, such that marriage and women may be used for competitive purposes in the interest of customary tradition, religion or the state. In the context of the Indonesian society, which is patriarchal and male-dominated, women will always be victims of the existing legal and social systems if special measures are not taken. For this reason, APIK and other women's groups have recommended that an Integrated Family Court System should be created to eliminate the partitions between civil and criminal justice, as well as divisions between religion, customs and state law.

Notes

1 Khofifah Indar Parawansa, Government policy in the effort to eliminate violence against women (Kebijakan pemerintah dalam upaya penghapusan kekerasan terhadap perempuan) as quoted by Munir, 2005: 9.

2 LBH APIK (Lembaga Bantuan Hukum Asosiasi Perempuan Indonesia untuk Keadilan/Indonesian Women's Association for Justice) is a legal aid society that provides free legal assistance to poor women and does advocacy work for legal reform. The 2004 DVA is a result of the advocacy of LBH APIK from 1995–2004.

3 This chapter is mainly based on a desk study on Cultural and Religious Barriers in Implementing the Domestic Violence Act in Indonesia supported by Cordaid. The project team consisting of Nursyahbani Katjasungkana and Sisca Dewi Noya would like to thank all research participants, one of whom is quoted in this chapter, for their courage and generosity. We hope that their voices, captured in this project, will help millions of women to exercise their rights and get access to justice.

4 In 2000, the Ministry for Women's Affairs was renamed as the Ministry of Women's Empowerment, under the progressive Muslim Minister Khofifah Indar Parawansa. In 2009, Children's Protection was added to the name.

5 According to Islamic law, a child can be breastfed by a woman other than the mother. The status of such a child is the same as a biological child.

6 The Indonesian Criminal Code is inherited from the Dutch Criminal Code that was introduced to Indonesia in 1915. It contains no specific article on domestic violence, but Article 356 under the assault chapter refers to an assault against wife, children or parents. The punishment is heavier than other forms of assault, for example someone who assaults anybody resulting in death could be jailed for nine years, but if the victim is the parent or wife or children of the perpetrator, the punishment could be up to twelve years.

7 As articulated in Article 4 of the DVA, the objectives of elimination of domestic abuse are to: (a) prevent all forms of violence within the household; (b) provide protection to victims of domestic abuse; (c) punish perpetrators of domestic violence and (d) maintain the wellbeing and unity of the family.

8 Rifka Annisa is a women's organization established in 1993 in Jogjakarta (Central Java). It provides legal services and has a crisis centre for victims of domestic violence. For further information about Rifka Annisa. See this link: http://lawforwo.multiply.com/journal/item/19/Rifka_annisaa_Comapny_Profile?&show_interstitial+1&u=%2Fjournal%Fitem.

9 See also *The Jakarta Post*, Wednesday, 4 February 2009: Divorce rate up 10 fold since reform era: Ministry. No author. Accessed 22 October 2012.

10 Cases of physical abuse can be proven by obtaining a 'Visum et Repertum', a request from the police to the medical law division of a government hospital. In cases of psychological abuse, one should be able to provide evidence by requesting a 'Visum et Psychiatricum' from the psychiatric law division of a government hospital or from other institutions that provide psychiatric services. A psychologist or psychiatrist can also be called at every stage of the investigation to examine and analyze both the victim as well as the perpetrator of the alleged abuse. However, based on past experiences, police, prosecutors and judges do not request a 'Visum et Psychiatricum'.

11 *The Jakarta Post*, Friday, 30 January 2009: 9. Domestic violence leads to aggression. No author. Accessed 22 October 2012.

12 APIK eventually compiled a book that listed domestic violence cases in which the perpetrators were never convicted. The compilation was published in a book entitled "Studi Kasus Kekerasan Domestic: Kejahatan yang Tak

Dihukum" (Case Studies on Domestic Violence: Crimes without Punishment (2004). This book was used as part of a campaign to lobby for the enactment of the DVA.

13 For a detailed analysis of this issue, see Munir 2005 and Munti 1997. The latter article was published in a Suara APIK bulletin that was part of the LBH APIK campaign that led to the enactment of the DVA.

14 *Uqud-u al-Lujain fi Bayan Huquqi Zaujain*, known as *Kitab Kuning* (called the Yellow Book because it is very old and its pages have turned yellow), has been analysed and re-written by Forum Kajian Kitab Kuning (Critical Analysis of Yellow Book) led by Sinta Nurriyah Abdurrahman Wahid (2005), which gives an alternative interpretation with a more equal relationship between husband and wife.

15 We extend our thanks to NOVIB, the Ford Foundation, USAID and other funding agencies and individuals/organizations, that we cannot list individually, for enabling APIK to produce a six-year strategic plan and formulate a draft of the DVA until it was enacted as the DVA No 23/2004.

16 This UN Framework has been tested in 5 provinces in Indonesia (see UNDP 2006). As a follow-up of this assessment, Bappenas (2009) discussed gender justice among other issues.

17 Although it was very difficult to obtain accurate sex-segregated data on the composition of law enforcement officers, the following figures indicate the imbalance in the structure and administration of law-enforcement institutions. The data below do not have the number and sex composition of court clerks who are influential in various stages of an abuse victim's legal process. The following data on the number of police officers, prosecutors and judges, including religious court judges, reflect the imbalance between the sexes that exists within the legal structure and court administration. The figures, compiled from a number of sources, are as follows: (a) number of police officers: 374,526 of whom 373,715 or 96.75 percent are men and 11,706 or 3.25 percent are women; (b) number of prosecutors: 7,698 of whom 5,490 or 71.31 percent are men and 2,208 or 28.68 percent are women (http://www.kejaksaan.go.id/unit_kejaksaan.php?idu=21&idsu=1&id=2). In the Attorney General's office alone, of 672 prosecutors, 500 (74.4 percent) are men and 172 (25.50 percent) are women; c) number of judges: 3,191 in district courts and 400 in the high courts. There are only 536 (16.8 percent) female judges in both the district and high courts d) number of judges in religious courts: 10,802 of whom 7,549 or 70 percent are men and 3,254 or 30 percent are women (Badan Pengadilan Agama 2008).

18 Data were obtained from a researcher at the Centre for Human Rights Studies, Padang University. The results of this investigation were requested by the Judicial Commission to evaluate the promotion of judges; for this reason, the researcher requested that his/her name be excluded.

19 Article 5 of CEDAW requires countries to address and change social and customary patterns that reinforce the stereotyping of women and traditional gender roles or that promote the relative superiority or inferiority of either of the sexes.

20 The appropriate term is polygyny because the right to polygamy (marriage to many partners) is only given to husbands and not to wives.

21 In 2006, 879 divorce requests were submitted by wives who gave polygamy

as the primary reason to end the marriage. In 2008, the number of divorces increased substantially to 5,944, as reported by the Division of Religious Courts of the Supreme Court (Vice Chair of Supreme Court Justice's presentation, 16 September 2009). Meanwhile, LBH APIK Jakarta noted that the number of abuse cases caused by polygamy increased sharply from 16 in 2007 to 87 in 2008 (Jakarta Post 2 April 2009). However, divorce caused by polygamy can be considered an honourable solution, according to the words of God: "And if the two divorce, God will give enough to each one from His compassion. And God's compassion is great, is wise." (An Nissa, Paragraph 130). In addition, "a wife must be treated well in marriage, but also treated well in divorce." (al-Baqarah, Paragraph 231). This rule differs from the cultural norms and hadith (traditional) teachings that are commonly taught: that divorce is taboo, that it is despised by God and it angers God. This widespread teaching causes such fear among women that they are reluctant to ask for divorce even though they are abused (Surin: 1978: 54–57).

22 The complete resolution of the Constitutional Court can be accessed through the following website: www.bkkbn.go.id 4 September 2007; for a more complete analysis see http://jurnalhukum.blogspot.com/2007/10/konstitusi-poligami-dan-kebebasan.html.

23 See also Mulia 2012.

24 Committee Recommendations to CEDAW 1998, presented in the 18th CEDAW Plenary Meeting Januari–Februari 1998. (Rekomendasi Komite PBB tentang penghapusan diskriminasi terhadap perempuan sidang XVIII; 19 Januari - 6 Februari 1998). Translated and published by LBH APIK, undated.

25 In a discussion with the author on a TV talk show, Puspo Wardoyo admitted that he married each of his wives to help him manage his restaurants. It is clear that his Quranic justification for polygamy is merely a pretext.

26 The Constitutional Court verdict number 46/PUU-VIII/2010, 17 February 2012. The verdict can be accessed via: http://www.mahkamahkonstitusi.go.id/putusan/putusan_sidang_46%20PUU%202010-TELAH%20BACA.pdf

27 The Jakarta Post 17 April 2012: Paternity ruling to apply in rape case. http://www.thejakartapost.com/news/2012/04/07/paternity-ruling-apply-rape-cases.html.

28 For further discussion on the Constitutional Court judgment number 46/PUU-VIII/2010, 17 February 2012, see Rasyid, Chatib (2012: 18) on children born out of wedlock.

29 Information based on cases dealt with by LBH APIK Jakarta.

30 See report on Budget Analysis of MDG Programs, Jakarta: Bappenas 2009.

31 With the enactment of the Anti-Pornography Law, the public, in particular women, can be accused of a crime because of their body movements, clothing or their sexual orientation and gender identity.

References

Bappenas (Badan Perencanaan Pembangunan Nasional, the National Development Planning Body). (2009). *A National Strategy on Access to Justice (Strategi Nasional Akses terhadap Keadilan)*. Jakarta: Bappenas.

Irianto, Sulistyowati and Antonius Cahyadi (2008). *Runtuhnya Sekat Perdata dan*

Pidana; studi peradilan kasus kekerasan terhadap perempuan (The breakdown of the separation between civil and criminal court; a study on the judicial treatment of cases of VAW). Jakarta: Yayasan Obor Indonesia.

Kartini Asia Network/APIK (2007) Hegemoni Heteronormativitas: Membongkar Seksualitas Perempuan yang Terbungkam (Heteronormativity hegemony: Dismantling Women's Silenced Sexuality) with Introduction by Saskia E. Wieringa, Nursyahbani Katjasungkana and Irwan Hidayana. Jakarta: Kartini Network.

Katjasungkana and Damanik (2004). *Kekerasan Domestik, Kejahatan yang tak Dihukum (Domestic Violence Case Studies: Crimes not convicted)*. Jakarta: LBH APIK Jakarta/Novib.

Katjasungkana, Nursyahbani. (2004). 'Gender and Transformative Legal Aid' in Karen Mokate (ed.), *Women's Participation in Social Development (experiences from Asia, Latin America and the Caribbean)*. Washington: Inter American Bank, pp. 147–162.

Katjasungkana, Nursyahbani and Damanik (eds). 2004 *Studi kasus kekerasan domestik: Kejahatan yang tak dihukum* (case studies on domestic violence, crimes without punishment. Jakarta: LBH APIK Jakarta.

Komnas Perempuan 2011). Annual Report on Violence Against Women. Jakarta: Komnas Perempuan

Kurz, D. (1989) Social perspectives on wife abuse: Current debates and future directions. *Gender and Society*, 3(4): 489–505.

Mulia,Musdah. (1999) *Pandangan Islam tentang Poligami* (Islamic's Perspectives on Polygamy). Jakarta: Solidaritas Perempuan — Lembaga Kajian Agama dan Gender — The Asia Foundation.

Mulia, Musdah. (2012). Contesting fundamentalism; humanizing women. Nursyahbani Katjasungkana and Saskia E. Wieringa, eds, *The Future of Asian Feminisms: Confronting Fundamentalisms, Conflicts and Neo-Liberalism.* Newcastle upon Tyne: Cambridge Scholars Publishing. pp. 284–300.

Munir, Lily Zakiyah. (2005). Domestic Violence in Indonesia, *Muslim World Journal of Human Rights*, volume 2, Issue 1, pp. 1–37.

Munti, Ratna Batari. (1997). *Pemukulan Istri dalam Perspektif Islam* (Wife Battering from the Perspective of Islam) in *APIK Bulletin nr 5*: 7–9.

Oakley, Ann. (1974). *The sociology of housework*. New York: Pantheon Books.

Oakley, Ann. (1976). *Woman's work: the housewife past and present.* New York: Vintage Books.

Rasyid, Chatib (2012*). Akibat hukum terhadap anak luar kawin pasca putusan Mahkamah* Konstitusi (legal impact of constitutional court's ruling on children born out of wedlock). Yogyakarta: Total Media.

Surin, Bachtiar FA (1978). Terjemah dan tafsir ak-Quran, huruf Arab dan Latin (Translation and interpretation of the Quran, in Arabic and Latin script.

Talib, M. (1996). 40 *Tanggungjawab Istri terhadap Suami*, (40 Obligations of Wives toward their Husbands) Jakarta: Irsyad Baitus Salam.

UNDP. (2006). Programming for Justice: Access for All — A Practioner's Guide to a Human Rights Based Approach to Access to Justice, Asia Pacific Rights and Justice Initiative. Bangkok: UNDP Regional Center.

Wahid, Sinta Nurriyah Abdurrahman. (2005). *Kembang Setaman Perkawinan* (Flowers in the Garden of Marriage). Jakarta: Penerbit Buku Kompas.

Wieringa, Saskia and Virginia Vargas. (1998) The Triangle of Women's

Empowerment. In Geertje Lycklama a Nijeholt, Virginia Vargas, and Saskia Wieringa (ed), (1998) *Women's Movements and Public Policy in Europe, Latin America and Carribean*. New York and London: Garland, pp. 3–25.

Wilujeng, Henny, Attashendartini Habsyah and Dhevy Setya Wibawa. (2005). *Dampak Pembakuan Peran Gender terhadap Perempuan kelas bawah di Jakarta* (The Impact of Standardization of Gender Roles on Low-income Women in Jakarta), Jakarta: APIK.

CHAPTER

9

Reflections on Domestic Violence as Gender-Based Violence in European Legal Developments

RENÉE G. RÖMKENS

Domestic or intimate partner violence is no longer what it used to be. In the wake of the second feminist movement of the 1970s, violence against women (VAW) was put squarely on the political agenda. It was politicized as a violation of women's bodily integrity, directly related to the historically rooted and socially and culturally sanctioned inequalities in power relations between women and men. Violence against women was exposed as a form of discrimination against women. This perspective reflects a paradigm shift and evoked nothing less than a historical transformation. The issue changed from a private problem to a public concern, *inter alia* a state concern. Over the past decades, a formidable body of research has been developed in academia, often inspired by the work of women's grassroots organizations and NGOs including Amnesty International, Human Rights Watch, WHO, and the UN Special Rapporteur on violence against women in the field of violence against women. A wide range of data has been gathered, demonstrating the widespread prevalence and severity of domestic violence and violence against women.

In the international legal and policy field of violence against women, the feminist perspective on violence against women has been very influential in agenda setting. To a large extent, the feminist perspective, where violence against women and girls is contextualized in an analytical framework of gender-based power differentials, has been mainstreamed. VAW is by now widely considered to be a form of *discrimination* by men against women since it is a consequence of and sustained by unequal power relations[1]. This social and politico-legal understanding of violence against women finds its concise translation in the concept of gender-based violence, which is the accepted term, referring to "violence directed against a woman because she is a woman and that affects women disproportionately" (UN General Recommendation 19, 1992, rt 6). In 1993, the historical UN Declaration of Violence against Women added a second pillar to the international legal foundation of the concept by acknowledging that violence against women is not only a form of discrimination but also a *violation of fundamental human rights of women.*

At a time when the epidemic proportions of violence against women and girls are becoming increasingly evident, the gender-based and discriminatory analysis underlying this analytical transformation is under siege. A paradox is noticeable: while the concept of gender-based violence seems to gain ground — also in international human rights law in which this perspective is increasingly legally anchored — the claim that domestic violence is not a form of discrimination since it affects women and men is voiced with increasing loudness. For a while, this claim was considered marginally relevant, as an anti-feminist backlash without a convincing empirical evidence base. However, more recently it seems that this perspective is gaining influence, despite its flawed evidence base. This provides food for thought.

This chapter addresses how the claim of gender neutrality in domestic violence, and some even claim gender equality, currently operates in some European international human rights legislative developments. Without aiming to be exhaustive, this chapter provides a socio-legal perspective on how academic controversies play out in recent developments in lawmaking within the Council of Europe (CoE) in the field of domestic violence.

After a brief presentation of the *vox populi* in Europe through recent survey data on people's attitudes towards domestic violence against women, the debate contesting the gender inequality in domestic violence will be outlined. Against this backdrop, some current European developments in international law, as developed by the CoE, are discussed as an illustration of the ambiguity in the recognition of the gender-based nature of domestic violence.

News in Europe: Shifting attitudes towards domestic violence

In 2010, the EUROBAROMETER, a European Union (EU)-wide survey among almost 27,000 inhabitants of the twenty-seven Member States (MS), was dedicated to domestic violence.[2] This was a follow-up to a similar survey in 1999 among the then fifteen EU MS, allowing a comparison in results for this first generation EU MS.[3] We will present the general data for the current twenty-seven EU MS below, and where relevant will specify comparisons for the fifteen "old" EU MS. The survey questions address *"domestic violence against women"*, without any further elaboration of the gender based-nature of domestic violence.

The outcome indicates that interesting changes took place over time. The *attitudes* toward domestic violence against women have become tougher in Europe over the past ten years. In 2010, 84 percent of all respondents found domestic violence unacceptable under all circumstances and thought it should always be punishable by law, up from 63 percent in 1999. An attitude of "law and order" seems to have gained ground. However, the contrast between attitudes towards physical and sexual violence is striking. Across the EU, almost 20 percent still consider sexual violence against a woman *not* a very serious offence. Three in four respondents (76 percent) know about laws prohibiting domestic violence and over two-third (69 percent) know about social and legal support measures for victims of domestic violence.

On the level of *personally knowing* a victim or perpetrator, one in four respondents reported knowing a woman in their family or circle of friends who had suffered domestic violence (up from 19 percent in 1999). One in five knew someone who *committed* domestic violence (up from about 14 percent in 1999). A growing number of people apparently now notice and acknowledge domestic violence when they are confronted with it, although numbers vary widely between MS.[4] Interestingly, domestic violence is a better hidden secret among men since more women than men report knowing a perpetrator or a victim (29 percent and 21 percent, respectively).

While domestic violence is becoming more widely known, the question is whether it actually is less of a private problem for those directly concerned. Does it mean that the victim or perpetrator themselves speak openly about it? Upon closer examination, the picture is more complex. Knowing a victim or perpetrator in one's close environment does not mean that it has been a topic of conversation. The number of respondents who had heard directly about domestic violence from friends or family has actually on average *decreased* over the past ten years among the majority of (first generation, "old") EU MS. Again, here stark differences are seen between countries. With Spain, Denmark and Germany being the exceptions, within all other countries families speak *less* about it (an average drop of over 5 percent on a total average of 18 Percent). As for friends as a source of information, a similar drop in many countries is visible, with only two countries showing a remarkable increase (Spain and Greece; for Spain this might be directly related to major legal changes implemented during the past decade).[5]

These quantitative data raise various interesting questions when we look at it from the perspective of the public–private dichotomy. Maybe it has only become easier to discuss domestic violence in general, as a public concern in public media, often debating how the state or semi-public institutions have to take responsibility. Could the public discourse, in which perpetrating domestic violence has increasingly fallen into disgrace, unintentionally foster an increase of private shame? Has the transformation of domestic violence into a subject of public concern and moral rejection paradoxically fostered a renewed privatization? Alternatively, maybe the public and the private domain are on an individual experiential level as separated as they have been, notably when it comes to personally painful experiences. Maybe the level of secrecy and shame about violence from loved ones does not so easily change when it hits one personally. The finding that more people report personally knowing someone who suffers from domestic violence among family or friends, while less people seem to have actually heard about it from their family or friends than from others, is no contradiction.

After all, mass-media have been the most cited source of information by respondents. People might have learned to be better able to recognize a victim or a perpetrator from a distance.[6] The recognition of the gender-based nature of domestic violence has not been addressed in this EUROBAROMETER survey. All questions related to domestic violence were framed as domestic violence against women. However, when briefly looking at the results on people's opinions regarding the causes of domestic violence, a striking finding is presented. It is interesting to note that people could give more than one (pre-structured) answer to the question on causes and most did. Besides the well-known causes that people attribute domestic violence to, such as alcohol, drugs, unemployment and poverty, almost two-thirds believed that it was caused by "the way women are viewed by men" and by "the way power is shared between the sexes". Admittedly, these two items can be understood very differently since the framing of the answer does not indicate any substantive or normative position concerning the views themselves or the direction of the power-sharing that is considered a cause of violence. So, we can hardly interpret these results as an unequivocal sign of a widely shared concern about gender inequality. However, the answering item "provocative behavior of women" is remarkably clear in wording on who is to blame for the violence: the victim. More than half (52 percent) of all respondents agree with this option. We can conclude that the widely spread attitude of the unacceptability and criminalization of domestic violence against women apparently goes together with widespread victim blaming as well. So much for ambiguity in attitudes on the popular level!

Gender analysis under siege

The feminist perspective on domestic violence developed in the 1970s. At its core is the analysis of violence as a form of abuse that is directly related to the inequality of women versus men and that can affect any and all women. This has been a subject of critique from various angles.

First of all, from within the feminist community (here the term community refers to feminists as an epistemic community), it was argued that a more sophisticated and differentiated analysis was required to understand the different risks in victimization. Are some women more at risk than others and why? How do individual, psychological variables, for example victimization during childhood, interact with more structural social economic factors such as unemployment, level of education, etcetera? Since the 1970s, feminist analyses on causes and consequences of domestic violence and violence against women in general have obviously evolved in an effort to address the challenging question of differences and diversity in victimization between and among women (and *mutatis mutandis* regarding perpetration by men). One important strand of feminist criticism that began in the 1980s was voiced by women of colour, mostly African-American, British and Asian scholars and activists. The call to pay more attention to the impact of racial and ethnic differences between women has been ongoing. Feminist scholarship and activism is increasingly addressing the issue of diversity and the concept of intersectionality is widely used as an analytical tool (see Crenshaw 1989. For a recent intersectional analysis of data on spouse killing, see Römkens & Lahlah 2011). In responding to the call for an intersectional analysis that does justice to the differences in women's vulnerability to violent victimization, we need to, when looking at the role of gender, simultaneously take into consideration how gender intersects with and is constituted by other foundational social markers such as ethnicity, class, religion, age or sexual orientation. The perspective of intersectionality has proven to be theoretically fruitful, although it remains empirically difficult to capture (Sokoloff & Dupont 2005; Verloo 2006; Nixon & Humphreys 2010). Yet, it is crucial in order to produce meaningful knowledge in light of today's complex challenges where violence against women is a phenomenon simultaneously affected by different variables related to globalization and increasing flows of migration (trafficking of women, sexual harassment and violation of female migrant workers, child sex tourism and child prostitution; see Rijken & Römkens 2010).

On a policy level, the success of the feminist perspective and agenda setting is visible in how it has affected existing policy frameworks and professional domains. The topic of domestic violence or intimate partner violence is receiving increasing attention in fields such as social work, health care or the criminal justice system. The success of mainstreaming implies collaboration with institutions that are not unequivocally wedded to the feminist message, which positions domestic violence as a form of violent discrimination against women. This inevitably means that in the process of mainstreaming, both on the level of state policies and in its implementation in the field, the original feminist analysis has become diluted (Hearn & McKie 2008). It is no coincidence that the change in terminology from wife abuse to the gender-neutral term of domestic violence or intimate partner violence (or its linguistic equivalent, since this gender neutralization can be seen in different languages) coincides with the mainstreaming of the issue during the 1990s. In the wake of the mainstreaming of domestic violence, it has been increasingly positioned as a criminal, legal, and more generally, a social or moral concern. It has even become one of the favourite subjects of the political conservative right wing. After all, violence in the home undermines family life, creates social instability, is morally objectionable to most people and illegal anyway. So who would not oppose domestic violence? The relatively successful mainstreaming of domestic violence has come at a price. Although the underlying initial feminist analysis has fostered an increasing gender awareness in the mainstream, the issue has become vulnerable to erosion and dilutions as a family concern due to its mainstreaming. It is noteworthy that domestic violence has been mainstreamed much more effectively than, for example, sexual violence which has by now become marginalized again as a subject of state responsibility (Bumiller 2008).

Secondly, with the diminishing influence of the feminist movement in the twenty-first century, the feminist perspective in general and in the field of domestic violence in particular, has come under attack (Walby 2011). It comes as no surprise then that a new post- and anti-feminist critique is currently directed against the feminist analysis of domestic violence as a gendered phenomenon (Johnson 2005). On the level of popular cultural ideology, a revival of traditional if not hierarchical gendered discourse can be witnessed, paradoxically reasserting women's agency by holding her accountable, if not blameworthy, for sexual dating violence, for example (Roiphe 1994). It is remarkable that sexual violence against women is increasingly constructed as a problem that women (and female children) either make up or provoke. In a post-feminist era, the acknowledgement of feminine vulnerability does not fit very well with a claim to girl power or women being finally emancipated and liberated. For different political reasons, the blatant anti-feminist father's rights movement is another voice that joined the anti-feminist critique. Basically, their claim is that feminists are discriminating against men and undercutting their rights. (Girard 2009).

Thirdly, and not unrelated to the former two developments, the gender-neutralizing perspective (fuelled by anti-feminist rhetoric) with respect to domestic violence in particular has grown in influence, certainly among social scientists but also in the professional field of women's shelter movements. Considering the social sciences as part of a knowledge-producing machinery that inevitably is operating on the nexus of many truth claims as well as ideologies (Foucault 1980). Intimate partner violence has become the area to launch the claim to gender neutrality ("it's inherent to the family system") (Hearn & McKie 2008). In the face of all empirical evidence on violence against women, including domestic violence, it is remarkable that domestic violence is singled out as an exception to the rule that violence against women is a form of gender-based discrimination.

To summarize: in general, two main perspectives on intimate partner violence can currently be distinguished — violence as a form of gender-based abuse and control and violence as a family problem. Both positions differ fundamentally in their underlying epistemological and theoretical premises and methodological approach. It is no surprise then that they produce different empirical data. On the one hand, intimate partner violence as a form of abusive control positions it in a relational context where its micro-dynamics are intricately related to a wider social and cultural context of power differentials and subsequent dynamics, which in most societies position men as potentially being in some form of control over women. From this perspective, empirical research is required to deploy a method that is adequate to capture the intersecting impact of the meso- and macro-dynamics of gender inequality as well as other social markers of inequality. Intimate partner violence is essentially conceptualized as one form of abusive control. In relationships, where the violence becomes repetitive, it becomes part of a pattern of controlling behaviours towards women. Not the violent incidents as such, but if and how the violence becomes part of this pattern, is the focus of analysis. The family (or "systemic") violence position, on the other hand, takes as a starting point that violence and aggression are essentially human behaviours common to everybody and in no way gender specific. Therefore, there is no need for a method that should presume any gender differences with regard to the way intimate partner violence is either expressed or reported in research settings. It is the family and relational systemic setting that deserves attention. The method of data collection is usually a highly standardized instrument that does not address the wider power context, leading to what some argue are biased results (Archer 1999, Simpson & Christensen 2005).

Whereas the first perspective yields results that underline the disproportionality in prevalence as well as severity of women's compared to men's victimization, from the second perspective empirical results are produced where most of the violence in couples is mutual and comparable in prevalence rates. The conclusion is that, in fact, a new gender equality is emerging in the use of intimate partner violence between women and men. If nothing else, these debates illustrate that conducting research into the nexus of violence and heterosexual intimacy is asking for trouble, or to put it more eloquently: it is one of those areas that from an epistemological perspective is *essentially contested*.

To make any valid empirical interpretation of women's and men's violence directed at an intimate partner, it seems a preliminary requirement is to position the violence in the wider context that *seems* to affect it, that is, gender-related inequalities. Only by collecting data on that potential connection can we test the hypothesis on whether and how the violence is related to that context. Assuming it is unrelated is a peculiarly uncurious and *ipso facto* unscientific approach. It boils down to putting the rabbit (gender neutrality) in the (research-)hat, only to let the rabbit out at the end of the process as — aha! — the result of the research instead of a not-so-transparent preliminary conceptual decision. Only by explicitly addressing the issue can we achieve a valid assessment of the meaning of the differences in severity of the violence and its dynamics (being defensive or offensive) (Dobash et al. 1992, Römkens 1997). A body of research by now illustrates that it is possible to distinguish intimate controlling and unilateral violence on the one hand from so-called common-couple and often mutual violence on the other (*inter alia* Römkens 1997; Walby & Jonathan 2004; M. P. Johnson 2006; Johnson et al. 2008). Taking differences in severity and in mutuality into account, gendered patterns of intimate partner violence persist: women suffer more severe (in terms of injury) and more frequent violence, and more forms of economic and (notably) sexually violent, abusive and controlling behaviours from men than men suffer from women or from other males for that matter (for example, Catalano et al. 2009; Lauritsen & Heimer 2009; WHO 2010). Women are more fearful than men as a consequence of the abuse. Note also that women are more often than men the victim of homicide committed by their male (ex-)partner (Johnson H. 2006; Römkens & Lahlah 2011).

The fact is that women and men use violence in relationships. The question is: what kind of violence is committed and how severe is it. Most importantly, does the violence affect a substantive enough group to represent either a public health problem or a criminal and safety problem of such a magnitude that it requires the state's intervention. Taking care of violent relationship troubles — how painful they can be is illustrated by the high divorce rates — is essentially not the states' responsibility unless we are dealing with a structural problem. Men's victimization at the hands of their female partner, although clearly occurring, is neither a public health nor a safety concern affecting large numbers of men in society comparable to the numbers of affected women. Therefore, it does not seem to qualify as a public concern, nor as a form of discrimination, unlike a substantive part of women's victimization at the hands of known men.

The initial politicized feminist analysis of domestic violence represented a meta narrative, where a strategic concept of sameness was deliberately put forward. All women were portrayed as "subordinated" and running the risk of becoming victims of male violence. After several decades of research and after having arrived in the post-feminist era of the early twenty-first century, this is politically and scientifically no longer a satisfying analysis.[7] The current challenge is to acknowledge and investigate the differences both between and among men and women — including women's use of violence. When researching violence, we need to carefully look at how gender intersects with other major social markers such as ethnicity, class, age and sexual orientation in order to demonstrate and explain which differences in vulnerability between women and men are at stake. The analysis of the gender-specific nature and the disproportionality with which women and girls face violence will become even more necessary as a valid and reliable empirical basis for adequate policy and legal measures that address violence against women.

Council of Europe: International legal developments

The impact of these competing discourses concerning the gender-based nature of domestic violence has clearly reached beyond academia. [8] A good example can be seen in the developments contributing to the 2011 CoE *Convention on prevention and combating violence against women and domestic violence (the* "Istanbul Convention").[9]

The CoE has been very active, for over a decade, in promoting a coherent human rights and gender-based approach to VAW. Given the CoE's essential human rights identity that comes as no surprise.[10] Since the mid-1990s, the CoE produced a series of recommendations, indicators and other non-binding documents that set guidelines for how progress in addressing violence against women might be made. Several studies have been commissioned by the CoE in the field of VAW (for example, Hagemann-White,2010; Kelly 2008). The Recommendation Rec (2002) 5 on the Protection of Women against Violence (adopted by the Committee of Ministers in April 2002) is the first (non-binding) dedicated instrument on VAW recommending that MS "*review their legislation and policies*", guaranteeing women *inter alia* the recognition, enjoyment, exercise and protection of their human rights and fundamental freedoms. The Recommendation requires MS to exercise *due diligence* to prevent, investigate and punish acts of violence, whether those acts are perpetrated by the state or private persons, and provide protection to victims.

The CoE's strong commitment translated into establishing the *Task Force on Violence against Women, including Domestic Violence.* Between 2006 and 2008, it launched a series of campaigns,[11] conferences and activities to raise awareness. In its 2008 *Final Activity Report,* the CoE Task Force strongly endorsed the development of binding legal instruments that aim to regulate prevention, protection and punishment in the area of violence against women.[12] Note that in the definition of the scope of the Task Force, the concept "domestic violence" is positioned as a distinct form of violence against women ("VAW, *including* domestic violence").

Meanwhile, the CoE called on MS in 2008 "to step up implementation of the standards to fight violence against women".[13]

After having established the feasibility of a CoE convention against domestic violence (Römkens & Letschert 2007), the CoE decided in 2009 to take a historical step towards developing a new and binding European instrument.[14] In 2011, this resulted in the *Convention on preventing and combating violence against women and domestic violence.* As of 11 May 2011, the convention was open for signing and ratification. The convention requires ten ratifications before entering into force. As of October 2012, twenty-three states had signed and one (Turkey) had ratified the convention. The convention will be the first European international binding document to address VAW as a human rights violation *and* as a form of (gender-based) discrimination. The instrument defines in detail the range of integrated legal and other measures states are required to take to meet their obligations to prevent, protect and prosecute violence against women with "due diligence". In that respect, the convention will be the first regional binding instrument that takes the identification of state obligations a crucial step further compared to the only other international legal instrument addressing VAW (the *Inter American Convention on the prevention, punishment and eradication of violence against women*, Belem do Para,1994, twenty-five articles). The CoE convention specifies in greater detail (eighty-eight articles) the different kinds of measures states are expected to take (*inter alia* data collection, prevention, protection and support, legislative measures, investigative and prosecutorial measures, etcetera). It also includes the setting up of a monitoring mechanism, which is an important step towards holding MS accountable for implementing the convention *de facto* and *de jure*. The convention definitely goes beyond the traditional criminal legal response and lays out an integrated approach to VAW where the state is obliged to respond with specified and detailed measures in the realms of prevention, protection and prosecution.

In the preamble, the convention is squarely positioned in the context of existing international human rights standards as laid down in, *inter alia,* the UN Conventions on Civil and Political Rights, on Economic, Social and Political Rights as well as the UN Convention to End All forms of Discrimination against Women (CEDAW), the Convention on the Rights of the Child, the Convention on Rights of Persons with Disabilities and the Rome Statute on the International Criminal Court. The convention text *per se* is the result of long and fierce debates and negotiations during eleven, often heated, three-day meetings between 2009 and 2011 between the forty-seven MS.

The convention is a landmark instrument in its recognition of VAW as a form of gender-based violence directly related to discrimination. This is a historical achievement. However, a profound ambiguity has entered the convention precisely when it comes to domestic violence against women. This is not unrelated to the academic debate sketched earlier in this chapter.

The title of the convention clearly sets apart domestic violence as a *different* form of violence than "violence against women". Unlike the definition of VAW as laid down in the appendix of the CoE Ministers' Recommendation 2002(5), which guided earlier on the CoE Task Force, domestic violence is now no longer part of the wider concept of VAW (replacing the "including" with "and"). Domestic violence is explicitly positioned as a non-gendered form of violence since some domestic violence also affects men and children. The text of the convention reflects this hybrid conceptualization in various places. For example, in article 1, on the purposes of the convention, paras 1a and 1b put a clear emphasis on violence against women in the context of discrimination. Yet both in para 1a and in para 1c, domestic violence is also carefully positioned as being distinct from VAW. Para 1a reads: "*[The purposes of the Convention are] to protect women against all forms of violence and prevent, prosecute and eliminate violence against women* ***and*** *domestic violence*" (emphasis added), followed by 1b "*to contribute to the elimination of all forms of discrimination against women and promote substantive equality between women and men, including by empowering women*". Para 1c then continues with a third purpose (to) "*design a comprehensive framework, policies and measures for the protection of and assistance to all victims of violence against women* ***and*** *domestic violence*" (emphasis added). In article 1 of the Explanatory Report of the Convention, it becomes clear that the reference to domestic violence includes "children, men and the elderly".

The ambiguity concerning the recognition of domestic violence as a form of gender-based violence and discrimination is even more obvious when comparing article 1 concerning "purpose" with the article regarding the scope of the convention (article 2). "*Parties are encouraged to apply the Convention to all victims of domestic violence. Parties shall pay particular attention to women victims of gender-based violence in implementing the provisions of this Convention.*" Here, the convention simultaneously positions domestic violence as a gender-neutral phenomenon, while acknowledging that domestic violence affects women disproportionally. This implies a departure from the CoE's earlier recognition of the gender-based nature of domestic violence. It is also in contrast with accepted international binding definitions of gender-based violence. Since *discrimination* of women in the context of inequality in power relations between men and women is one of the constitutive elements of this convention, it is internally contradictory, and from an international human rights law perspective illogical and without legal ground, to position domestic violence against men within its realm.

In light of the CoE's task to protect and uphold human rights, this indicates a change in perspective. It tends to gravitate towards an approach towards domestic violence as a moral concern of a humanitarian nature, instead of as a violation of human rights. With this extension of the convention's scope, it goes against standards that have been firmly set by now in international law, notably CEDAW, where violence against women is defined as a form of gender-based discrimination.

Gender and domestic violence: revisiting an area of contestation

That this ambiguous positioning of domestic violence as both gender-based and gender-neutral entered the convention is directly related to the ongoing debate on the so-called gender neutrality of domestic violence as presented earlier in this chapter. The claim of gender neutrality of domestic violence was brought forward by a substantive minority of MS, notably from various first-generation EU MS. Referring to "scientific research", representatives insisted that the scope of the convention be extended to include male victims of domestic violence. The debate saw a mix of so-called scientific claims (referring to data indicating the equality in prevalence of "common couple's violence" of women against men) and more principled arguments about the perceived necessity of gender neutrality and objectivity of law. The argument that domestic violence against women is a form of discrimination against women, unlike domestic violence against men, was considered irrelevant by proponents of this extension, ignoring existing international legal standards as contained *inter alia* in CEDAW and ignoring the recent case law of the European Court of Human Rights (ECtHR (see below). Various women's NGOs as well as Amnesty International, having observer status to the commission, have voiced strong concerns during the negotiations about the extension of the scope of the convention.[15]

The extension of the scope of the convention and the arguments brought forward to support it could not contrast more with recent jurisprudence from the ECtHR. The scientific experts on the committee presented the landmark case of June 2009 of Opuz v. Turkey, pointing to the incompatibility of extending the convention's scope with the existing standards upheld by the court.[16] In this case, the complainant had been severely abused for many years during which she had requested police protection many times, in vain. In the end, she was severely injured and her mother killed by her ex-husband; she claimed that Turkey had violated its obligation to protect the right to life (article 2), the right to be free from torture (article 3) and to be free from discrimination (article 14 European Convention of Human Rights, ECHR). The court explicitly acknowledged, for the very first time, that it "*had to have regard to the provisions of more specialised legal instruments and decisions of international legal bodies*" (para 51). Explicitly referring to CEDAW, which defines violence against women as a form of discrimination, and to the Inter-American Convention on violence against women, the European Court concluded that domestic violence is a form of discrimination and that it is the duty of states, under the due diligence principle, to take measures to provide protection and avoid risk for the victim in cases where the state "knew or ought to have known" of a "real and immediate risk to the life of an identified individual(s) from the criminal acts of a third party". Interestingly enough, in this case, scientific data played an important role as well, indicating that domestic violence affects women primarily. The court concluded that "*supported by unchallenged statistical information, the existence of a prima facie indication that the domestic violence affected mainly women and that the general and discriminatory judicial passivity in Turkey created a climate that was conducive to domestic violence*" (para 64).

It is remarkable that the CoE MS struck a compromise and, ignoring this ruling, decided to include domestic violence within the convention's scope as a gender-neutral form of violence, while admitting that domestic violence affects women disproportionately and again leaving it to states to decide whether to apply the convention to men, children and the elderly. The denial of the relevance of the European Court's binding ruling reflects a serious affront from within the very organization that is expected to uphold the court's jurisprudence. On a more mundane level, it illustrates how (international) lawmaking is very much the result of political compromise where many often want to have the cake and eat it too. The future will tell what this implies for the international legal protection it can offer women and men.

Conclusion

Many in Europe are in a state of confusion and ambiguity when it comes to recognizing the public nature of private violence against women by their partners or ex-partners. Domestic violence is currently at risk of being singled out as gender neutral, if not privatized again as a family issue. It leads to a paradox: while in the international human rights based legal and policy field, the perspective on violence against women as a violation of fundamental women's, and therefore human, rights has been mainstreamed, Europe is ambiguously backtracking at the same time.

Two important requirements flow from the long-established recognition of violence against women as a violation of human rights — the need for an integrated state response that goes beyond criminalization and includes preventive and protective support measures and the recognition, in legal and policy based measures, that violence against women is *discriminatory* violence intrinsically related to gendered inequality between men and women.[17]

The recognition of the gendered nature of the most prevalent form of VAW, domestic violence, has weakened in the 2011 CoE Convention on preventing and combating violence against women and domestic violence. It underlines how human rights law is subject to multiple and politically inspired interpretations when it comes to the question of domestic violence as a form of discriminatory violence. With an eye to the efforts to develop regional instruments in Asia, there are lessons to be learned when looking at Europe. Domestic violence is at risk of being neutralized and, in a way, privatized again. The public–private dichotomy reflects deeply rooted traditional values that are useful for many different political agendas. A discursive collusion is taking place, where politicians and social scientists tune in to produce a siren's song of gender neutrality and equality in the home, precisely with respect to domestic violence (of all things for men and women to be equal in!). Current European developments illustrate the competition of frames of meanings that are attached to the use of a human rights perspective to frame VAW, as if it is more a socio-political rather than a more or less solid international legal frame. Human rights are no longer the exclusive domain of international public law. The human rights perspective is increasingly embraced worldwide to frame the political and legal battles of violence against women (see Merry 2006). It demonstrates that law is a living thing, subject to interpretation and not only of legal experts. This politicization may have fostered a different consequence: the weakening of international legal standards. Vigilance is, therefore, required.

From a theoretical perspective, these developments also illustrate Foucault's analysis of how law has long lost its all-powerful disciplinary position (Foucault 1980; Hunt & Wyckham 1994; Smart 1995). However, it is still unique in its powers, and it will be interesting to see what the eventual impact of the recent jurisprudence of the ECtHR will be on the eventual direction of the CoE convention. Violence against women has become the domain of many social and political actors aiming to regulate the field and in doing so, discipline citizens. It has become part of a wider social engineering agenda, aiming to move citizens towards non-violence against women. A governance perspective, emphasizing the dispersed nature of power that the various disciplinary regimes enact, not necessarily in concordance with each other, is helpful to analyze the unintended effects of some discursive strategies. It illustrates how crucial decision-making processes in legislative domains are indeed no longer exclusively in the hands of the state nor of the legislative bodies, or any single decision-making institution for that matter. Many different actors, including civil society, shape social and political developments that determine the ultimate structure of legislation in the field of violence against women.

This is history in the making. The recognition, under human rights law, of the discriminatory nature of violence against women, including domestic violence, has been a major transformation and is a strategic asset. Domestic violence is not only to be considered a public concern but one that is intimately connected to behaviours of gendered individuals operating under regimes of various inequalities. It is crucial that feminist scholars, activists and NGOs remain vigilant in constructing the manner in which violence against women is transformed into a subject of state concern.

Notes

1 CEDAW Convention (1979) *General recommendation # 19*. This is adopted in core documents of the CoE as well as the EU.

2 EUROBAROMETER 2010: The multi-stage random sample consisted of respondents (fifteen years and older) who were interviewed face-to-face in their home (via CAPI-Computer Assisted Personal Interview). In the fall of 2010, the EU MS had a total of almost 407,000,000 inhabitants aged fifteen years and above.

3 In 1999, the EU MS consisted of Austria, Belgium, Denmark, Luxemburg, Netherlands, Finland, France, Germany, Greece, Spain, Italy, Ireland, Portugal, Sweden and the United Kingdom. After 1999, twelve Central and Eastern European countries joined the EU: Bulgaria, the Czech Republic, Cyprus, Estonia, Hungary, Latvia, Lithuania, Malta, Poland, Romania, Slovakia and Slovenia.

4 For example: In the UK, Latvia and Sweden 38–39 percent of respondents knew a female victim of domestic violence, in contrast to 16 percent in Germany and Italy and 11 percent in Bulgaria (EUROBAROMETER 2010: 24).

5 In 2004, Spain introduced its Organic Law on gender-based violence.

6 These data deserve careful analysis which goes beyond the scope of this chapter. It reflects the diversity of developments within the EU in this field. Any generalization regarding the EU requires this caveat: it is a union in diversity holding twenty-seven countries, almost as many different national languages, and a multitude of social, cultural, ethnic and historical legacies that bind or divide, or both, depending on whom you ask.

7 What is striking is that the plea for diversity has been voiced and practiced for a long time within feminist research, yet the anti-feminist positions refer to the "feminist" positions as if they are on a unitary monolithic ideology.

8 See the Canadian veto of the Ontario Domestic Violence Law (Girard 2009) or the threat of cutting funding (2010) of Women's Aid in the UK if they would not open their shelters for male victims.

9 For the adopted convention text and explanatory memorandum, see http://www.coe.int/t/dghl/standardsetting/violence/default_EN.asp

10 The CoE is a human rights based transnational organization, encompassing forty-seven MS (besides the twenty-seven EU countries, it includes all the former Soviet Republics and Central and Eastern European States). As a human rights based legislative body it has the power to issue binding instruments, like a convention, but in the end it has less of a direct impact on unwilling MS due to the relative lack of sanctioning mechanisms of the CoE compared to the EU. The European Court of Human Rights can hold the CoE MS accountable and convict MS but it has no enforcement mechanism other than "naming and shaming" through its case law. As a political-economic union, the EU has, in areas specified in the EU Treaties (notably the Amsterdam and Lisbon Treaty), a direct and binding legislative and/or policy impact on its MS and is monitored by the European Commission.

11 http://www.coe.int/t/dc/campaign/stopviolence/default_en.asp, accessed 12 October 2012

12 http://www.wave-network.org/imges/doku/coe_tf_final_activity_report_08.pdf Last accessed 19 October 2012.

13 These standards were agreed by the CoE's Committee of Ministers in November 2007 and the measures called for by the Parliamentary Assembly in its 2004 and 2007 resolutions. http://assembly.coe.int/ASP/Press/StopPressView.asp?ID=2018

14 CAHVIO Committee (Ad Hoc Committee on preventing and combating VIOlence against women and domestic violence). The author was appointed as independent scientific expert (criminology) to the Drafting Committee by the CoE Secretary General. Professor Christine Chinkin was appointed to the CAHVIO Committee as international law expert. Both experts took part in the CoE drafting commission meetings and the (eleven) CAHVIO meetings of the committee between April 2009 and January 2011.

15 EPAC/EWL: *Women's NGOs call on the Council of Europe to move towards a strong Instrument on Violence against Women*. http://www.coe.int/t/dghl/standardsetting/convention-violence/CAHVIO/STATEMENT-270409.pdf. Also: Amnesty International, *Council of Europe don't waste this opportunity*. http://www.unhcr.org/refworld/docid/4c7f63f32.html

16 See Opuz v. Turkey (Appl No 33401/02). ECHR, 9 June 2009.

17 CEDAW (1979) *General recommendation #19*. This is adopted in core documents of the CoE as well as the EU.

References

Archer, J. (1999) 'Assessment of the reliability of the conflict tactics scales: A meta-analytic review.' *Journal of Interpersonal Violence*, 14 (12), 1263–1289.

Bumiller, K. (2008) *In an abusive state. How neo-liberalism appropriated the feminist movement against sexual violence*. Durham/London: Duke University Press.

Catalano,S., E. Smith, H. Snyder, M. Rand (2009) 'Female victims of violence.' Bureau of Justice Statistics. Selected findings. September, 2009.

CEDAW Convention (1979) *General recommendation #19*. This is adopted in core documents of the Council of Europe as well as the EU.

Crenshaw, K. (1989) *Demarginalizing the Intersection of Race and Sex: A Black Feminist Critique of Antidiscrimination Doctrine, Feminist Theory, and Antiracist Politics*. Chicago Legal Forum 1989: 139–67.

Dobash, R. P., Dobash, R. E., Wilson, M. & Daly, M. (1992) 'The myth of sexual symmetry in marital violence.' *Social Problems*, 39(1), 71–91.

EUROBAROMETER 344/Wave 73.2 (2010). *Domestic violence against Women*. Brussels: TNS Opinion & Social. (Survey at the request of the Directorate-General for Justice, Freedom and Security of the European Commission).

Foucault, Michel (1980) 'Two lectures' in Colin Gordon (ed) *Power/Knowledge: Selected Interviews and Other Writings* 1972–1977. pp. 78–108. Brighton: Harvester Press.

Girard, A. (2009) 'Backlash or equality? The influence of men's and women's rights discourses on domestic violence legislation in Ontario.' *Violence against women*. 15(1), pp. 5–22.

Hagemann-White, C. (2010) *Protecting women against violence. Analytical study of the results of the third round of monitoring the implementation of Recommendation Rec (2002) 5 on the protection of women against violence in Council of Europe member states*. Strassbourg: Council of Europe Directorate General of Human Rights.

Hagemann-White, C. (2006) *Combating violence against women: Stocktaking study on the measures and actions taken in Council of Europe members states.* Council of Europe, DG Human Rights/Equality Division: Strasbourg.

Hagemann-White, C. (2010) *Stocktaking study on the measures and actions taken in Council of Europe members states.* Council of Europe, DG Human Rights/Equality Division: Strasbourg.

Hearn, J. & McKie, L. (2008) 'Gendered policy and policy on gender: The case of domestic violence.' *Policy & Politics*, 36 (1), 75–91.

Hunt, A. & Wyckham, G. (1994) *Foucault and Law: Towards a Sociology of Law as Governance.* London, Chicago, Illinois: Pluto Press.

Johnson, H. (2006) *Measuring violence against women. Statistical trends 2006.* Ottawa: Statistics Canada.

Johnson, H., Ollus, N., Nevala, S. (2008) *Violence against women, an international perspective.* New York: Springer.

Johnson, M.P. (2005) 'Domestic Violence: It's Not About Gender — Or Is It?' *Journal of Marriage and Family.* 67(5), 1126–1130.

Johnson, M. P. (2006). 'Conflict and control: Gender symmetry and asymmetry in domestic violence.' *Violence Against Women*, 12 (11), 1003–1018.

Kelly, L. (2008) *Combating violence against women: minimum standards for support services.* Council of Europe, DG Human Rights/Equality Division: Strasbourg.

Lauritsen, J.L., K. Heimer (2009). *Gender and Violent Victimization, 1973–2005.* Washington DC: National Institutue of Justice.

Merry, S. E.(2006) *Human rights & gender violence. Translating international law into local justice.* Chicago: University of Chicago Press.

Nixon, J. & C. Humphreys (2010) 'Marshalling the evidence: Using intersectionality in the domestic violence frame.' *Social Politics.* 17(2), 137–143.

Roiphe, K. (1994) *The morning after. Sex, fear and feminism*, Little, Brown & Company.

Rijken, C. & Römkens, R. (2010) 'Vulnerability in a globalized world: The case of human trafficking'. In: J. Van Dijk & R. Letschert (eds) *Globalisation, human security & victims.* pp. 73–99. New York: Springer.

Römkens, R. (1997) 'Prevalence of wife abuse in the Netherlands. Combining quantitative and qualitative methods.' *Journal of Interpersonal Violence.* 12(1), 99–125.

Römkens, R., R. Letschert (2007) *Feasibility study for a convention against domestic violence.* Strasbourg: Council of Europe Directorate General of Human Rights and Legal Affairs.

Römkens, R., E. Lahlah (2011) 'Particularly violent. The discursive construction of Muslim culture as a risk factor'. In: S. Condon, M. Schroettle, T. Ravi (eds) *Violence against women and ethnicity. Commonalities and differences*, pp. 79–96. Opladen: Barbara Buddrich Publishers.

Simpson, L. E.; Christensen, A. (2005). 'Spousal Agreement Regarding Relationship Aggression on the Conflict Tactics Scale-2.' *Psychological assessment: a journal of consulting and clinical psychology.* 17(4): 423–432.

Smart, C. (1995) *Law, crime and sexuality. Essays in feminism.* London/Thousand Oaks/New Delhi: Sage Publ.

Sokoloff, N. & I. Dupont (2005) 'Domestic Violence and the Intersection of Race, Class and Gender: Challenges to Understanding Violence against Marginalized

Women in Diverse Communities.' *Violence against Women.* 11(1), pp. 38–64.
Verloo, M. (2006) 'Multiple Inequalities, Intersectionality and the European Union.' *European Journal of Women's Studies* 13(3), 211–228.
Walby, S. (2011) *The future of feminism.* Polity Press: Cambridge.
Walby, S. Jonathan A. (2004) *Domestic Violence, Sexual Assault and Stalking. Findings from the British Crime Survey. Home Office Research Study 276.* London: Home Office Research, Development and Statistics Directorate.
World Health Organization and London School of Hygiene and Tropical Medicine (2010) *Preventing intimate partner and sexual violence against women: taking action and generating evidence.* Geneva: WHO.

The Editors and Contributors

Cheryll Alipio is a former Postdoctoral Fellow at the Asia Research Institute of the National University of Singapore. She received both her MA and PhD degrees in Anthropology from the University of Washington, Seattle, and her BA degrees in Anthropology and Psychology, with a minor in Women Studies from the University of California, Davis. Her dissertation, *Affective Economies: Child Debts, Devotions, and Desires in Philippine Migrant Families*, explores the intergenerational and gendered transfers, relations, and dynamics of children and youth in the midst of transnational migration and Christianity.

Zarizana Abdul Aziz is a human rights lawyer from Malaysia who has been training lawyers, civil society advocates, religious scholars and government officials in several countries. She was President of the Women's Crisis Centre (now Women's Centre for Change) and provided legal and emotional support to victims of VAW. She was involved in legal and legislative reform initiatives on gender equality and anti-violence in Timor Leste, Bangladesh, Indonesia, Malaysia and recently in constitutional dialogues in the Middle East post-Arab Spring. She chairs Women Living Under Muslim Laws and is researching 'Due Diligence and State Responsibility to End Violence against Women: Standards and Indicators'.

Narayanan Ganapathy is an Associate Professor in the Department of Sociology at the National University of Singapore, and Adjunct Professor in the School of Justice, Queensland University of Technology, Brisbane, Australia. His research and teaching interests are criminology, sociology of crime and deviance, sociology of law and policing, juvenile justice, criminal gangs and domestic violence. He is on the Editorial Boards of the *European Journal of Criminology, International Journal of Comparative and Applied Criminal Justice* and the *Asian Journal of Criminology*. Along with several journal articles and book chapters, he has written the book *Policing Marital Violence in Singapore* (2008), Leiden: Brill.

Nursyahbani Katjasungkana is a human rights lawyer with three decades experience in women's rights and environmental issues. She is active in the field of legal and legislative advocacy, training and conducts policy research and analysis. She was member of the People Consultative Assembly (1999–2004), an elected Member of Parliament (2004–2009) before acting Vice Chair of the National Awakening Party (2004–now). She is developing community-based legal aid and paralegal training to the community, especially to women survivors of VAW.

Maznah Mohamad is an Associate Professor with the Departments of Malay Studies and Southeast Asian Studies at the National University of Singapore. She teaches and researches in the area of gender, family and the politics of Islam and ethnicity in Malaysia and Southeast Asia. She has published *Feminism and the Women's Movement in Malaysia* (co-authored, 2006), and *Changing Marriage Patterns in Southeast Asia: Economic and Socio-Cultural Dimension* (co-edited, 2011).

Amrita Nandy is a doctoral candidate at the New Delhi-based Jawaharlal Nehru University where she is researching women's non-normative choices vis-à-vis motherhood, mothering ideologies and the family. Through her work with the UN, various NGOs and the government, she is involved with many socio-political campaigns in the South Asia region. As a freelance journalist, she writes for various national English dailies, magazines, news agencies and blogs in India. Amrita has a Master's in Women's Studies from the University of Oxford, U.K.

Renée Römkens is the Director of Atria, Institute on Gender Equality and Women's History, Amsterdam. She has published widely on gender and victimization, notably on the impact of legal regulation of violence against women in the home. Her current research work focuses on European developments in regulation of VAW. As an academic expert she has worked for the European Commission (European Institute on Gender Equality), Fundamental Rights Agency, the UN Special Rapporteur on VAW and the Council of Europe, most recently for the Commission that drafted the CoE Convention on Violence Against Women and Domestic Violence (2011).

Saskia E. Wieringa is an honorary Professor at the University of Amsterdam, holding the Chair on Women's Same-Sex Relations Crossculturally. From 2005 till 2012, she was the Director of Aletta, Institute for Women's History in Amsterdam. She is also the co-founder and presently secretary of the Kartini Asia Network. She has a long experience of activism in both the women's and third world solidarity movements. Since the late 1970s, she has done research on women's movements, sexual politics and same-sex relations in many parts of the world, particularly in Indonesia and has authored and (co-)edited over 30 books and 200 articles.

Index